Road to October 7

**Erik Skare** is a historian at the University of Oslo and the author of the award-winning *A History of Palestinian Islamic Jihad: Faith, Awareness, and Revolution in the Middle East.* He specializes in Palestinian history with a particular focus on religion and secular politics. Skare has published extensively on Palestinian Islamism and resistance, and his work has been cited in the *Washington Post*, *Le Monde diplomatique*, and other international news outlets.

# Road to October 7

## A Brief History of Palestinian Islamism

Erik Skare

**VERSO**
London • New York

First published by Verso 2025
© Erik Skare 2025

The manufacturer's authorized representative in the EU for product safety
(GPSR) is LOGOS EUROPE, 9 rue Nicolas Poussin, 17000, La Rochelle, France
contact@logoseurope.eu

The moral rights of the author have been asserted

1 3 5 7 9 10 8 6 4 2

**Verso**
UK: 6 Meard Street, London W1F 0EG
US: 207 East 32nd Street, New York, NY 10016
versobooks.com

Verso is the imprint of New Left Books

ISBN-13: 978-1-80429-788-9
ISBN-13: 978-1-80429-789-6 (UK EBK)
ISBN-13: 978-1-80429-790-2 (US EBK)

**British Library Cataloguing in Publication Data**
A catalogue record for this book is available from the British Library

**Library of Congress Cataloging-in-Publication Data**

Names: Skare, Erik, author.
Title: Road to October 7 : a brief history of Palestinian Islamism / Erik
  Skare.
Description: London ; New York : Verso, 2025. | Includes bibliographical
  references and index.
Identifiers: LCCN 2024054612 (print) | LCCN 2024054613 (ebook) | ISBN
  9781804297889 (trade paperback) | ISBN 9781804297902 (ebook)
Subjects: LCSH: Islam and politics—Palestine. | Palestinian
  Arabs—Politics and government—20th century. | Palestinian
  Arabs—Politics and government—21st century.
Classification: LCC DS119.7 .S583 2025 (print) | LCC DS119.7 (ebook) |
  DDC 956.9405/5—dc23/eng/20250121
LC record available at https://lccn.loc.gov/2024054612
LC ebook record available at https://lccn.loc.gov/2024054613

Typeset in Minion Pro by MJ&N Gavan, Truro, Cornwall
Printed and bound by CPI Group (UK) Ltd, Croydon, CR0 4YY

*For my daughters,*
*my sweet, sweet girls,*
*whom I love more than life.*


*In loving memory of Kjetil Selvik*

[We] must grasp the truth, 'Political power grows out of the barrel of a gun.'

Our principle is that the Party commands the gun, and the gun must never be allowed to command the Party.

– Mao Zedong

# Contents

*List of Illustrations*                                      ix
*List of Abbreviations*                                      xii
*Key Figures*                                                xiii
*Timelines*                                                  xv
*Acknowledgements*                                           xvii

Introduction                                                  1

1  The Solution Is Islam                                      11

2  Reviving the Caliphate                                     43

3  Rise of the Vanguard                                       60

4  Peace, Blood, and Twisted Metal                            93

5  Guns and Governance                                       128

6  Prelude                                                   165

7  Road to October 7                                         199

*Appendix*                                                   206
*Index*                                                      211

# Illustrations

## Plates

1 Hassan al-Banna visiting Muslim Brotherhood branch in Gaza City, March 19, 1948
2 Muslim Brotherhood scouts in Gaza before the 1948 Palestine War
3 Ismail Abdel Aziz al-Khalidi, co-founder of the Muslim Brotherhood in the Gaza Strip
4 Members of the Tawhid Association, 1949
5 Ahmad Yassin as a teacher, late 1950s
6 Ahmad Yassin on excursion with Muslim Brotherhood to one of Gaza's beaches, late 1950s/early 1960s
7 Ahmad Yassin in an orange field in Beit Hanoun, 1961
8 Taqi al-Din al-Nabhani, founder of Hizb al-Tahrir
9 Fathi al-Shiqaqi, co-founder and first PIJ secretary-general
10 Co-founders of PIJ as students in Egypt, 1970s
11 Fathi al-Shiqaqi and Ramadan Shallah in exile after the former's deportation to Lebanon
12 Last known photograph of Fathi al-Shiqaqi from visit to Libya, 1995
13 Abdel Aziz al-Rantisi as a young student, 1980s
14 Hamas activist, late 1980s
15 Hamas demonstration in commemoration of the assassination of Hassan al-Banna, 1989

16  Imad Aql, co-founder of Hamas's Izz al-Din al-Qassam Brigades and
    Muhammad Deif's mentor
17  Poster advocating for the release of the imprisoned Ahmad Yassin
18  Muhammad Deif holding the passport of kidnapped Israeli soldier
    Nachshon Wachsman, 1994
19  Muhammad Deif
20  Leader of the al-Qassam Brigades, Salah Shahada, posing with three
    suicide bombers
21  Yahya Ayash, chief bomb maker of Hamas, mid-1990s
22  Mahmoud Saqr al-Zatma, chief PIJ bomb maker
23  Yahya Sinwar at the Islamic University of Gaza, November 15, 1980,
    with Dr Ma'mun Abu Amir
24  Hamas graffiti from the First Intifada
25  Ramadan Shallah receiving his doctorate in economics from Durham
    University in 1990
26  Ziyad al-Nakhala and Ramadan Shallah at the funeral of Fathi
    al-Shiqaqi

## Figures

3.1  Geographical distribution of Gazan PIJ martyrs, 1985–99          76
3.2  Geographical distribution of Gazan al-Qassam martyrs,
     1988–99                                                         77
3.3  Geographical distribution of PIJ martyrs, 1985–99              83
4.1  Number of Hamas and PIJ attacks, 1986–99, with moving
     average                                                        114
5.1  Militants joining the Qassam Brigades and PIJ, 1986–2004       133
5.2  Geographical distribution of PIJ martyrs, 2000–5               134
5.3  Geographical distribution of al-Qassam martyrs, 2000–5         135
5.4  Number of al-Qassam and PIJ martyrs, 2000–5                    151
6.1  Gazan kinship clusters in the Qassam Brigades, 1988–2006
     (> 4)                                                          169
6.2  Gazan kinship clusters in the Qassam Brigades, 2007–22
     (> 4)                                                          170
8.1  Militants joining the Qassam Brigades and PIJ, 2007–22         209

## Tables

3.1  Education level of PIJ martyrs, 1985–99                              80
3.2  10 most common occupations, PIJ, 1985–99                         80
3.3  Most common known education specializations, PIJ, 1985–99    81
4.1  Education level of al-Qassam martyrs, 1988–99                  100
4.2  Regional distribution of Islamist martyrs, 1985–2022           101
5.1  PIJ's cooperation with other armed factions, 2000–6             137
6.1  Occupation distribution in the Qassam Brigades and PIJ,
     2007–22                                                                    171

# Abbreviations

| | |
|---|---|
| APF | Alliance of Palestinian Forces |
| DFLP | Democratic Front for the Liberation of Palestine |
| EIJ | Egyptian Islamic Jihad |
| EU | European Union |
| IS/ISIS | Islamic State |
| PA | Palestinian National Authority |
| PFLP | Popular Front for the Liberation of Palestine |
| PFLP-GC | Popular Front for the Liberation of Palestine – General Command |
| PIJ | Palestinian Islamic Jihad |
| PLA | Palestine Liberation Army |
| PLC | Palestinian Legislative Council |
| PLF | Palestine Liberation Front |
| PLO | Palestine Liberation Organization |
| PPSF | Palestinian Popular Struggle Front |
| PRC | Popular Resistance Committees |
| RCC | Revolutionary Command Council |
| TRO | Ten Resistance Organizations |

# Key Figures

List of key figures ordered alphabetically by last name.

Abu Marzuq, Musa     (1951–present)     Deputy chairman Hamas political bureau

Abu Shanab, Ismail     (1950–2003)     Hamas deputy leader

Abu Tayr, Muhammad     (1951–present)     Hamas senior member

Aql, Imad     (1971–1993)     Co-founder al-Qassam Brigades

Arafat, Yasser     (1929–2004)     Co-founder and Fatah leader

Awda, Abdel Aziz     (1950–present)     Co-founder and PIJ spiritual leader

Ayash, Yahya     (1966–1996)     West Bank leader al-Qassam Brigades

Badran, Husam     (1966–present)     Field commander al-Qassam Brigades

Deif, Muhammad     (1965–2024)     Leader al-Qassam Brigades

Haniyeh, Ismail     (1962–2024)     Chairman Hamas political bureau

Issa, Marwan     (1965–2024)     Deputy leader al-Qassam Brigades

al-Ja'bari, Ahmad     (1960–2012)     Deputy leader al-Qassam Brigades

| al-Khalidi, Ismail | (unknown–2022) | Co-founder Gazan Muslim Brotherhood |
| al-Khawaja, Mahmoud | (1960–1995) | First leader PIJ military wing (Qassam) |
| Mansur, Jamal | (1960–2001) | Hamas senior member |
| al-Maqadma, Ibrahim | (1952–2003) | Co-founder al-Qassam Brigades |
| Mishal, Khalid | (1956–present) | Chairman Hamas political bureau |
| al-Nabhani, Taqi al-Din | (1909–1977) | Founder Hizb al-Tahrir |
| al-Nakhala, Ziyad | (1953–present) | Third PIJ secretary-general |
| al-Rantisi, Abdel Aziz | (1947–2004) | Co-founder and Hamas leader |
| Rayan, Nizar | (1959–2009) | Hamas and al-Qassam senior member |
| Shahada, Salah | (1953–2002) | Co-founder al-Qassam Brigades |
| Shallah, Ramadan | (1958–2020) | Second PIJ secretary-general |
| al-Shiqaqi, Fathi | (1951–1995) | First PIJ secretary-general |
| Sinwar, Yahya | (1962–2024) | Co-founder Majd and Hamas leader |
| al-Wazir, Khalil | (1935–1988) | Co-founder Fatah |
| Yassin, Ahmad | (1936–2004) | Co-founder and Hamas spiritual leader |
| Yazouri, Ibrahim | (1941–2021) | Co-founder Hamas |
| al-Zahar, Mahmoud | (1945–present) | Hamas senior member |

# Timeline (1928–1979)

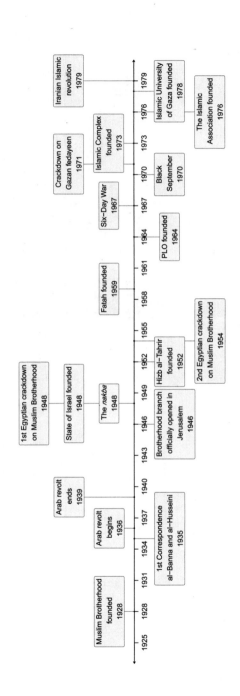

# Timeline (1980–2023)

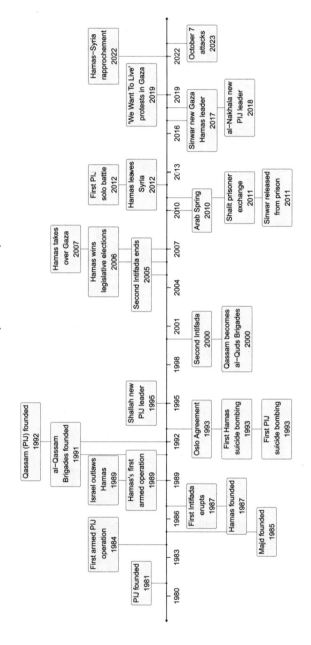

# Acknowledgements

This book started from a conversation with Sebastian Budgen, the editorial director at Verso Books, which sparked the idea for this project. I am thankful for his support and guidance as the book took shape. I extend my gratitude to the entire team at Verso Books, who assisted with practical matters, proofreading, typesetting, and indexing. Their expertise and attention to detail were invaluable. October 7 made me put my existing research projects on hold, and I am thankful to my colleagues at the Department of Culture Studies and Oriental Languages who allowed me to fully withdraw to my office to write this book. I have also benefited tremendously from the help and comments of my colleagues, in and outside of Oslo. Jacob Høigilt, Brynjar Lia, Ragnhild Johnsrud Zorgati, Colin Powers, and Kjølv Egeland provided thorough feedback on the draft manuscript. I am also thankful to the anonymous reviewers whose insightful feedback and constructive criticisms significantly enriched this manuscript. Truls Tønnessen's invitation to present my initial analysis at the Norwegian Institute of International Affairs (NUPI) was equally helpful, thanks to the extensive and insightful comments and questions raised there. Similarly, my lecture on the updated Palestinian Islamist martyr dataset at the T. E. Lawrence Program at All Souls College, University of Oxford, hosted by Thomas Hegghammer, provided valuable perspectives informing this book. The discussion and feedback from the audience were particularly beneficial.

Al-Zaytouna Centre for Studies and Consultation and Dr Muhsin Salih granted me and Verso Books permission to republish several photos of the Gazan Muslim Brotherhood from the 1940s to the 1960s. They were incredibly forthcoming, and I am deeply appreciative of their support. I am equally grateful to Dr Ahmad Ma'mun for letting me and Verso republish the photo of his father, Dr Ma'mun Abu Amir, and Yahya Sinwar at the Islamic University of Gaza in 1980. Dr Bilal Shalash, researcher at the Arab Center for Research and Policy Studies, Doha Institute, also shared sources and photos with me, and I hope to repay him in due course.

Needless to say, any mistakes, errors, or inaccuracies in this book are my responsibility alone.

# Introduction

So Gaza could not be contained after all. When the Palestinian militants breached the wall on October 7, 2023, Gaza had been under blockade for sixteen years. Nearly 80 per cent of Gaza's population depended on aid, two-thirds faced food insecurity, and almost half suffered from multi-dimensional poverty. More than half of its population was unemployed, exceeding 70 per cent for its youth population.[1] By 2023, the majority of Gazans under thirty had never seen the world outside, and a sixteen-year-old would have experienced four wars and a countless number of skirmishes, airstrikes, and cross-border armed confrontations. Gaza would not – could not – remain isolated indefinitely.

The militants did not limit their violence to Israeli military targets, however. Clear visual recordings showed how a Thai worker was decapitated with a garden hoe. Another clip depicted a father and his two sons hunted down in their pyjamas, 'upsetting in part because it showed a relationship between parent and child'.[2] In a separate incident, Palestinian militants found a girl – no more than nine years old – hiding under a table. They executed her after briefly consulting one another.[3] With the

---

1  Yazan Ajamieh et al., *West Bank and Gaza: Selected Issues* (Washington, DC: International Monetary Fund, 2023), 5–6.

2  Graeme Wood, 'A Record of Pure, Predatory Sadism', *Atlantic*, October 23, 2023, theatlantic.com.

3  Rory Carroll, 'Israel Shows Footage of Hamas Killings "to Counter Denial of Atrocities"', *Guardian*, October 23, 2023.

killing of the elderly, with parents shot in front of their children, and with 'bloody rooms crowded with massacred civilians', the attacks caused global shock and outrage.[4] These were acts, Azmi Bishara rightfully argues, that cannot be defended by the legitimate right to resist.[5] If anything, October 7 reveals how suffering does not turn the victim into a moral agent.

What ensued was a relentless bombing campaign against the Gaza Strip. Over 75,000 tons of explosives have been dropped on a besieged population as of this writing, exceeding the combined tonnage used in the bombings of Dresden, Hamburg, and London during the Second World War.[6] More than 40,000 have been killed, which by conservative estimates could rise to 186,000.[7] An already vulnerable infrastructure – electricity, water, sewage, and sanitation – has either been severely damaged or destroyed.[8] Israeli authorities have meanwhile 'deliberately blocked' humanitarian aid to the civilian population of Gaza by turning away supply trucks, killing aid workers, and razing agricultural structures.[9] Journalists, ambulances, and universities have not been spared.[10] Famine, disease, and the resurgence of polio have taken hold.[11] Terms like 'scholasticide', 'medicide', 'domicide', 'urbicide', 'ecocide', and 'genocide' have

---

4   Quoted in Diakonia International Humanitarian Law Centre, '2023–2024 Hostilities and Escalating Violence in the oPt | Account of Events', January 12, 2024, diakonia.se.

5   Azmi Bishara, *Moral Matters in Hard Times* (Doha: Arab Center for Research and Policy Studies, 2023), 8.

6   '200 Days of Israel's War on Gaza', *al-Jazeera*, April 23, 2024; *Britannica*, 'Bombing of Dresden', last updated August 2, 2024, britannica.com; 'The Bombs, Their Meaning, and the Consequences Today', Universität Hamburg, July 24, 2023, uni-hamburg.de; *Britannica*, 'The Blitz', last updated August 31, 2024, britannica.com.

7   Rasha Khatib et al., 'Counting the Dead in Gaza: Difficult but Essential', *Lancet* 404, no. 10449 (2024): 237.

8   Scott Neuman et al., 'In Gaza, Months of War Have Left Palestinians with Barely the Necessities to Survive', NPR, June 1, 2024, npr.org.

9   Brett Murphy, 'Israel Deliberately Blocked Humanitarian Aid to Gaza, Two Government Bodies Concluded. Antony Blinken Rejected Them', *ProPublica*, September 24, 2024, propublica.org.

10   'Gaza: UN Experts Decry Bombing of Hospitals and Schools as Crimes against Humanity, Call for Prevention of Genocide', Office of the United Nations High Commissioner for Human Rights, October 19, 2023, ohchr.org.

11   'Gaza: Israeli Aid Obstruction Inflaming Polio Outbreak', Human Rights Watch, August 26, 2024, hrw.org.

been invoked as descriptive, analytical, or legal categories to capture the extent of Gaza's suffering.[12] The devastation has been accompanied by an Israeli double speech. On the one hand, 'we're doing everything we can to get civilians out of harm's way'; on the other, 'there are no innocent civilians' in Gaza.[13]

This book is not about October 7, nor is it about its aftermath. It is about its prelude, its broader historical context. It is a history of how a once-marginal phenomenon became one of the main currents in Palestinian politics and resistance. It is the account of how a group of Palestinians went from rejecting the feasibility of violence to organizing suicide bombings against cinemas, night clubs, and coffee shops. It is also the tale of adolescent love in the alleyways of Khan Younis and the execution of collaborators in the markets of Gaza City. Of political pragmatism and of ideological intransigence. Of those who rose to prominence and of those who fell into obscurity. It analyses the catalysts for a day when everything changed.

It is also a story about suffering. It is the account of the children who were born refugees and who grew up in the slums of Gaza. About the poverty, humiliation, and pain inflicted upon them. About their loss of loved ones – fathers, mothers, brothers, sisters, daughters, sons – and how they inflicted that agony upon others. It narrates how their experiences shaped them, hardened them, and made them organize new insurgent movements when those who came before grew tired after decades of struggle in exile, who yielded and entered negotiations with Israel. Their choices took them to the depth of Israeli prisons, to the no-man's-land of southern Lebanon, to Florida and Malta, and to a Gazan tunnel network spanning more than 500 kilometres below the houses of Gaza.

Going back eighty years may seem excessive. Yet, how we understand armed movements and their preferred tactics depends on the analytical

12   'UN Experts Warn International Order on a Knife's Edge, Urge States to Comply with ICJ Advisory Opinion', Office of the United Nations High Commissioner for Human Rights, September 18, 2024, ohchr.org; Louis Milan et al., '"Reasonable Grounds" to Believe Israel Is Committing Genocide in Gaza, UN Expert Says', CNN, March 27, 2024, cnn.com.

13   Quoted in Avner Gvaryahu, 'The Myth of Israel's "Moral Army"', Foreign Affairs, March 4, 2024, foreignaffairs.com; David Ingram, 'Israeli Government Sparks Outcry with X Videos Saying "There Are No Innocent Civilians" in Gaza', NBC News, June 14, 2024, nbcnews.com.

starting points of our inquiry. 'Conflict does not play out on a blank slate', Staniland writes, 'that actors can make and remake as they wish.' To limit our focus to particular eruptions of violence, such as that of October 7, is to miss deeper structural patterns that limit and constrain the actors involved as 'politics do not start – or stop – when the first bullet is fired'.[14] Armed movements, including Palestinian Islamist currents, do not operate in a void. Instead, they reflect broader societal patterns and developments. While the emergence of Palestinian Islamic Jihad (PIJ) in the early 1980s reflected the loss of faith in the Palestine Liberation Organization (PLO) in general and the de-secularization of the Palestinian–Israeli conflict in particular, its irrelevance in the 1990s was an indication of Palestinian hopes of peace negotiations. While the Palestinian aspirations for a sustainable peace and viable two-state solution made Hamas vacillate in its approach to electoral participation in the 1990s, it turned to armed operations with renewed force when Oslo took its final breath in 2000.

Some of the reactions to October 7 reveal how a longer view on Palestinian Islamism remains relevant, as they appear to assume Islamist ideology was the key cause and determinant. Hamas is, it is claimed, nothing more than a spoiler espousing a genocidal ideology.[15] Incapable of rational cost–benefit calculations, the movement is blindly driven by religion and an anti-Semitic and anti-Western ideology. Its violence is merely a part of an Iranian strategy in the region.[16] In fact, #HamasIsISIS.[17] PIJ, on the other hand, has since the 1990s been portrayed as one of the most extreme and uncompromising Palestinian factions. PIJ is simply more militant, it rejects political participation and diplomatic dialogue, and it has adopted an unequivocal Palestinian identity.[18] We will see that, in fact, Palestinian Islamism is far more complex and dynamic.

---

14   Paul Staniland, *Networks of Rebellion: Explaining Insurgent Cohesion and Collapse* (London: Cornell University Press, 2014), 218–19.

15   Bruce Hoffman, 'Understanding Hamas's Genocidal Ideology', *Atlantic*, October 10, 2023, theatlantic.com.

16   American Jewish Committee, 'What Hamas Is Hiding', *Global Voice*, October 7, 2023, ajc.org; '10 Things to Know about Hamas', Foundation for Defense of Democracies, October 16, 2023, fdd.org.

17   Monica Marks, 'What the World Gets Wrong about Hamas', *Time*, October 30, 2023, time.com.

18   Jason Burke, 'What Is Palestinian Islamic Jihad and What Is Its Relationship with Hamas?', *Guardian*, October 18, 2023; Shaul Mishal and Avraham Sela,

The vast majority of research has focused on Hamas, its history, its violence, its social services, its political thought and practice, and its governance project in Gaza.[19] PIJ has received less attention, although there is a growing literature on the group.[20] There exists no history of Palestinian Islamism that integrates and synthesizes this knowledge production into a coherent understanding. The research on Hamas, PIJ, and Hizb al-Tahrir remains concentrated for the most part in knowledge silos. These silos necessarily limit our understanding of how Palestinian Islamism has developed through the interplay and competition of its components, why some of its representatives succeeded and why some failed, and why some engaged in violence while others prioritized proselytizing. In short, we fail to grasp how Palestinian Islamism is a far more heterogeneous phenomenon than commonly assumed.

This book attempts to address this problem by exploring three main lines of inquiry. The first is empirical. What are the main Palestinian Islamist currents and how do they differ from, and relate to, each other? What are their views on the state, elections, democracy, and violence? And

*The Palestinian Hamas: Vision, Violence, and Coexistence* (New York: Columbia University Press, 2006), 32.

19    See, for example, Khaled Hroub, *Hamas: Political Thought and Practice* (Washington, DC: Institute for Palestine Studies, 2000); Azzam Tamimi, *Hamas: Unwritten Chapters* (London: Hurst, 2009); Mishal and Sela, *The Palestinian Hamas*; Beverley Milton-Edwards and Stephen Farrell, *Hamas: The Islamic Resistance Movement* (Cambridge: Polity Press, 2010); Sara Roy, *Hamas and Civil Society in Gaza: Engaging the Islamic Social Sector* (Princeton, NJ: Princeton University Press, 2011); Jeroen Gunning, *Hamas in Politics: Democracy, Religion, Violence* (London: Hurst, 2009); Björn Brenner, *Gaza under Hamas: From Islamic Democracy to Islamist Governance* (London: I. B. Taurus, 2017); Erik Skare, 'Texts or Praxes: How Do We Best Understand Hamas and Palestinian Islamic Jihad after October 7?', *CTC Sentinel* 16, no. 10 (2023): 34–9.

20    See Meir Hatina, *Islam and Salvation in Palestine* (Tel Aviv: Moshe Dayan Center for Middle Eastern and Africa Studies, 2001); Wissam Alhaj, Nicolas Dot-Pouillard, and Eugénie Rebillard, *De la théologie à la libération? Histoire du jihad islalmique palestinien* (Paris: La Découverte, 2014); Erik Skare, *A History of Palestinian Islamic Jihad: Faith, Awareness, and Revolution in the Middle East* (Cambridge: Cambridge University Press, 2021); Erik Skare, *Palestinian Islamic Jihad: Islamist Writings on Resistance and Religion* (London: I. B. Taurus, 2021); Antonella Acinapura, 'A Framing-Sensitive Approach to Militant Groups' Tactics: The Islamic Jihad Movement in Palestine and the Radicalisation of Violence during the Second Intifada', *Critical Studies on Terrorism* 16, no. 1 (January 2, 2023): 123–45.

what is their solution? The second line of inquiry is explanatory. How did Palestinian Islamism emerge in the Occupied Palestinian Territories and how did it develop? How does competition between movement wings and factions, coupled with external factors, determine violence and policy choices? And how has Hamas's evolution from a clandestine armed group to a governing authority influenced Palestinian Islamism overall? The last is analytical. Why did Palestinian Islamism bifurcate between the West Bank and Gaza? Why do we have PIJ when we have Hamas? Why have some Palestinian Islamist movements succeeded while others have failed? Last but not least, why did October 7 happen?

The main argument of this book is that Palestinian Islamism has been continuously shaped and determined by the fierce discussions and competition between moderates and hardliners about the way forward. These discussions have largely been settled by external drivers – intra-Palestinian competition, Israeli violence and repression, or shifts in the regional power balance. Heightened Israeli repression, for example, has traditionally strengthened Hamas hardliners' bid to escalate in kind, while protracted warfare and civilian suffering have helped moderates convince hardliners that a ceasefire is necessary. PIJ has played its own role in shaping this dynamic as an accelerating driver – and as a hardliner in its own right. It was the spectacular violence of PIJ in the mid-1980s that forced Hamas into existence, and its uncompromising stance – unencumbered by the inconvenient responsibilities of governance – was a thorn in Hamas's side as the latter struggled to maintain its ethos as a resistance movement when ruling Gaza in the 2010s.

The division between hardliner and moderate is neither dichotomous nor is it inflexible. It is constantly in flux and is marked by both 'conflict and cooperation, of rivalry and collaboration, of antagonism and limited partnership'.[21] The back-and-forth nature in the strength and weakness of moderates versus hardliners has traditionally given this dynamic a cyclical nature – each cycle lasting between five and ten years. Such cycles signify a decisive change in *emphasis* maintaining a duality between wings rather than representing singular shifts. This dynamic is evident from the violence imposed by the hardliners from 1989 to 1994, followed by a reversion to social work from 1995 to 2000, and from the terror balance

---

21   Shaul Mishal, 'The Pragmatic Dimension of the Palestinian Hamas: A Network Perspective', *Armed Forces and Society* 29, no. 4 (July 1, 2003): 573.

intended to out-suffer Israelis in the Second Intifada to Hamas's dogged attempt to maintain calm with Israel from 2007 to 2017. October 7 was, *in extenso*, not inevitable. The attack happened because moderates in Hamas had few, if any, victories to show for since 2006. They were consequently sidelined by those in the movement advocating the use of extreme force to break the Palestinian impasse.

The primary goal of this book is to compile and synthesize existing research to present a comprehensive analysis of the conditions and drivers spawning and shaping contemporary Palestinian Islamism. As such, I integrate scattered pieces of knowledge with my own perspective and interpretation of events as they unfolded. The bibliography demonstrates how this work stands on the shoulders of those who came before. Still, as this study began to take shape, certain empirical gaps in the literature were filled, and I gradually began to incorporate my own data from ongoing and parallel research projects between pages, paragraphs, and sentences to provide a more comprehensive, albeit brief, account of the phenomenon we today refer to as Palestinian Islamism. Parts of earlier research have similarly found their way into this manuscript. Bits and pieces of my *A History of Palestinian Islamic Jihad*, as well as a segment from my article 'Controlling the State in the Political Theory of Hamas and Palestinian Islamic Jihad', are scattered, in modified form, in the latter half of this book.[22]

An important source of information was the Palestinian Islamists' own writings. Though we often refer to their violence, Palestinian Islamist movements have a significant literary production on religion, political theory, morals and ethics, Palestinian society, colonial history, and their conflict against the Israeli occupation. The works of Fathi al-Shiqaqi, Ramadan Shallah, Ibrahim al-Maqadma, Jamal Mansur, and Taqi al-Din al-Nabhani, to mention just a few, consist of several thousands of pages of text. Finding and collecting these sources took years of archival research, online searches, and assistance from Palestinian colleagues.

Another crucial historical source was Palestinian Islamist memoirs and biographies. The historical works of senior PIJ members Yusuf Arif al-Hajj Muhammad and Anwar Abu Taha were particularly useful. So

---

22    Skare, *A History of Palestinian Islamic Jihad*; Erik Skare, 'Controlling the State in the Political Theory of Hamas and Palestinian Islamic Jihad', *Religions* 12, no. 11 (November 16, 2021): 1010.

were the autobiographies of al-Qassam commander Husam Badran and PIJ commander Thabit Mardawi, senior Hamas members Abd al-Aziz al-Rantisi and Muhammad Abu Tayr. Even Yahya Sinwar has published an autobiographical novel in which he describes life in Gaza as a child and his later involvement in the Muslim Brotherhood, in Majd, and in prison. 'The imagination in this work lies only in transforming [the narration of events] to fulfill the form of a novel and its conditions,' Sinwar writes in the preface. 'Everything else is real. I lived through it, and I heard [the rest] from those who experienced it along with their families and neighbors.'[23] Although this ambiguous form of the text precludes a detailed account of Sinwar's life and upbringing, I have nevertheless treated it as a primary source because it is written by someone inside of Hamas and its security apparatus and because it offers a description of life in Gaza from the 1960s to the 1980s.

I also collected the socio-economic data and geographical distribution of 4,037 Islamist militants killed between 1985 and 2022, based on martyr biographies published by the Qassam Brigades of Hamas and the Quds Brigades of PIJ. To my knowledge, this includes every militant killed in the ranks of Hamas and PIJ as reported by the movements themselves. All martyr biographies were collected online using open-source material and all information used in the dataset is publicly available. I employed two websites to collect data on PIJ. The first was the Mujhat al-Quds Foundation, a PIJ institution for the interests of 'the families of the martyrs and prisoners of all Palestine'.[24] The second was the martyr biographies published on the official website of PIJ's al-Quds Brigades (saraya.ps). For Hamas militants, all information was collected from the official website of the Qassam Brigades (al-qassam.ps). The appendix provides a discussion of the information gaps and biases in the dataset, in addition to the availability of sources and citation style.

Difficult choices were made to ensure that this book remained a *brief* history. It is the prerogative of the reader to disagree with these decisions. I have seldom agreed with myself when prioritizing events, analytical frameworks, or aspects of Islamist political behaviour. The social services and welfare infrastructure of Hamas, the Islamic movement in Israel, or the historical roles and legacies of Izz al-Din al-Qassam and Abdallah

---

23  Yahya Sinwar, *al-Shawk wa-l-qaranful* (n.p., 2004), 2.
24  Muhjat al-Quds, 'Man Nahnu?', *Muhjar al-Quds*, April 27, 2014.

Azzam could have been included – or received greater attention – in a different study.[25] I hope the reader will appreciate the need to prioritize although remaining critical.

When tracing the events and historical development of Palestinian Islamism, the premise of this study – the epistemic framework – is that we *can* confidently say something about the past. While narratives are open to interpretation, they are not open to any interpretation. Some are necessarily more persuasive than others,[26] and 'while perfect certainty is never achievable, there are gradations of plausibility – some kinds of evidence are better than others, some kinds of interpretations are easier to support'.[27] Although there are contradictory reports about the disputes among Palestinian Islamists in the 1980s, we may confidently suggest that it did not centre on the right of return for the Palestinian refugees. When Iran cut funding to PIJ in 2015, we may suggest with equal confidence that the discord was not about opposition to Israel.

While historians may differ in their interpretations of the past and their selection of sources, one may nevertheless make credible claims about the past as it *was* in order to obtain a greater understanding of the present as it *is*. This is not to assert perfect certainty, but rather that a reasonable accuracy of historical analysis is achievable. In this sense, as Eric Hobsbawm points out, to study history is to remove the blindfolds of self-justifying myths of the present – to challenge those notions and structures we regard as self-evident.[28] If it were impossible to produce a true account of the past, or at least an accurate one, then demystification of self-evident structures of the present would be equally fruitless. As Ellen Meiksins Wood sardonically commented on the postmodern turn:

25   For an analysis of Hamas's social services, see Roy, *Hamas and Civil Society in Gaza*; for the Islamic movement in Israel, see Tilde Rosmer, *The Islamic Movement in Israel* (Austin: University of Texas Press, 2022); for an analytical account of Izz al-Din al-Qassam, see Mark Sanagan, *Lightning through the Clouds: Izz al-Din al-Qassam and the Making of the Modern Middle East* (Austin: University of Texas Press, 2020); for the authoritative work on Abdallah Azzam, see Thomas Hegghammer, *The Caravan: Abdallah Azzam and the Rise of Global Jihad* (Cambridge: Cambridge University Press, 2020).

26   Richard J. Evans, *In Defense of History* (New York: W. W. Norton, 1997), 189.

27   Martha Howell and Walter Prevenier, *From Reliable Sources: An Introduction to Historical Methods* (Ithaca, NY: Cornell University Press, 2001), 79.

28   Eric Hobsbawm, *On History* (New York: New Press, 1997), 36.

'There may never be a revolutionary reconstruction of society, but there can always be a ruthless deconstruction of texts.'[29]

While this may seem to favour normative presuppositions in historical research, 'We historians operate in the grey zone where the investigation of what is – even the choice of what is – is constantly affected by who we are and what we want to happen or not to happen: this is a fact of our professional existence.'[30] It is, in a sense, this presupposition Marc Bloch refers to when he wrote that there must be a 'guiding spirit' to give the research of the historian a sense of direction.[31] What matters then is not to pretend presuppositions do not exist in historical research (or any other field for that matter), but, rather, to present accurately and honestly what sources were employed, how they were read, and how analyses were produced by them. I have attempted to do so to the best of my abilities.

29    Ellen Meiksins Wood, *Democracy against Capitalism: Renewing Historical Materialism* (New York: Verso, 2016), 10.

30    Hobsbawm, *On History*, 24.

31    Marc Bloch, *The Historian's Craft* (Manchester: Manchester University Press, 1992), 54.

# 1

## The Solution Is Islam

Today, we may take for granted that Palestinian Islamist groups participate in the armed struggle. Hamas, the Islamic Resistance Movement, is perhaps the foremost representative of this trend. It was not always so, and Palestinian Islamists were initially reluctant to take up arms against the occupation. Change, they argued, came through the salvation of the individual who embraced the Islamic call and purified his heart; corruption and vice had to be cleansed from society before the Palestinians could liberate themselves. Why did the Palestinian Muslim Brotherhood prioritize social work and proselytizing?

This chapter examines the establishment and evolution of the Palestinian Muslim Brotherhood. It examines how a fragmented underground network of Islamists in the 1950s turned into one of the most prominent Palestinian political forces thirty years later. Despite their refusal to engage in armed struggle against the Israelis, we will see that the Palestinian Muslim Brothers were far from being pacifists. Physical assaults, intimidation campaigns, firebombs, and acid attacks were all part of their repertoire against political competitors. Their main adversary was not the Israeli occupier, however, but the Palestinian Marxists. The Palestinians were, as such, embroiled in their own culture war decades before the West.

## Genesis

> European 'civilization' . . . has developed in us a morbid mentality, a morbid taste and has made of us a morbid community that looks upon its own morbidity and decay as a thing of virtue and a sign of progress. Once corrupt, the greatest corruption is to regard one's corruption as good and desirable. – Hassan al-Banna[1]

Palestinian Islamism, as we recognize it today, did not appear in Palestine. Instead, its foundational roots grew out from Ismailia, a small northeastern Egyptian town founded in 1863 during the construction of the Suez Canal. There, on the west bank of the canal, the nucleus of the Muslim Brotherhood was founded in 1928 by Hassan al-Banna, a twenty-two-year-old preacher and schoolteacher. Al-Banna's following consisted of no more than six dedicated individuals at the time. From the 1930s, however, the Brotherhood would develop into 'the mother organization of all modern Islamist movements'.[2]

The Muslim Brotherhood was typical of its time as far as it was a grievance-based movement, and it mirrored a wave of Islamic thinkers who, from the late nineteenth century, began articulating 'a religiously based critique of the contemporary Muslim world'.[3] Al-Banna, like his contemporaries, vehemently opposed the continued presence of British soldiers and the persistent foreign intervention in Egyptian political affairs, although Egypt's 1922 declaration of independence formally abolished the protectorate.[4] His assignment to teach Arabic in Ismailia from

---

1   Quoted in Richard P. Mitchell, *The Society of the Muslim Brothers* (Oxford: Oxford University Press, 1969), 224.

2   Brynjar Lia, *The Society of the Muslim Brothers in Egypt: The Rise of an Islamic Mass Movement* (Reading: Ithaca Press, 1998), 1.

3   Steven Brooke and Neil Ketchley, 'Social and Institutional Origins of Political Islam', *American Political Science Review* 112, no. 2 (May 2018): 379.

4   Though Egypt gained trappings of formal independence, the British retained rights to protect their interests, greatly restricting sovereignty. M. W.

1927 only strengthened his sense of injustice. Ismailia's landscape was shaped not merely by British military camps but also by the Suez Canal Company, with complete foreign control of public utilities and the opulent homes of foreigners overlooking the miserable dwellings of their workers. 'Even the street signs . . . were written in "the language of the economic occupation".'[5] From the early and mid-1930s, the Muslim Brotherhood was firmly anticolonial, and it became increasingly vocal in its opposition.[6]

The Muslim Brotherhood was also a revivalist movement. The impasse of the Islamic world, its backwardness and regression, was primarily caused and driven by its spiritual decline. With blind adaptation of European systems and laws, with the spread of corrupting popular culture undermining traditional values, and with the spread of gender-mixing, alcohol, gambling, and prostitution, colonial control was augmented by a perceived spiritual enslavement betraying the country's Islamic identity and heritage.[7] 'Explaining to their fellow Muslims the utter humiliation and disgrace the Islamic world had been forced to endure,' Lia narrates, 'they exhorted them to wake up and divest themselves from their apathy and inaction.'[8] Only by returning to a truly Islamic way of life could they regain past glory with true prosperity and development. If Western colonialism was the problem, then Islam was the solution.

Providing a religious framework to understand the malaise, al-Banna and his acolytes promoted a view of Islam as both 'religion and state'. Religion was not just a matter of private belief or a prayer ritual, but a complete system of life governing the individual and his relationship with the outside world, social values, and, equally important, law and politics.[9] The Brotherhood did not present an elaborate political programme or a blueprint for the future organization of society as much as they focused on the centrality of Islam. 'Those who think that these teachings are

---

Daly, 'The British Occupation, 1882–1922', in M. W. Daly, ed., *The Cambridge History of Egypt*, vol. 2, *Modern Egypt* (Cambridge: Cambridge University Press, 1998), 250.

5    Mitchell, *The Society of the Muslim Brothers*, 7.

6    There are disagreements about the early Brotherhood's anticolonial stance, as it received Suez Canal Company funding in 1931. See Lia, *Society of the Muslim Brothers in Egypt*, 41.

7    Wickham, *The Muslim Brotherhood*, 22.

8    Lia, *Society of the Muslim Brothers in Egypt*, 83.

9    Wickham, *The Muslim Brotherhood*, 23.

concerned only with the spiritual or ritualistic aspects are mistaken in this belief,' al-Banna wrote in 1938, 'because Islam is a faith and a ritual, a nation and a nationality, a religion and a state, spirit and deed, holy text and sword . . . the Glorious Qur'an . . . considers [these things] to be the core of Islam and its essence.'[10] This Islam, he proclaimed, was a religion that was alive, not dead; flexible, not ossified; moving, not stagnant; and with a focus on renewal, instead of an unquestioning acceptance of conventions. Religion had to be continuously adapted to the current age and conditions instead of blindly emulating tradition.

A fundamental aspect of al-Banna's practice was thus the moral upbringing of Brotherhood members. The early training of the Brothers revolved around reciting and memorizing the Quran, discussing and commenting on religious texts, in addition to learning Islamic history and the life and virtues of Prophet Muhammad. Conveying his teaching in a simplified and pedagogical manner, with a focus on the practical and spiritual aspects of the faith, al-Banna aimed to raise a new generation of Muslims who understood their religion correctly.[11] This committed class of followers would then set forth, traversing the countryside, frequenting coffee shops and mosques and propagating their calls in the homes, clubs, and workplaces of their fellow Egyptians. Within a decade, the Muslim Brotherhood had established hundreds of branches across Egypt. Brothers paraded publicly, raised funds, and set up social services for the needy, while continuously spreading al-Banna's revivalist message.[12] By 1949, their membership ranged between 300,000 and 600,000 followers, which, if correct, means that 3 per cent of Egypt's total population were Muslim Brothers.[13]

The influence of the Muslim Brotherhood also began expanding beyond Egypt's borders. By 1937, the movement had established several branches in Sudan, Saudi Arabia, Syria, Lebanon, Morocco, Bahrain, Syria, Djibouti, and, not least, in Palestine. In fact, al-Banna had sent telegrams to the Grand Mufti of Jerusalem, Hajj Amin al-Husseini, in 1935, and his brother, Abdel Rahman, was warmly received by al-Husseini

---

10    Quoted in Mitchell, *The Society of the Muslim Brothers*, 232–33.

11    Lia, *Society of the Muslim Brothers in Egypt*, 37.

12    Neil Ketchley, Steven Brooke, and Brynjar Lia, 'Who Supported the Early Muslim Brotherhood?', *Politics and Religion* 15, no. 2 (June 2022): 388–416.

13    Brooke and Ketchley, 'Social and Institutional Origins of Political Islam', 380.

in Jerusalem that same year. The Brotherhood's pro-Palestinian fervour was not so much driven by its religious prominence as by the movement's anticolonial credentials. Naturally, Palestine was the focal point of this effort, although Libya, Syria, and Morocco also received attention.[14]

The Muslim Brotherhood's concern for the Palestinian cause only strengthened when the Great Palestine Revolt erupted in 1936. Recognized as the first sustained Palestinian insurrection, the Revolt was a response to the Zionist movement's pronounced aspirations and efforts to establish a Jewish State in Mandate Palestine. Attempting to gain control over a country that already had a much larger and antagonistic indigenous population, the Jewish minority's principal strategy to strengthen the Yishuv was through further immigration, which would gradually 'overwhelm the native majority' demographically.[15] Between 1922 and 1940, the Jewish population thus increased from 83,790 to 467,000, nearly one-third of the total population. Jewish landholdings similarly rose from 148,500 acres to 383,500 in the same period (roughly one-seventh), and Tel Aviv developed into an all-Jewish city of 150,000 inhabitants.[16] Initially commencing as a series of violent acts carried out by another religious revivalist, Izz al-Din al-Qassam, and his followers from 1935, the insurgency developed into a guerrilla war against British convoys and installations following the publication of the Peel Report on July 7, 1937.[17]

Mobilizing both Egyptian Muslim and Coptic public opinion for the Palestinian cause, al-Banna praised the heroic efforts of their Muslim and Christian Palestinian brethren who united to defend the holy places of Islam. The Palestinians were now, he proclaimed, playing their part in the anti-imperial struggle of the Islamic and Arab homeland.[18] Convening a conference in March 1936, the Egyptian Brothers collected donations

---

14    Israel Gershoni, 'The Muslim Brothers and the Arab Revolt in Palestine, 1936–39', *Middle Eastern Studies* 22, no. 3 (1986): 369; Lia, *Society of the Muslim Brothers in Egypt*, 155–6.

15    Benny Morris, 'Revisiting the Palestinian Exodus of 1948', in Eugene L. Rogan and Avi Shlaim, eds, *The War for Palestine: Rewriting the History of 1948*, 2nd ed. (Cambridge: Cambridge University Press, 2007), 39.

16    *Britannica*, 'The Arab Revolt', last updated August 20, 2024, britannica.com.

17    Ilan Pappé, *A History of Modern Palestine* (Cambridge: Cambridge University Press, 2004), 106.

18    Gershoni, 'The Muslim Brothers', 371.

for the Palestinian General Strike and actively supplied moral and material aid to Palestinians through the Palestine Piaster campaign. Issuing pamphlets and declarations, the Brotherhood denounced the British and called for a boycott of Jewish goods and journals in Egypt. They also sent telegrams to the High Commissioner in Palestine and the British foreign minister, as well as the Secretariat of the League of Nations to protest British policies in Mandate Palestine. Some Brothers were reportedly also successful crossing the border and joining Palestinian guerrilla fighters.[19]

There are differing accounts concerning when the Muslim Brotherhood was formally established in Mandate Palestine, and information is sparse. Some assert that the first official Palestinian branches were inaugurated in Gaza and in Jerusalem after the Second World War in 1946.[20] Others refer to documents and correspondence that show Brotherhood activity in Jerusalem, Jaffa, Lydda, and Ramla well before 1946. Lia, for example, refers to a 1937 Brotherhood survey revealing the existence of several Brotherhood branches within Mandate Palestine indicating a semi-formal organizational footprint in the 1930s.[21]

There are also disagreements about the type of Brotherhood activities in this period. Hroub maintains that the heightened 'political awareness and nationalistic spirit' of the Palestinian Muslim Brotherhood resulted in their political activities taking precedence over proselytizing and social services. Mishal and Sela, however, argue that the Palestinian Brothers generally focused on 'social and cultural activities and, unlike their colleagues in Egypt, refrained from active involvement in politics or violence.'[22] According to Ismail Abdel Aziz al-Khalidi, one of the first founders of the Muslim Brotherhood in the Gaza Strip, their activities were primarily social and cultural in this period, and they organized charitable services, scouting activities, and sporting events.[23]

---

19    Khaled Hroub, *Hamas: Political Thought and Practice* (Washington, DC: Institute for Palestine Studies, 2000), 12–13.

20    Ibid., 15; Jean-Pierre Filiu, 'The Origins of Hamas: Militant Legacy or Israeli Tool?', *Journal of Palestine Studies* 41, no. 3 (June 2012): 56; Mohammed K. Shadid, 'The Muslim Brotherhood Movement in the West Bank and Gaza', *Third World Quarterly* 10, no. 2 (April 1988): 659.

21    See Hroub, *Hamas*, 15; Lia, *Society of the Muslim Brothers in Egypt*, 155.

22    Hroub, *Hamas*, 17; Shaul Mishal and Avraham Sela, *The Palestinian Hamas: Vision, Violence, and Coexistence* (New York: Columbia University Press, 2006), 16.

23    Ismail Abdel Aziz Khalidi, '60 'aman fi jama'at al-Ikhwan al-Muslimin', 2010.

It is at any rate evident that the mid-1940s marked a fertile period for the Palestinian Brotherhood branches. Partly driven by an appreciation for the early support and solidarity of the Egyptian Brotherhood, the movement spread rapidly throughout Mandate Palestine. Although the Brotherhood attracted ordinary Palestinians, the movement had from the onset an elitist and thus an urban appeal; the clergy from Palestinian notable families were the first to join the Jerusalem branch and al-Hajj Amin al-Husseini was named its local leader.[24] The Brotherhood branches in Gaza City were symptomatically located in the wealthiest neighbourhoods, and its leaders were judges, notables, and members of Gaza's chamber of commerce.[25] By 1947, there were between twenty-five and thirty-eight Palestinian branches with a membership ranging from 12,000 to 20,000.[26]

The Palestinian Muslim Brotherhood was not independent, however, and it acted as a de facto satellite for its Egyptian mother organization. Decision-making and policy planning, for example, were centrally located in Cairo, and the Egyptian leaders disseminated their dictates to branches outside Egypt without local consultation. The role of the external branches, whether in Palestine or elsewhere, was merely to spread the overall message of the Brotherhood, engage in social services, and to teach the values of the Quran to the local population.[27] Presumably, geographical proximity mattered for Egyptian–Palestinian ties, as well, and the Gazan branches were regularly visited by their Cairene Brothers from the central headquarters. Even al-Banna visited Gaza in 1948, as 'Palestine became [his] main theater of mobilization.'[28]

By 1939, the Great Palestine Revolt had been decisively crushed through the violent coercion of the Palestinian population. Based on their experiences from the North Indian counter-insurgency, the British used collective punishment, civilian property destruction, aerial bombings of dissident Palestinian villages, assassinations, torture, and mass arrests to

---

24    Beverley Milton-Edwards and Stephen Farrell, *Hamas: The Islamic Resistance Movement* (Cambridge: Polity Press, 2010), 33; Ziad Abu-Amr, 'Hamas: A Historical and Political Background', *Journal of Palestine Studies* 22, no. 4 (1993): 6.

25    Milton-Edwards and Farrell, *Hamas*, 32; Filiu, 'The Origins of Hamas', 57.

26    Abu-Amr, 'Hamas', 7.

27    Beverley Milton-Edwards, *Islamic Politics in Palestine* (London: I. B. Tauris, 1999), 34.

28    Filiu, 'The Origins of Hamas', 57.

put down any remaining resistance.[29] In terms of military losses, over 10 per cent of the male Palestinian population was killed, wounded, imprisoned, or exiled by the end of the revolt. Economically, the Palestinians suffered from several self-inflicted wounds. While the strikes inadvertently strengthened the Jewish economy, they dealt a blow to Palestinian citrus exports, quarrying, transportation, and industry. Many Palestinian landowners were forced to sell land to Jewish settlers in an effort to mitigate their deteriorating economic conditions. Politically, the traditional Palestinian leadership shattered over tactics – divisions the British were eager to exploit to their own advantage. Indigenous leaders were exiled by the colonial power, and some, like Hajj Amin al-Husseini, fled. Palestinian society effectively fragmented between urban factions, rural clans, and individual leaders.[30] Given how the power balance between the Palestinians and the Jewish settlers had shifted even further in favour of the Yishuv by 1939, Khalidi concludes that the uprising 'fell victim both to failures at the top . . . and to profound weaknesses at the base.'[31]

Because the grievances of the Palestinian indigenous population and the territorial aspirations of the Zionist movement were irreconcilable, the British counter-insurgency did little more than set the stage for new waves of unrest. While the Palestinians were key organizers of the insurgency of the 1930s, a decade later it was primarily Jewish paramilitary groups like Irgun and Lehi that used violence to advance their campaign for statehood. Assassinating British officials, bombing police stations, mining railroads, and kidnapping soldiers – the violence had by 1947 become intolerable for the British, which by then had more soldiers stationed in Palestine than in the Indian subcontinent.[32] The Jewish insurgency was coupled by the emergence of Palestinian guerrillas, and the Muslim Brotherhood had by then also begun mobilizing for war at mosques, religious festivals, and meetings.[33] By July 1947, the

---

29   See, for example, Jacob Norris, 'Repression and Rebellion: Britain's Response to the Arab Revolt in Palestine of 1936–39', *Journal of Imperial and Commonwealth History* 36, no. 1 (March 2008): 25–45.

30   Rashid Khalidi, 'The Palestinians and 1948: The Underlying Causes of Failure', in Rogan and Shlaim, *The War for Palestine*, 26–7.

31   Ibid., 28.

32   Pappé, *A History of Modern Palestine*, 121.

33   Jean-Pierre Filiu, *Gaza: A History* (Oxford: Oxford University Press, 2014), 59.

British had had enough. Deciding to withdraw, they deferred the future of Palestine to the newly established United Nations. 'Partition was the fashionable diplomatic solution of the period for a host of seemingly intractable situations, including in Germany, India, and Korea,' Kimmerling and Migdal write. 'None of these other cases managed to forestall international war or repeated diplomatic crises, and Palestine was no exception.'[34]

Civil war erupted the day after the United Nations adopted the Palestine partition plan, Resolution 181, and there were momentary triumphs and setbacks for both sides in the first few months of fighting. Al-Banna dispatched three battalions to Palestine in April 1948, and guerrilla fighters affiliated with the Muslim Brotherhood quickly launched a campaign of attrition against Jewish settlements in Gaza and in the Negev. Still, they never played a significant role and they suffered heavy losses in the fighting.[35] The only Islamic group that had some impact was the popular militia of al-Husseini, the 'sacred jihad' group, which operated in Jerusalem, Ramla, Lydda, and Jaffa.[36] Besides, the Brotherhood volunteers in the 1948 Palestine War were primarily Egyptian, and the Palestinian branches were never employed by Cairo for intelligence gathering or logistical support due to the centralized nature of the movement. This left the Palestinian Brotherhood 'weak in the face of the upheaval wrought by the . . . Arab-Israeli war of 1948–1949', and the movement was effectively marginalized by the Arab armies.[37] From March until mid-May 1948, the superiority of the Jewish armed forces proved decisive as they conquered a series of Palestinian towns, cities, and villages. Unable to prevent the loss of a homeland, Palestinian society had in effect begun to disintegrate when the 1948 Palestine War, the second phase, erupted on May 15.[38]

---

34    Baruch Kimmerling and Joel S. Migdal, *The Palestinian People: A History* (Cambridge, MA: Harvard University Press, 2003), 146–7.

35    Wickham, *The Muslim Brotherhood*, 26; Filiu, *Gaza*, 59.

36    Mishal and Sela, *The Palestinian Hamas*, 16.

37    Milton-Edwards, *Islamic Politics in Palestine*, 34; Filiu, 'The Origins of Hamas', 57.

38    Rashid Khalidi, 'The Palestinians and 1948', 13.

## Turning inwards

Historical Palestine was unrecognizable when the war ended in January 1949. Out of the 850,000 Palestinians who once lived in the territories designated by the UN as a Jewish state, only 160,000 stayed on, or nearby, their land. Those who remained became a Palestinian minority in what today is known as Israel. The rest were expelled or fled under the threat of expulsion, and thousands were killed in massacres.[39] To ensure a state that was exclusively Jewish 'not only in its socio-political structure but also in ethnic composition', Jewish armed forces carried out what Ilan Pappé describes as a 'systematic eviction of the Palestinians', utilizing intimidation campaigns, military sieges, bombings, arson, and widespread violence to forcibly remove Palestinian inhabitants from their homes.[40] In some instances, Israeli bulldozers flattened Palestinian villages and turned them into new Jewish settlements or cultivated lands. Palestinian neighbourhoods in mixed towns were similarly destroyed, and new settlements received Hebrew versions of their original Arabic names. The Palestinian village of Lubya, for example, was now Lavi.[41]

The Palestinian social fabric disintegrated. Gaza's population tripled in less than a year – from 80,000 to nearly 300,000. The economy of Gaza City, once a prosperous market town, was devastated; it became almost entirely dependent on imports.[42] The first refugees were housed in mosques or in the homes of the original Gazan population. The wave was too great, however, and with only a few hundred tents available, they found cover under palm trees, on beaches, or in orchards. Flour provision was limited and far from sufficient. The result was a humanitarian crisis. Approximately ten children died daily from hunger, cold, or disease.[43]

Although the West Bank experienced an influx of refugees as well, the two regions exhibited clear structural differences. One difference was

---

39   Pappé, *A History of Modern Palestine*, 137.
40   Ilan Pappé, *The Ethnic Cleansing of Palestine* (London: Oneworld, 2006), 15; Ilan Pappé, *The Biggest Prison on Earth: A History of the Occupied Territories* (London: Oneworld, 2017), 9.
41   Pappé, *A History of Modern Palestine*, 138.
42   Filiu, Gaza, 69–70; Beryl Cheal, 'Refugees in the Gaza Strip, December 1948–May 1950', *Journal of Palestine Studies* 18, no. 1 (1988): 139.
43   Filiu, *Gaza*, 70–1.

geographical, as the West Bank was fifteen times larger than the Gaza Strip. Although the population of the West Bank was almost twice that of Gaza, the population density of the latter was nearly nine times higher. The geographical differences were compounded by demography; 70 per cent of Gaza's population were now refugees, compared to 20 per cent in the West Bank. While the latter were fully integrated and economically absorbed, the Strip's limited resources and small size prevented any similar integration. Class realignments were 'superimposed with traumatic effect' in the post-1948 period, and the Gazan refugees – coping with their displacement – clung to traditional forms of social organization and authority. This insular turn precluded the formation of new social and political structures in Gaza, which hindered 'the emergence of an effective indigenous leadership capable of articulating the refugees' needs and interfacing with Gaza's non-refugee population'.[44] Whereas the Gaza Strip experienced greater isolation and faced more restrictions on interactions with the rest of the Arab world, the West Bank was, in contrast, continuously exposed to foreigners.[45]

Equally important, Gaza fell under Egyptian administration and the West Bank was annexed by the Jordanian Hashemite Kingdom from 1949. The differences in Egyptian and Jordanian political aspirations meant that the two regions were exposed to two different types of repression. Politically, the Egyptians imposed a number of repressive measures on the Gazans with the prohibition of the formation of labour unions, political parties, or local organizations. Egyptian authorities similarly decreed the dissolution of the Muslim Brotherhood in December 1948 after discovering a number of arms caches they feared were intended for armed revolution.[46] The Jordanians were far more lenient towards the Palestinians in the West Bank. To avoid popular resistance and maintain political legitimacy, the Hashemite rulers initially allowed a West Bank opposition and administration.[47]

---

44   Sara Roy, 'Civil Society in the Gaza Strip: Obstacles to Social Reconstruction', in August Richard Norton, ed., *Civil Society in the Middle East*, vol. 2 (Leiden: Brill 1995), 227.

45   Ibid., 227.

46   Wickham, *The Muslim Brotherhood*, 26.

47   Avraham Sela, 'The West Bank under Jordan', in P. R. Kumaraswamy, ed., *The Palgrave Handbook of the Hashemite Kingdom of Jordan* (Singapore: Palgrave Macmillan, 2019), 287.

Culturally, the Egyptian authorities stressed the existence of a Palestinian national identity and the temporary nature of its control over Gaza. The Jordanians, in contrast, repressed any such notions, granted full citizenship to West Bank Palestinians, and attempted to consolidate a shared Hashemite identity.[48] Because the Gaza Strip never experienced the same institutional development as in the West Bank, the political culture there turned more confrontational and aggressive, which 'consistently used violence rather than debate to mediate conflict and political action'.[49] The geographical, demographic, political, and cultural differences between the Gaza Strip and the West Bank led to the development of two distinct forms of Palestinian Islamism over the next four decades. Because their political fates were intrinsically connected to their different geographical realities, Palestinian Islamism bifurcated.

The Muslim Brotherhood in the West Bank, for example, merged with the Jordanian Brothers, and effectively became the Muslim Brotherhood in Jordan. Although there was some de facto autonomy in coordinating activities on the ground, its sixteen West Bank branches – such as those in Jerusalem, Hebron, Nablus, and Jenin – operated without any sense of organizational independence under the Amman headquarters. Senior positions remained firmly in the hands of Jordanian Brothers, and senior West Bank members had to travel to Amman to consult the central leadership if they wished to implement new strategies or revise policies in their local communities.[50]

The integration into the Jordanian structure thus shaped the political strategies and opportunities of the West Bank Brothers. The Jordanian Brotherhood enjoyed cordial relations with the Hashemite authorities as a force of 'loyal opposition', and it pursued its activities openly and legally. Although there were periods of friction regarding Jordan's close ties with the United States or its liberal stance on Islamic law, a symbiotic relationship nevertheless developed between the two. The Muslim Brotherhood eagerly participated in parliamentary elections, for example, also when the elections were boycotted by the Palestinian nationalists in 1962.[51] The lenient approach was partly premised by the non-political approach of the West Bank Brothers; the Jordanian Muslim Brotherhood

---

48   Ibid., 279, 283.
49   Roy, 'Civil Society in the Gaza Strip', 226.
50   Milton-Edwards, *Islamic Politics in Palestine*, 60.
51   Shadid, 'The Muslim Brotherhood Movement', 661–2.

acted primarily as a religious and educational organization and focused on spreading Islamic literature, organizing social activities, and prose-lytizing.[52] The Brothers were also seen by the authorities as a viable tool against competing political currents such as the communists, Baathists, and Nasserists, and the Brotherhood organized support for King Hussein against 'those whom it termed suppressive elements', while praising his defence of Islam.[53]

In some aspects, Milton-Edwards contends, the Muslim Brotherhood in the West Bank aligned more closely with Hassan al-Banna's principles than its more intransigent counterpart in Gaza. Al-Banna was a teacher and a preacher, and his revivalist message was based on the education of the masses. Emancipation could only be achieved through the liberation of the Muslim mind. Based on their aspirations for the Islamic renewal of Palestinian society, the main activities of the West Bank branches were accordingly teaching and education. 'The issue of national liberation through the revolutionary Arab nationalist vanguard did not concern [them]. There was no call for arms, just a call on Muslims to return to the mosque and pray.'[54] If anything, the West Bank brothers were *less* militant than al-Banna who, after all, visited Gaza in 1948 to mobilize for armed action.

Unlike the West Bank and Amman, the Muslim Brotherhood in Gaza did not enjoy organic ties to Cairo. Communication between the two effectively ceased when the Brotherhood was banned in December 1948.[55] Although the ban affected the manoeuvrability of the Gazan Brothers, they largely circumvented repression for the next six years by reopening their branch as the Tawhid Association in 1950 under the leadership of Zafer al-Shawa. Another branch headed by Omar Sawan opened shortly thereafter under the traditional Brotherhood moniker, and the two worked in parallel with 'approximately the same goal'.[56] The isolation of Gaza afforded the Brothers there with a greater degree of

---

52   Ziad Abu-Amr, *Islamic Fundamentalism in the West Bank and Gaza* (Bloomington: Indiana University Press, 1994), 4; Hroub, *Hamas*, 19–20.

53   Azzam Tamimi, *Hamas: Unwritten Chapters* (London: Hurst, 2009), 20; Shadid, 'The Muslim Brotherhood Movement', 661.

54   Milton-Edwards, *Islamic Politics in Palestine*, 61.

55   Sara Roy, *Hamas and Civil Society in Gaza: Engaging the Islamist Social Sector* (Princeton, NJ: Princeton University Press, 2011), 21.

56   Al-Aziz Khalidi, '60 'aman fi jama'at al-Ikhwan al-Muslimin'.

independence, which allowed the movement to engage in political work, social initiatives, and the provision of medical and educational services to displaced Palestinians.

The Gazan counterpart made 'strong inroads in the Gaza Strip' the first years following the 1948 Palestine War, and, with few viable competitors, the movement soon developed into one of the main political players in the Strip. The growth of the Brotherhood was additionally driven by the long-time conservatism of the Strip and the support it had garnered from its military involvement against the British.[57] The distinct features of the Brotherhood in the West Bank and Gaza – one in loyal opposition and the other unable to strike an alliance with centralized power – remained once the two regions were 'united' by the Israeli occupation in 1967, and the two largely failed to behave as a 'Palestinian-Islamic movement within an explicit area of Palestinian politics' over the following two decades.[58]

Although the Gazan Brothers began solidifying their presence, the Free Officers Coup on January 26, 1952, soon challenged their influence. The Muslim Brotherhood supported the coup initially – buoyed by their close ties with several Egyptian officers and hopeful that the new regime would align with their own aspirations for Egypt. The relationship soon soured, however, as the Brotherhood was the only realistic opposition force to the newly established Revolutionary Command Council (RCC) and a rival for political power. The two could not coexist. The Free Officers proved to be a formidable challenge for the movement. Outlawing the Brotherhood in 1954 after a Muslim Brother's failed assassination attempt on Egyptian president Gamal Abdel Nasser, the RCC executed six of its leaders and arrested thousands of its members.[59]

The crackdown on the Muslim Brotherhood necessarily had an impact on Gaza. As in 1949, Egyptian authorities dissolved the Gazan Brotherhood, confiscated its assets, and banned its publications, though it did not arrest its members. The legal front of the Gazan Muslim Brotherhood, al-Shawa's Tawhid Association, was banned in 1958.[60] In an attempt to avoid

---

57    Hroub, *Hamas*, 23.

58    Roy, *Hamas and Civil Society in Gaza*, 21.

59    For the authoritative account on the Muslim Brotherhood and state repression in Egypt, see Abou El Zalaf, *The Muslim Brotherhood and State Repression in Egypt: A History of Secrecy and Militancy in an Islamist Organization* (London: I. B. Tauris, 2024).

60    Filiu, 'The Origins of Hamas', 60.

provoking further punitive measures, the Gazan Brotherhood survived by turning inwards. The Brotherhood avoided any work deemed too political and hence subversive, and al-Khalidi describes their activities from 1954 as 'monotonous': secretly organizing study circles and readings of the Quran in the private homes of members and distributing the occasional leaflet criticizing Gazan government officials. Showing little interest in confronting the Egyptian regime or Israel, 'the activities of the [Brotherhood] preachers were limited to the official Friday sermons, which most speakers delivered as a work duty, devoid of any enthusiasm and sincerity touching the hearts'.[61] With their recruitment efforts effectively curtailed, and with 'thousands of its members' emigrating to the Gulf or to Jordan to avoid repression, the Muslim Brotherhood in Gaza would remain both numerically and politically insignificant for over a decade.[62]

The Nasserist regime also posed an ideological challenge to the Muslim Brotherhood. While Gazan Islamists attributed the Palestinians' defeat in 1948 to their spiritual decline, their revivalist call found little resonance amid the widespread allure of Nasser's pan-Arabism. 'No other Arab leader approached his status, and no other Arab leader aroused such high expectations', and the 1956 Suez Crisis further enhanced Nasser as a pan-Arab hero who stood up against both Israel and the Western imperial powers.[63] From the late 1950s, Palestinians associated liberation with Arab Baathism, Nasserism, nationalism, and leftist ideals rather than Islamism.[64] Even Hamas and Palestinian Islamic Jihad (PIJ) cadres such as Musa Abu Marzuq, Mahmoud al-Zahar, and Fathi al-Shiqaqi were ardent Nasserists in their teens before they were swayed by religion beginning in the late 1960s.[65]

Egyptian rule similarly had an indirect secularizing impact on the Gaza Strip, which further limited the reach of the Brotherhood, and – although

61    Al-Aziz Khalidi, '60 'aman fi jama'at al-Ikhwan al-Muslimin'.
62    Abu-Amr, *Islamic Fundamentalism*, 9; Milton-Edwards, *Islamic Politics in Palestine*, 54.
63    Cleveland and Bunton, *A History of the Modern Middle East*, 312–13.
64    Milton-Edwards and Farrell, *Hamas*, 36.
65    Shaker al-Jawhari, *Musa Abu Marzuq: Mishwar hayat: Dhikriyat al-luju' wa-l-ghurba wa sanawat al-nidal* (Beirut: Markaz al-zaytuna li-l-dirasat wa-l-istisharat, 2019), 72; Erik Skare, *A History of Palestinian Islamic Jihad: Faith, Awareness, and Revolution in the Middle East* (Cambridge: Cambridge University Press, 2021), 15; Milton-Edwards, *Islamic Politics in Palestine*.

it still played a role in Palestinian society – religion was largely confined to the private realm. Instead of serving as a launching pad from which the Islamic message could spread to the masses, Gaza became a weekend getaway for middle-class Egyptians who flocked to the Strip to enjoy nightclubs, casinos, restaurants, and hotels once evening fell. A segment of the Palestinian refugee population also gained access to higher education abroad, and with urban influence from Cairo, Damascus, and Amman, young Gazan men commonly donned shirts and trousers in Gaza, whereas women were occasionally seen sporting miniskirts and short dresses.[66]

The Gazan Muslim Brotherhood did not just lose its senior members and cadres. Its turn inwards also meant that its young guard began defecting from the movement. Many of the Fatah founding members – such as Khalil al-Wazir (Abu Jihad), Salah Khalaf (Abu Iyad), and Salim al-Za'nun – had joined the Brotherhood starting in the mid-1940s. Believing that freedom was not granted but taken, these young activists pressured their local leaders to engage in direct action against the Israelis. In the early 1950s, they established two clandestine military bodies, the Youth of Revenge and the Battalion of Right. Yet, 'dissatisfied with the timidity of the Brotherhood leadership', Sayigh writes,

> al-Wazir used his position . . . to build a parallel network. He set about forming secret cells in preparation for independent military operations, and sternly shunned those of his colleagues who saw Palestine 'as only one of many issues, and who wanted us to concentrate on general Islamic themes only'.[67]

The dissolution of the Muslim Brotherhood in 1954 led to a formal split between the young and old guards, as the former realized the movement could no longer serve as an effective framework for armed Palestinian struggle. Initially attempting to extricate the movement from its impasse by putting it back on the nationalist road of armed liberation, al-Wazir and his compatriots proved unsuccessful. Believing that a precarious situation could always deteriorate further, the senior echelons of the Brotherhood argued they had to remain steadfast and prepare the masses.

---

66  Milton-Edwards, *Islamic Politics in Palestine*, 53–4.
67  Yezid Sayigh, *Armed Struggle and the Search for State: The Palestinian National Movement, 1949–1993* (Oxford: Oxford University Press, 1997), 81–2.

What mattered was the survival of the Gazan Brotherhood. Only when their revivalist mission had succeeded could they liberate Palestine with the support of the entire Islamic world.[68]

Offering a retrospective justification for the Brotherhood's passivity in the mid-1950s, al-Khalidi writes: 'The Brotherhood objected to the plan and methodology [of al-Wazir and Arafat] because they were based on unrealistic fantasies, and it would thus not lead to [liberation]. [The Muslim Brothers] saw it as opening a battle without [the required preparations].'[69] From the Youth of Revenge and from the Battalion of Right came the Palestinian National Liberation Movement, Fatah, in 1959. As we will see later in this study, splitting from the quietist Muslim Brotherhood to pursue armed action made the early formation of Fatah conspicuously similar to the emergence of another Palestinian faction, PIJ. The strategic role of violence was always a fault line in the Palestinian struggle.

Suffering from Egyptian state repression and ideological marginalization, and losing both its old guard to emigration and its young guard to the Fatah nucleus, the Gazan Muslim Brotherhood found 'unlikely bedfellows' in the 1950s.[70] There were several instances of uneasy cooperation between the Islamists and the communists in this period. Both organizations joined forces to organize protests in 1955, for example, against the joint UN–Egyptian relocation plan to resettle Palestinian refugees in the Sinai Peninsula.[71] They also joined the civil resistance against the four-month-long Israeli occupation of the Gaza Strip in 1956.[72] These were momentary alliances, however, and nothing more than marriages of convenience contingent upon mutual concerns and shared grievances rather than any ideological alignment or cordial relations. Indeed, there was fierce competition between the Gazan Islamists and communists, and therefore no love lost between them.

The animosity between the two was partly based on the historical distrust of the Palestine Communist Party because it had endorsed partition in October 1947. The professed secularism of the Marxists also lent a decidedly ideological dimension to the conflict, and the Islamists perceived communism as a clear corrupting influence in Islamic society:

---

68  Hroub, *Hamas*, 26.
69  Al-Aziz Khalidi, '60 'aman fi jama'at al-Ikhwan al-Muslimin'.
70  Milton-Edwards and Farrell, *Hamas*, 35.
71  Hroub, *Hamas*, 24.
72  Filiu, 'The Origins of Hamas', 60.

'For many of its followers, Marxist thought is nothing but the pursuit of personal desires . . . [permitting him] to live unrestrained and without the controls that Islam has long cared for and preserved.'[73] Typical of the movement's discourse at the time, Ibrahim al-Maqadma proclaimed in 1988 that

> Communism is found to be intimately linked to Judaism. It is no coincidence that Karl Marx, Lenin, Trotsky, and other leaders of Communist thought were Jews . . . [The Jews] depended on Freud to demolish morality by attributing all human behavior to instincts, like animals. They used Marx to eradicate the remaining vestiges of religion with his comprehensive system, which reduced humans to materialistic beings solely concerned with seeking sustenance.[74]

Anticommunism remained a constant for the Muslim Brotherhood. The adversary of the Gazan Muslim Brotherhood in the 1950s was, as such, not Israel but the Marxists. '[Egyptian repression of the Brotherhood] opened the door for the communists and the proponents of atheism and vice to run rampant', al-Khalidi writes about the 1950s, when they 'exploit[ed] the government's monitoring and tracking of Muslim Brotherhood members'.[75] Meeting in one of the Brothers' homes, al-Khalidi and the few cadres still remaining in Gaza discussed how they could oppose the communist activity in Gaza and defeat the perceived red menace. 'We talked about our discussions with the communists and advised each other on how to respond to them, what books we should read to strengthen our arguments in defense of Islam, and how to silence its enemies.'[76]

One solution was practical. Providing books to students, inviting children to the mosques, and setting up sports activities on the beaches for volleyball, weightlifting, and swimming, they attempted to keep Palestinian youths away from the leftists. The Brotherhood organized vacation camps for the Gazan youth 'to keep them away from corruption and

---

73   Muhammad Abu Tayr, *Sayyidi Umar: Dhikriyat al-shaykh Muhammad Abu Tayr fi al-muqawama wa thalatha wa thalathin 'aman min al-i'tiqal* (Beirut: Markaz al-Zaytuna li-l-Dirisat wa-l-Istisharat, 2017), 79.

74   Al-Maqadma, *Ma'alim fi al-tariq li-tahrir Filastin*, 42.

75   Al-Aziz Khalidi, '60 'aman fi jama'at al-Ikhwan al-Muslimin'.

76   Ibid.

harmful habits such as smoking, and engaged in social services for the needy with the financial assistance of expatriates in the Gulf.[77]

Another solution was organizational. By the 1950s, the Brotherhood was no longer a fully functioning organization but a loose network of Brothers. When their clandestine activity began, there was one Brotherhood group in Gaza City, one in Deir al-Balah, one in Khan Younis, and another in Rafah. Although they all knew about each other, they worked independently, in parallel, and in an uncoordinated manner. Meeting in Khan Younis in 1962, they finally united under one organizational framework after years of preparatory work with coordinating, communicating, and constantly travelling between the Gazan districts.[78] With a clear sense of urgency, the Brotherhood began rebuilding their movement.

The fierce competition between the communists and Islamists from the 1950s mattered for the development of a distinct form of Islamism because the Muslim Brotherhood in Gaza was forced to reflect upon, and formulate, their own vision for Palestinian liberation in order to counter the reds. If the communists mobilized for a classless society free from capitalist exploitation, then the Islamists had to mobilize for a virtuous and harmonious society cleansed from vice and corruption, and one that was in adherence to God's commandments. In the West Bank, where the Palestinian Muslim Brotherhood remained in loyal opposition to the Jordanian rulers, Islamism remained conservative, stagnant, and inherently tied to elite power structures concerned with the preservation of traditional power and clan structure.[79] The evolution of the Palestinian Muslim Brotherhood, and later Hamas, was thus largely driven by political and social dynamics that were unique to the Gaza Strip.[80]

Although the Gazan Islamists must have felt weakened by the mid-1960s, they surely harboured a sense of optimism as well. If so, it was not unfounded. It remains doubtful, however, that the Gazan Muslim Brothers saw their fate as aligned with that of the Israelis, who initiated the military occupation of the West Bank and Gaza after the Six-Day War in 1967. Under new military rulers – who were more concerned about Palestinian guerrilla fighters than proselytizing Islamists – the Brotherhood could pursue its activities with far greater freedom in a

---

77   Ibid.
78   Ibid.
79   Milton-Edwards and Farrell, *Hamas*, 37.
80   Roy, *Hamas and Civil Society in Gaza*, 21.

new, and far more favourable, environment. This phase also enabled the rise of a prominent Gazan Islamist by the name Ahmad Yassin. This is where we turn next.

## Rebuilding a revivalist infrastructure

When Israel occupied Gaza after the Six-Day War in 1967, the Strip became a hotbed of armed Palestinian resistance, with its most intense period between 1969 and 1971. Although the Islamist wave in the Middle East is partly attributed to the fall of Nasserism, this was not immediately the case for the Palestinians. Instead, the Arab defeat of 1967 facilitated the rise of the Palestine Liberation Organization (PLO) and its military wing, the Palestine Liberation Army (PLA), which quickly grasped the opportunity to become the main representative of the Palestinian resistance. From the refugee camps of Gaza, the PLA employed bombs, grenades, and sabotage against Israeli targets and Palestinian collaborators. Unlike the West Bank, where a range of political forces had emerged under Jordanian rule, the Egyptians suppressed the development of any local leadership in Gaza; the only contenders there were now the Israeli occupation forces and the Palestinian guerrillas, and the overcrowded camps provided fertile ground for the PLO.[81]

The Israelis managed to regain control by early 1972, however, and weakened the resistance by killing a large number of Palestinian militants or systematically arresting them.[82] According to Israeli estimates, Israeli prisons held at least 2,800 Palestinian guerrillas and supporters by 1969; 1,828 others had been killed by 1970. Between March 1971 and January 1972, 100 more Palestinian guerrillas were killed and 1,000 others imprisoned. More than 2,500 Palestinian houses were also demolished in the Jabalya, Beach, and Rafah camps as part of the Israeli campaign, and 38,000 Palestinians were expelled, either to Sinai, to other parts of Gaza, or to the Dheisheh refugee camp in the West Bank.[83]

---

81    Sara Roy, *The Gaza Strip: The Political Development of De-development* (Washington, DC: Institute for Palestine Studies, 1995), 104; Milton-Edwards, *Islamic Politics in Palestine*, 75.

82    Roy, *The Gaza Strip*, 104.

83    Sayigh, *Armed Struggle and the Search for State*, 203, 287.

The Palestinian Muslim Brotherhood was 'virtually inactive' in this period due to Nasserist repression.[84] Yet, the defeat of the PLO guerrillas in 1972 marked a shift in Gaza's internal political landscape. The Muslim Brotherhood – refusing to engage in armed struggle and instead focusing on survival – was spared repression by the Israeli occupation authorities.[85] They would quickly resume the reconstruction of their movement, for which one young Palestinian Muslim Brother in Gaza, Ahmad Yassin, became the head architect.

Ahmad Yassin was born in 1936 in the Palestinian village of al-Jura, west of Majdal. Located on the southern coastal plain north of Gaza, and thought to have been built on the ruins of the Roman settlement of Jagur, nineteenth-century travellers' logs describe the area as particularly fertile, where sycamores, figs, pomegranates, citrus fruits, strawberries, almonds, apricots, and grapevines all flourished.[86] Growing up in a relatively affluent family on an orchard north of the village, Yassin had fond childhood memories of al-Jura, where he had enjoyed fishing and bird hunting.[87] If so, then Yassin's pastoral childhood mirrored the local economy, as al-Jura was a central fishing hub along the Palestinian coast and its village hunters travelled to the northern shores of Sinai to hunt quail.[88] Cooler than the inland, al-Jura also served as a summer resort for the inhabitants of Majdal, and it attracted visitors from neighbouring cities and villages who sought relief from the heat there with swimming, sport events, and religious festivals in the springtime.[89] With the Shrine of Hussein's Head – the holiest Shiite site in Palestine – located on a hilltop outside al-Jura, the area attracted pilgrims as well. Built by the Fatimids, the shrine allegedly housed the head of Husayn ibn Ali from approximately 906 CE to 1153 CE.[90]

84    Milton-Edwards, *Islamic Politics in Palestine*, 75.

85    Filiu, 'The Origins of Hamas', 63.

86    Avi (Avraham) Sasson, 'Historical Geography of the Palestine Southern Coastal Plain in the Late Ottoman Period – the Ashkelon Region as a Case Study', *Middle Eastern Studies* 55, no. 6 (November 2019): 980.

87    'al-Shaykh Ahmad Yasin: shahid ala asr al-intifada', episode 1, *al-Jazeera*, April 17, 1999.

88    Zochrot, 'al-Jura (Gaza)', zochrot.org; Sasson, 'Historical Geography of the Palestine Southern Coastal Plain', 980–1.

89    Zochrot, 'al-Jura (Gaza)'.

90    Michael Press, 'Hussein's Head and Importance of Cultural Heritage', *Ancient Near East Today* 11, no. 3 (2014).

Ahmad Yassin and his family were, like the other Palestinians in the area, not spared the destruction of the 1948 Palestine War and were expelled from their homes. 'The [Israeli] army's operations combined features of border-clearing and internal "cleansing",' Morris writes about Operation Yoav in November 1948, 'and nowhere was this clearer than in the area roughly between Majdal and the northern edge of the Gaza Strip.'[91] Yassin's family decided to leave the village as the battles between Jewish and Arab troops around al-Jura intensified and wait for the situation to stabilize. They split into two groups, with Yassin travelling with his mother and his brother to Gaza along the sandy shores of the Mediterranean. With little food, they ate what they found in passing orchards and fields before they reached the trees of Sheikh Ijlin in the southern parts of Gaza City.[92] 'The conditions were difficult and harsh,' Yassin described their first months in exile, 'but what should we do? Where should we live? We built a hut from straw and lived in it despite the winter and the cold . . . but praise be to God, He protected us with His grace.'[93] Though intended to be temporary, their flight from the hostilities of war turned permanent. Yassin and his family never resettled in al-Jura.

Photos of Yassin from the late 1950s show none of the frailty he would be known for forty years later. Nor is he in a wheelchair, despite having suffered spinal cord injuries from a sporting accident in 1952 that left him quadriplegic for the rest of his life. Instead, they depict a young, dapper man in his early twenties wearing a white shirt with rolled-up sleeves tucked into black pants. Handsome, with a short moustache and neatly trimmed hair, Yassin confidently locks arms with a friend on his left side as he looks into the camera. In another photo from 1961, now a teacher in his mid-twenties, Yassin stands to the far right, wearing a black jacket over a white sweater. He maintains the same penetrating gaze.

In some ways, the photos reveal the similarities between the young Ahmad Yassin and Hassan al-Banna. None of them enjoyed any formal religious credentials, and both were highly charismatic lay preachers. Yassin, a teacher like al-Banna, thrived on communicating directly with

---

91    Benny Morris, *The Birth of the Palestinian Refugee Problem Revisited* (Cambridge: Cambridge University Press, 2004), 517.

92    Atif Adwan, *al-Shaykh Ahmad Yassin: Hayatuhu wa jihaduhu* (n.p.: al-Markaz al-Filastini li-l-i'lam, 1991), 18–19.

93    'al-Shaykh Ahmad Yasin'.

those around him, preferring to speak rather than to write. He was a refugee like them, living in a poor neighbourhood, and he enjoyed 'a certain ordinariness which set him apart from many other political leaders in Gaza'.[94] Just as al-Banna spread his revivalist message to his followers in a pedagogical and simple manner, Yassin developed an everyday theology relevant to the ordinary lives of Gazans. His sermons did not deal with the esoteric jurisprudential issues that other religious scholars explored in their sermons. Instead, he addressed the problems of day-to-day life in Gaza.[95] '[Young men] would sit in a circle to read the Quran or study one of the religious books about the Prophet's biography, jurisprudence, or hadith,' Yahya Sinwar reminisced. 'Sheikh Ahmad [Yassin] would comment, explain, and tutor the youth [sitting] around him, and they would listen with understanding and eagerness. The sheikh would guide these young men who would spread out and then return with new youths to the mosque so that the circle would grow and expand.'[96]

Among Yassin's first recruits were Ibrahim al-Maqadma, Ismail Abu Shanab, and Musa Abu Marzuq, who were all in their teens when they first became acquainted with him. Abdel Aziz al-Rantisi, Yassin's protégé and close follower, came into the picture later. Others, like Fathi al-Shiqaqi and Abdel Aziz Awda, followed Yassin, but they left him to pursue their own political project, PIJ.[97] All of them had grown up in the Gazan slums with their parents telling them tales of their past lives. 'In our homeland,' al-Rantisi narrated, 'we lived a rich and prosperous life. A beautiful house in Yibna, still standing to this day, where I was born. A vast orchard surrounding the house on all sides.'[98] The idealized past stood in stark contrast to the poverty they experienced in childhood. The streets of the camps were filled with children whose heads were shaved to prevent the spread of lice and disease. Unable to afford a backpack, Abu Marzuq brought with him a repurposed flour sack on his first day of school – a relic of US food aid.[99] Similarly, when his brother travelled for work, the

94    Milton-Edwards, *Islamic Politics in Palestine*, 100–1.
95    Adwan, *al-Shaykh Ahmad Yassin*, 61.
96    Yahya Sinwar, *al-Shawk wa-l-qaranful* (n.p., 2004), 92.
97    Tamimi, *Hamas*, 21.
98    Abdel Aziz al-Rantisi, *Mudhakirat al-shahid al-duktur Abd al-Aziz al-Rantisi* (Cairo: Dar al-tawzi' wa-l-nashr al-Islamiyya, 2004), 30.
99    Al-Jawhari, *Musa Abu Marzuq*, 57–8.

seventeen-year-old al-Rantisi gave him his only pair of shoes so that his brother would not travel to Saudi Arabia barefoot.[100]

The experience of poverty was fuelled by the trauma of war. Both Abu Marzuq and al-Rantisi experienced the 1956 massacres when Israeli troops executed 275 Palestinian men in Khan Younis and, then, one week later, killed 111 more in Rafah camp – apparently as revenge for the raids into Israel by Palestinian guerrilla fighters.[101] Abu Marzuq recounted how, once the dust had settled, he witnessed a truck loaded with bodies being taken to a mass grave, and it had a profound impact on the five-year-old seeing how his neighbours and friends bid farewell to their loved ones.[102] Al-Rantisi, a nine-year-old at the time, would later describe how his father wailed once they learned that his uncle had been executed by the Israelis. 'I [could not] sleep for many months after that . . . It left a wound in my heart that can never heal.'[103] So, with bitterness and sorrow between every line of his memoirs, he summarized the Palestinian experience: 'I find that the suffering from the occupation of Palestine colours everything in our lives as a Palestinian people.'[104] Al-Rantisi became one of the staunchest hardliners within Hamas.

In 1968, when Yassin was elected the new leader of the Gazan Muslim Brotherhood, it was through a combination of ingenuity, discretion, and a lack of competitors. In order to avoid Egyptian repression, for example, Yassin disassociated from al-Kanz Mosque and worked independently of other Brothers in Gaza. Alone and from his home in Beach Camp, he carefully reconstructed Brotherhood cells through activities typical of the movement, such as summer camps, sports events, and Quranic study circles.[105] He was thus able to evade much of the harassment that

---

100   Al-Rantisi, *Mudhakirat al-shahid al-duktur Abd al-Aziz al-Rantisi*, 30–1.

101   Sayigh, *Armed Struggle and the Search for State*, 65; Rashid Khalidi, *The Hundred Years' War on Palestine: A History of Settler Colonialism and Resistance, 1917–2017* (New York: Metropolitan Books, 2020), 94; see also bullet point 23 in UNRWA Commissioner-General, *Special Report of the Director of the United Nations Relief and Works Agency for Palestine Refugees* (New York: United Nations, 1955); for a historical account of 1956, see Joe Sacco, *Footnotes in Gaza* (New York: Metropolitan Books, 2009).

102   Al-Jawhari, *Musa Abu Marzuq*, 54.

103   Quoted in Sacco, *Footnotes in Gaza*, ix.

104   Al-Rantisi, *Mudhakirat al-shahid al-duktur Abd al-Aziz al-Rantisi*, 29.

105   Adwan, *al-Shaykh Ahmad Yassin*, 37, 40.

other Islamists encountered from the Egyptians, and he was rewarded an assistant position to Zuhair al-Zuhri, leader of the Brotherhood branches in Gaza City, when the movement formally united its branches in 1962.[106] Co-founder of the Gazan Brotherhood Abdel Aziz al-Khalidi was the nominal head of the movement and responsible for its proselytizing efforts; he also decided to emigrate in 1968. The organizational void he left behind facilitated the rise of Yassin, whose influence had been boosted by over a decade of widespread communal contact and activities and the recruitment of a Brotherhood young guard.[107]

The rise of Yassin had a decisive impact on both the Muslim Brotherhood and Palestinian society. Organizationally, one of Yassin's first initiatives was renewing the movement. Frustrated by what he saw as the stagnation of the Gazan Brotherhood, and dissatisfied with an old guard content merely to read the Quran, he dismissed them from their positions. 'Honorably discharging' the old guard, Yassin crafted new roles that they would perceive as suitable to their stature; he assigned them to reconciliation and *zakat* committees, or tasked them with maintaining ties with village elders, merchants, and scholars in Gaza. Their vacated positions were then filled with energetic young men in their late teens and early twenties, whom he had recruited on the northern beaches outside of Gaza City and who were eager to fervently and boldly propagate the Islamic call.[108]

Operationally, Yassin was a key advocate for the Muslim Brotherhood to avoid politics and any confrontation with the Israeli occupation. For Yassin in the 1960s and 1970s, structural change was not implemented through direct action or political processes. Change came through the salvation of the individual who purified his heart by embracing the Islamic call. One by one, the moral foundation of Islamic society, the precondition for liberation, would be gradually constructed.[109] At its core, he aimed to counteract the perceived cultural and moral erosion of Palestinians under occupation, which rendered them weak in the face of oppression. Accordingly, senior Hamas member Muhammad Abu Tayr stressed the need for building a resilient Islamic identity among Palestinians:

---

106   Al-Aziz Khalidi, '60 'aman fi jama'at al-Ikhwan al-Muslimin'.
107   Adwan, *al-Shaykh Ahmad Yassin*, 54.
108   Ibid., 55–6.
109   Milton-Edwards and Farrell, *Hamas*, 39–40.

The occupation and its practices, the state of laxity and weakness, as well as the cultural contamination that the Palestinian cause has endured, have allowed the culture of occupation to take its place in people's lives. The culture of the occupation has imposed itself upon the people's homes, and some people have even invited the Zionists to join them for weddings and special occasions.[110]

Although he was spared its worst excesses, Yassin was not oblivious to the history and effects of Egyptian state repression. He feared that a premature conflict with the Israelis would attract a new crackdown on a movement still gaining its footing. Although Yassin had begun recruiting a young guard filling movement positions, the Brotherhood 'still did not have the organization that could bear the burden and strive'.[111] When the leftists and nationalists forged an anti-Israeli alliance following the occupation in 1967, it thus came as a shock to them when Yassin categorically refused to join and instead distanced the Muslim Brotherhood from nationalist agitation in favour of a strictly legalistic approach.[112] Patience was key.

There is no evidence to suggest, then, that Hamas was the creation of Israeli intelligence, although the Israeli occupation authorities left the Palestinian Muslim Brotherhood alone. The Israelis were, as demonstrated above, more preoccupied with crushing the PLO guerrilla fighters rather than wasting their energy on proselytizing Islamists. The perception that the Brotherhood posed little threat was further reinforced when Israeli forces seized Egyptian records, which revealed Fatah operatives but little to no operational Brotherhood activity after almost two decades under Egyptian administration.[113] Yassin and the Muslim Brotherhood, on the other hand, gave no greater recognition to the Nasserist regime – 'false prophets of liberation' – than to the representatives of the Jewish state, and the Israeli occupation did not alter the Muslim Brotherhood's longstanding preoccupation with education and nonconfrontational

---

110    Abu Tayr, *Sayyidi Umar*, 164.
111    'al-Shaykh Ahmad Yasin: Shahid ala asr al-intifada', episode 3, *al-Jazeera*, May 1, 1999.
112    Filiu, 'The Origins of Hamas', 62, 64.
113    Yezid Sayigh, 'Turning Defeat into Opportunity: The Palestinian Guerrillas after the June 1967 War', *Middle East Journal* 46, no. 2 (1992): 251.

activities.[114] While the Palestinian Muslim Brotherhood approached the occupation with strategic patience over the next two decades, the occupation authorities responded with conditional acceptance as long as the Islamists did not engage in violence against Israeli targets.

Socially, the Muslim Brothers commenced a mosque-building phase in the occupied Palestinian territories, doubling the number of mosques from 400 to 750 in the West Bank between 1967 and 1987. In Gaza, it tripled from 200 to 600.[115] The mosques were not merely an imposition of religious symbolism on Palestinian society but part of a comprehensive revivalist infrastructure instrumental to the Brotherhood's proselytizing efforts. Here, they invited Palestinian youths to listen to sermons and to study the Quran, to read Islamic books and literature in the newly established mosque libraries, and to use the facilities to prepare for exams.[116]

Structurally, key Brotherhood initiatives were formalized in 1973 with the establishment of the welfare network, the Islamic Complex, which provided charitable, medical, and educational services to the Palestinians in Gaza. Funded by Israeli authorities, Gulf donors, local supporters, and *zakat* committees, the Complex established nursery schools and kindergartens, religious schools, youth clubs, sports clubs, Islamic student societies, orphanages, day care centres, health clinics, and nursing homes, which spread throughout the Strip at the same pace as the mosques. Providing an umbrella for Brotherhood activities, the Islamic Complex was both an extension of Yassin's vision for correct practice and a direct response to the depressed socio-economic conditions experienced by Gazans. His followers – al-Rantisi, al-Maqadma, Mahmoud al-Zahar, and Ibrahim al-Yazouri – had all returned from their studies in Egypt or the United States as paediatricians, dentists, pharmacists, engineers, and educators. These were skills desperately needed by the Gazan community, and the Islamic Complex operated from some of the poorest areas in the Strip where the Muslim Brothers provided free medical consultations, dispensed medicine 'at cost or lower', circumcised boys without charge, and provided financial assistance to thousands of needy families.[117] Just as the teeming camps of Gaza had provided fertile soil for the PLO in the late 1960s, they now nurtured the communal activism of the

114    Filiu, 'The Origins of Hamas', 64; Hroub, *Hamas*, 29.
115    Hroub, *Hamas*, 31; Abu-Amr, *Islamic Fundamentalism*, 15.
116    Adwan, *al-Shaykh Ahmad Yassin*, 62–3.
117    Roy, Hamas and Civil Society in Gaza, 72–3, 75.

Brotherhood.[118] 'In a fairly short order', Roy observes, the Gazan Brotherhood was able to 'establish an infrastructure of social institutions based on
personal friendships, trust, and group solidarity, cementing its presence
and influence at the grassroots level in a manner other political groups
found difficult to match, let alone surpass'.[119]

The inroads of Yassin and his acolytes were equally driven by their
opponents' loss of momentum. Pan-Arabism was effectively undermined
by the Arab defeat in 1967 and experienced further decline when Gamal
Abdel Nasser died in 1970. The nationalist and leftist PLO forces were
equally weakened after Black September in 1970, after which the PLO
relocated to Lebanon via Syria. Its armed wing, the PLA, had been ground
to defeat in Gaza. The Popular Front for the Liberation of Palestine
(PFLP) suffered a leadership crisis in Lebanon. The Democratic Front
for the Liberation of Palestine (DFLP) had been militarily crushed in
Jordan, and the Popular Front for the Liberation of Palestine-General
Command (PFLP-GC) had mere nine members left in the Hashemite
Kingdom, 'all fugitives'.[120]

As Sayigh observes, while other guerrilla movements – and particularly Marxist ones – employed comparable crises to reassess political
programmes and modify their approaches to mass organization, the
Palestinians were unable to move on from erratic and fragmented cri-
tiques because proto-nationalism remained the primary source from
which all Palestinian guerrilla groups derived their understanding of
political and social processes. This was equally true for the Palestinian
left, as the formal assessment following Black September highlighted an
inability to propose solutions. Although the PFLP reaffirmed its commitment to a people's war, it failed to provide concrete strategies for how
Palestinian guerrillas could advance militarily or address the challenges
of the new phase. The DFLP, on the other hand, subtly aligned itself
with the PLO mainstream on practical matters in an attempt to regain
its footing.[121] Just as the Islamic Complex was carefully and meticulously
constructing its network of social welfare and proselytizing, Palestinian
revolutionary violence was losing traction.

---

118   Mishal and Sela, *The Palestinian Hamas*, 19.
119   Roy, *Hamas and Civil Society in Gaza*, 73.
120   Sayigh, *Armed Struggle and the Search for State*, 280.
121   Ibid., 273, 282.

As the Palestinian Muslim Brotherhood grew stronger from the late 1970s, they also became more confrontational. Although the movement primarily engaged in educational and social services, the Islamic Complex activists also used force against fellow Palestinians.[122] They torched cinemas, coffee shops, newspaper offices, billiard halls, and bars. They attacked shops selling alcohol, libraries spreading atheist literature, and ran intimidation campaigns against competitors.[123] Wedding celebrations deemed inappropriate – with alcohol, gender-mixing, singing, and dancing – were similarly assaulted, and the Brotherhood organized alternative, Islamic wedding ceremonies that instead sought 'the pleasure of God'.[124] Significant, and clearly patriarchal, efforts were made to engage Gazan women. These efforts aimed, in part, to organize women in grassroots institutions like the Young Muslim Women's Association and teach them sewing and embroidery, computer skills, religious education, and literacy.[125] It also meant policing and reforming social behaviour, segregating the sexes, and enforcing a perceived Islamic dress code.[126] Women were banned from swimming on the beach and those who refused to follow orders were, like political opponents, reportedly sprayed with acid.[127]

Because the primary concern of the Muslim Brothers was preventing corruption and vice in this period, their primary adversary was, as in the 1950s, the Palestinian Marxists. The Muslim Brotherhood's relationship with the PFLP was particularly volatile, and it deteriorated further when the Israeli occupation authorities formally recognized and legalized the Islamic Complex in 1978, five years after its foundation. Yassin used the momentum to encourage his followers to join labour unions, public institutions, and professional associations to deepen their influence through lawful institutionalization.[128] Because the leftists vied for similar influence in the social field, 'local health-care institutions soon became an arena of competition'.[129]

122   Milton-Edwards, *Islamic Politics in Palestine*, 104.
123   Milton-Edwards and Farrell, *Hamas*, 44.
124   Shadid, 'The Muslim Brotherhood Movement', 674; al-Aziz Khalidi, '60 'Aman fi jama'at al-Ikhwan al-Muslimin'.
125   Roy, *Hamas and Civil Society in Gaza*, 74.
126   Milton-Edwards, *Islamic Politics in Palestine*, 111.
127   Shadid, 'The Muslim Brotherhood Movement', 674.
128   Mishal and Sela, *The Palestinian Hamas*, 23.
129   Milton-Edwards, *Islamic Politics in Palestine*, 106.

This rivalry would inevitably involve the communist-affiliated Red Crescent organization in Gaza.[130] With the support of Fatah, which saw the leftists as annoying competitors in the national movement, an anti-Marxist front was built, and, in line with its legalist approach, the Islamic Complex nominated Ibrahim al-Yazouri as a candidate for the Red Crescent presidency in December 1979. Their aspirations were brutally crushed, however, when the leftist and committed secularist Haydar Abdel Shafi was re-elected with overwhelming majority by the organization's approximately 4,000 members. The Islamists, in turn, expressed their anger 'by ransacking the Red Crescent offices before moving on to cafés, cinemas, and drinking establishments in the town center'.[131] The Israeli soldiers stood by and watched as Palestinian strife intensified.

Despite bitter defeat, the Islamic Complex persisted in its efforts to legally institutionalize its presence in the Gaza Strip,[132] and conflict soon spread to the Islamic University of Gaza as a 'reflection of the more general political power-struggle occurring in Gaza Strip at the time'.[133] Although intended to be run according to Islamic principles, the university was under de facto PLO control once established in 1978, following Egyptian authorities' denial of Palestinian access to its higher education institutions for their protests against the Camp David Accords. Whereas Fatah and the Islamic Complex had struck an alliance to weaken the leftist currents, the Islamists soon turned against the followers of Arafat. Although confrontations between Islamist and nationalist students were an integral part of the power struggle, it was the financial mismanagement of the PLO that gave the Islamists their most notable victory. Unable to contribute its 'lion's share' of the university's budget, the PLO's shortfall was made up by the Muslim Brotherhood, whose representatives, in return, soon constituted the majority in the university's board of trustees.[134]

By 1983, the Brotherhood's imprint on the Islamic University of Gaza was evident, from the highest level to the lowest. Muhammad Saqr, a Brotherhood representative, was appointed university president, and its student group, the Islamic Bloc, won 51 per cent of the student election

---

130    Filiu, 'The Origins of Hamas', 65.

131    Ibid.

132    Mishal and Sela, *The Palestinian Hamas*, 23.

133    Michael Irving Jensen, '"Re-Islamising" Palestinian Society "from Below": Hamas and Higher Education in Gaza', *Holy Land Studies* 5, no. 1 (2006): 60.

134    Mishal and Sela, *The Palestinian Hamas*, 23–4.

votes that year.[135] Separate entrances for men and women were introduced, organized life at campus became dominated by Brotherhood activists, doormen and porters were paid to grow and maintain their beards, and 'leftists, liberals or progressives expressing a view that was in any respect contrary to that of the [Islamic Complex] were dealt with severely'.[136] The university's aim was no longer confined to providing its students with a formal education, but creating 'sound Muslims' by instilling the students with 'an organised way of thinking, a vigilant conscience, awareness, good conduct and holistic (that is to say Islamic) view of life'.[137]

In fairness, the Muslim Brotherhood did not monopolize intra-Palestinian violence, and it is striking how closely Islamist grievances mirrored leftist ones. Al-Khalidi, for example, narrates how Brotherhood members were subjected to physical abuse between May and June 1986. Yusra Hamdan, for example, a female student at the Islamic University of Gaza, was assaulted by two PFLP activists and had her face slashed with a scalpel – allegedly for being active in a women's Islamic advocacy group. Another Islamist activist, Zakariya Sinwar, similarly lost an eye after someone from the PFLP threw nitric acid on him, and leftists later stormed the pharmacy of al-Yazouri and beat him with a stick. Besides, whereas activists of the Muslim Brotherhood enforced an Islamic dress code on Gazan women, school principals of secularist orientations reportedly threatened to expel female students covering their hair on school premises, whether they did so voluntarily or not. While the Palestinian nationalists denounced the Israeli soldiers for standing by and watching Islamists setting Gazan establishments ablaze, al-Khalidi similarly complained that the Israelis 'neither punished the [leftist] attackers nor searched for them, sometimes even encouraging them, as when two youths from the PFLP attempted to run over Dr. Abdel Aziz al-Rantisi [with a car]'.[138] Decades before James Davison Hunter coined the term in 1991, the Palestinians contended with their own culture war.[139]

By the mid-1980s, the Palestinian Muslim Brotherhood had not just resurfaced in Gaza. It had grown to an extent previously unknown to

---

135    Filiu, 'The Origins of Hamas', 65.
136    Milton-Edwards, *Islamic Politics in Palestine*, 111.
137    Jensen, '"Re-Islamising" Palestinian Society "from Below"', 63.
138    Al-Aziz Khalidi, '60 'Aman fi jama'at al-ikhwan al-muslimin'.
139    See James Davison Hunter, *Culture Wars: The Struggle to Define America* (New York: Basic Books, 1991).

the Palestinian Islamists. Its rise was less about a genuine Palestinian longing for the establishment of an Islamic state, Roy concludes, and more about the Muslim Brothers' ability to transform into a critical, at times indispensable, social actor through the provision of essential health and educational services. Although the Brotherhood was a polarizing force, the movement also 'empowered the [Gazan] poor and provided them with a greater sense of equity and fairness in a system that had extremely limited options'.[140] Indeed, although there were other Islamist movements attempting to gain similar traction in Palestinian society, they largely failed because they were unable to address Palestinian grievances. In the next chapter, we will thus turn to Hizb al-Tahrir, whose revivalist mission failed miserably.

---

140    Roy, *Hamas and Civil Society in Gaza*, 75.

# 2

# Reviving the Caliphate

When thinking about Palestinian Islamism, one may conjure the image of Ahmad Yassin, the strategist behind the Palestinian Muslim Brotherhood and the spiritual leader of Hamas. Others may recall Fathi al-Shiqaqi, who opposed the quietist Brotherhood line and who opened an Islamist front in the armed Palestinian struggle. Abdallah Azzam, meanwhile, mobilized the Afghan Arabs and is considered the godfather of global jihadism. Whether we can reduce Palestinian Islamism to one individual or not, it is evident that the phenomenon has fostered several important ideological thinkers, political organizers, and militant agitators. Taqi al-Din al-Nabhani was not one of them.

This chapter examines the Palestinian Islamist political party Hizb al-Tahrir (the Liberation Party), founded in Jerusalem in 1952. It examines the thought of its leader, al-Nabhani, his analysis of the perceived impasse in the Muslim world, and the solutions he proposed. We will see that Hizb al-Tahrir fundamentally differed from any other Palestinian Islamist movement. It did not bother with the armed struggle. Neither did the party believe in social services or proselytizing perceived Islamic values from which a pious society would gradually emerge from below. The sole purpose for Hizb al-Tahrir was re-establishing the Islamic state. The length of this chapter is proportional to the party's success; it is the shortest in the book. Why, then, was Hizb al-Tahrir never an appealing alternative to the Palestinians? And what does that tell us about Palestinian Islamism?

## Ignoring Palestine

Re-establishing the Islamic State is a duty upon all the Muslims . . . The Muslims remain sinful until they begin working towards re-establishing the Islamic State so they can pledge their oath of allegiance to a Caliph who will implement Islam and carry its call to the world. – Taqi al-Din al-Nabhani.[1]

Reports differ on when Taqi al-Din al-Nabhani was born in Ijzim, a Palestinian village approximately twenty kilometres south of Haifa. While some sources suggest he was born as early as 1905, others propose 1909.[2] All the same, it was at a time when the Mutasarrifate of Jerusalem – the Ottoman district encompassing Jerusalem, Hebron, Jaffa, Gaza, and Beersheba – had taken an irreversible step into the modern world. As Khalidi narrates, although the district remained predominantly rural, cash crops and wage labour had already begun to make their mark with an emerging and developing capitalist economy, as did the concentration of land ownership in the hands of a few. Centre or periphery – towns, cities, and villages – all were increasingly intertwined with the rest of the capitalist world via the telegraph, steamships, and railroads. Literacy had begun to spread, and a decidedly modern mode of education was introduced. Printed books and newspapers presented new ideas about the world, and about progress and the way forward. The rise of the working class, a sense of nationhood (no longer just Ottoman but now also Palestinian) and shifting gender consciousness meant that new forms of

---

1 Taqi al-Din Nabhani, *al-Dawla al-islamiyya* (Beirut: Dar al-umma li-l-taba'a wa-l-nashr wa-l-tawzi', 2002), 239.

2 See, for example, David Commins, 'Taqī al-Din al-Nabhānī and the Islamic Liberation Party', *Muslim World* 81, nos 3–4 (1991): 194; Suha Taji-Farouki, *A Fundamental Quest: Hizb al-Tahrir and the Search for the Islamic Caliphate* (London: Grey Seal, 1996), 1.

identities appeared. Most, if not all, of these appropriated an inherently modern meaning, although Palestinians retained a pride in their religious affiliation and origins.[3] 'It is clear,' he writes, 'that by the first part of the twentieth century there existed in Palestine under Ottoman rule a vibrant Arab society undergoing a series of rapid and accelerating transitions.'[4] Al-Nabhani's family was firmly rooted in the fading traditions of the old world. His father was a distinguished scholar of Islamic law and affiliated to the educational administration. The maternal grandfather of al-Nabhani, Yusuf, was a Sufi scholar and head judge in the Ottoman courts who enjoyed close links to the Ottoman political classes. Receiving private lessons from these mentors and paternal figures to supplement his early education, al-Nabhani became an Islamic scholar himself after receiving formal training in Islamic jurisprudence at the prominent al-Azhar University in Egypt. Upon returning to Mandate Palestine and working as a teacher until 1938, al-Nabhani was first appointed as a legal assistant in the Islamic court system, and he later became a mufti (an Islamic jurist) at the Ramla Islamic court.[5] Al-Nabhani would, by all means, have been part of an urban elite were it not for the fall of the Ottoman Empire and the establishment of the State of Israel. It is difficult not to view his subsequent ambitions to revive an idealized past as motivated in part by the legacy of his family and its associated privileges and political influence.

Ijzim, like the other Palestinian villages discussed thus far, was destroyed in 1948. Yet the triangular region south of Haifa – with Ijzim, Ayn Ghazal, and Jaba' – was able to withstand attacks until late July.[6] Ijzim held out the longest among the coastal pockets of resistance, and a small number of armed villagers fought against hundreds of Israeli soldiers. Between 130 and 200 villagers were killed in the battle for the village, during which Jewish troops brought in the air force to quell the defence. The rest of Ijzim's population was expelled to Jenin in the northern West

3    Rashid Khalidi, *The Hundred Years' War on Palestine: A History of Settler Colonialism and Resistance, 1917–2017* (New York: Metropolitan Books, 2020), 17–19.

4    Ibid., 20.

5    Hasan Azad, '(Im)Possible Muslims: Hizb Ut-Tahrir, the Islamic State, and Modern Muslimness' (PhD diss., Columbia University, 2017), 31–2; Taji-Farouki, *A Fundamental Quest*, 1.

6    Zochrot, 'Ijzim', zochrot.org.

Bank once the dust had settled.[7] In its place, the *moshav* community Kerem Maharal was established by a group of Jewish Holocaust survivors from Czechoslovakia in 1949.[8]

The dissolution of the Ottoman Empire in 1922, its replacement by the Arab states, and the establishment of the State of Israel had a significant, yet by no means uniform, impact on the emergence and development of political movements and ideological currents in the region. As the old world lay in ashes, there was a need to comprehend the scope of the catastrophe and seize the opportunities it presented, as a way of forging a path through the impasse. The choices made were, as noted, just as much driven by political pragmatism as by ideological conviction. For the Gazan Muslim Brotherhood, the Palestinian Marxist became the short-term antagonist who spread corruption and vice in society. Their West Bank Islamist counterpart merged with the Jordanian branch and served as loyal opposition to political power.

The *nakba* had a similarly deep impact on political leaders, thinkers, and philosophers. One of them was the Palestinian nationalist leader Musa Alami, who argued that the Arab defeat of 1948 was caused by the lack of Arab unity, the weaknesses of Arab governments, and an absence of a political consciousness in the Arab masses. Triumph could only be achieved by Arab unity and by comprehensively reforming the mode of governance so that it became 'rational in its policy and scientific in administration, and concerned with the welfare of the people'.[9] Syrian political thinker Constantin Zurayk arrived at a similar conclusion. The Arabs could only succeed, he explained, if there was a complete change in the Arab way of life, as there existed no Arab nation in the real sense of the word. Although this change required social development, it depended primarily on intellectual change among the masses, with the Arab becoming a part of the world in which he lived in both fact and in spirit. This transformation could not be accomplished by the masses themselves; it could only be spearheaded by an intellectual elite capable of seeing the world clearly.[10]

---

7   Ilan Pappé, *A History of Modern Palestine* (Cambridge: Cambridge University Press, 2004), 196.

8   Claims Conference, 'Survivor Story: Shoshana Ceizler', January 20, 2017, claimscon.org.

9   Albert Hourani, *Arabic Thought in the Liberal Age 1798–1939* (Cambridge: Cambridge University Press, 2012), 355.

10   Ibid., 354.

Al-Nabhani was thus part of a broader idealist trend when he began diagnosing the malaise of the Muslims and the way forward in the early 1950s. Material driving forces – economic development, class struggle, technological advancement, or environmental factors – creating and shaping social structures, political systems, and human behaviour are noticeably absent in his political thought. Instead, he stressed the importance of ideas, ideology, and values – a metaphysical spirit – as the key to human behaviour, society, and politics. According to al-Nabhani, the Islamic creed helped explain both the past glory of the Caliphate and its downfall, and it was the key to reviving it once more. 'The Islamic State is based on the Islamic ideology and derives its strength solely from that ideology,' al-Nabhani professed. 'It is the main cause of progress and prosperity and the basis of its existence . . . Islam made all this possible as the driving force behind the state.'[11] The strength of the Islamic state had waned because the understanding of Islam deteriorated, divine rules were misapplied, and the strong faith of Muslims was extinguished. This led their state 'away from the right path and to its weakness and disintegration'.[12]

The rise of Europe was similarly not seen as the product of material change. It was facilitated by European philosophers, writers, and intellectuals transforming European concepts and adopting 'a specific viewpoint concerning life'. With a transformation of European thought and values, the Europeans correspondingly transformed their lives, which 'catapulted the industrial revolution into motion'.[13] Indeed, while the Ottomans did not understand their religion properly, the Europeans 'became the possessor of an ideology' and 'a specific system' under whose shadow the Muslims now found themselves.[14]

That is not to say that al-Nabhani ignored colonial invasions and warfare, and he does refer to the French and British military campaigns. Yet for him, colonialism was a cultural invasion just as much as it was a military one, if not more so. Worse than the military defeat of the Ottoman Empire was the deculturalization of Islamic lands. European missionary campaigns, ('invasions', he termed them) introduced nationalism with the formation of a Balkan identity and a Turkish one, as well as Arab,

---

11    Al-Din Nabhani, *al-Dawla al-islamiyya*, 169.
12    Ibid., 172.
13    Ibid., 179.
14    Ibid., 180.

Kurdish, and Armenian identities. Socialism and communism were similarly introduced as Ottoman politicians were poisoned by foreign ideologies. Missionary schools further introduced syllabi promoting Western philosophy, thought, and culture, which westernized Islamic intellectuals in thought and in practice.[15] 'The objective of this curriculum was to produce individuals with a Western personality,' al-Nabhani proclaimed, '... which would naturally lead to the separation of religion from the state.'[16] Young Muslims began adapting and emulating a European, and disbelieving, lifestyle. They no longer viewed Islam as a complete system of life but rather as a source of spiritualism. European colonialism essentially conquered the Islamic world culturally before it could do so politically and militarily.[17]

The Muslim Brotherhood and Palestinian Islamic Jihad (PIJ) also attributed deculturalization at the hands of Western colonialism as one cause for the decline of past greatness. Yet al-Nabhani's idealist understanding of history and its driving forces, coupled with his strict elitism, resulted in a prescription different from the other Palestinian Islamists. For him, the Brotherhood's work to alleviate poverty, misery, corruption, and vice in society was all a distraction. Muslim piety was commendable, he argued, but it was not sufficient for a people in a given society to be sincere Muslims if they lived under a non-Islamic system. On the contrary, the one-sided focus by some Islamists to promote personal morality and piety was at best misguided because it reduced religion to spiritual guidance while ignoring the broader aspects of the faith and their inherently political implications.[18] Because Islam was a comprehensive creed, ideology, and system of life, 'the Islamic society is brought into being when ... the Islamic system is implemented on the people ... For a [Muslim] person together with another [Muslim] person constitute only a group, and they do not make a society.'[19] At worst, these pious proselytizers were unwitting tools of imperialism because they were engaged in mere benevolent cultural societies without any political ambitions threatening the status quo.[20]

---

15    Ibid., 183, 201–2, 206.
16    Ibid., 231.
17    Ibid., 181, 201.
18    Ibid., 232.
19    Taqi al-Din Nabhani, *Nizam al-Islam*, 6th ed. (n.p.: Manshurat Hizb al-Tahrir, 2001), 37–8.
20    Commins, 'Taqī al-Dīn al-Nabhānī and the Islamic Liberation Party', 202.

Al-Nabhani similarly showed little interest in Palestine as a distinct territorial unit to be liberated from usurpation. Because Islam considered the Islamic community to be an indivisible whole, and because 'Islam does not allow making Islamic lands into countries', there was no political or religious difference between the district of Hijaz or Turkey, or between the district of Jerusalem or that of İskenderun.[21] Palestine was a province like any other province, and Hizb al-Tahrir never bothered with the Israeli–Palestinian conflict in practical terms. Not because Palestine was irrelevant, but because its liberation was long-term, collective, and possible only under the banner of the caliphate once established on Muslim lands. The party therefore never organized demonstrations against the Israeli occupation, and the followers of al-Nabhani's line gave the conflict no greater attention even when violence escalated. They focused on Russia, Myanmar, Syria, and Uzbekistan instead.[22]

Although Ahmad Yassin, PIJ's Fathi al-Shiqaqi, and al-Nabhani all argued that the Palestinians had to resume an Islamic way of life, each of them had a vastly different understanding of what that meant. For al-Nabhani, man required a complete system to organize life if he was to achieve harmony and bliss. Because human nature was inherently flawed and prone to self-interest, any human-made system would be marred by contradictions and biases, and it would lead to misery, corruption, and inefficiency regardless of its capitalist, communist, or nationalist ideological underpinning.[23] The Islamic ideology, however, was necessarily rational and in man's best interest as it came from God.[24] Islam was diagnostic, prognostic, prescriptive, and redemptive. 'There is only one way to attain our revival,' he proclaimed, 'which is the resumption of the Islamic way of life. There is no way to resume the Islamic way of life except through establishing the Islamic state.'[25] The state was the means with which the system would be implemented from the top down. Personal piety was relied on, but it was correct legislation that in the end ensured

---

21    Al-Din Nabhani, *al-Dawla al-islamiyya*, 216, 246.

22    Jacob Høigilt, 'Prophets in Their Own Country? Hizb al-Tahrir in the Palestinian Context', *Politics, Religion and Ideology* 15, no. 4 (October 2014): 514–15.

23    Al-Din Nabhani, *Nizam al-Islam*, 71.

24    Ibid., 25.

25    Ibid., 60.

the collective compliance with Islam.[26] The individual could only be reformed once society was reformed.[27]

In keeping with the party's idealism, the establishment of the Islamic state did not depend on altering existing social structures or material conditions. Rather, the solution to humanity's predicaments lay in the masses gaining a profound understanding of the universe, man, and life itself.[28] Seeking to ground his pan-Islamism in reason and evidence, al-Nabhani believed faith in God could be reached logically.[29] Indeed, 'only a clear understanding of Islam will bring back the Islamic state', whose source was Islamic jurisprudence.[30] This was convenient, of course, given that al-Nabhani was a jurist, and it was correspondingly the responsibility of an enlightened vanguard – comprised of individuals who 'have understood Islam and who sincerely believe' – to disseminate the Islamic call and inspire the rest of society to re-establish the Islamic state through a radical transformation of its mentality and culture.[31] From being an idea in the mind of the vanguard to an ideology manifest in society as a whole, a popular movement would emerge to establish an Islamic state in a given society through a bloodless coup d'état. From the establishment of an Islamic state in one society, it would spread outwards – either by spreading the call or by the use of force – to other societies until Islam had triumphed globally.[32] There was no need for social services or armed struggle, according to al-Nabhani. The strength of the Islamic thought was sufficient.[33] What mattered, then, was to radically and comprehensively change one thought and to replace it with another:

> Society is like water in a large kettle. If anything is placed beneath the kettle that causes the temperature to drop, then the water freezes and transforms into ice. Similarly, if corrupted ideologies are introduced

---

26   Ibid., 35.

27   Al-Din Nabhani, *Mafahim Hizb al-Tahrir*, 6th ed. (n.p.: Manshurat Hizb al-Tahrir, 2001), 64.

28   Al-Din Nabhani, *Nizam al-Islam*, 5–6.

29   Høigilt, 'Prophets in Their Own Country?', 508.

30   Al-Din Nabhani, *al-Dawla al-Iislamiyya*, 174; al-Din Nabhani, *Nizam al-Islam*, 56–7.

31   Al-Din Nabhani, *Mafahim Hizb al-Tahrir*, 72.

32   Al-Din Nabhani, *al-Dawla al-islamiyya*, 250–1.

33   Ibid., 248.

into a society, then it would freeze in corruption and continue to deteriorate and decline . . . If flaming heat was put under the kettle, on the other hand, the water would warm and boil before emitting a dynamic and forceful steam. Similarly, if a correct ideology was introduced into a society, it would act as a flame whose heat would bring society to its boiling point and transform it into a dynamic force. The society would then implement the ideology and carry its call to all other societies.[34]

In the Islamic state envisioned by al-Nabhani, the caliph would bear the full responsibility for enforcing all aspects of Islamic law, encompassing rituals and moral conduct. This law would govern key societal domains such as the economy, education, gender relations, and foreign policy. Al-Nabhani argued that individuals would not enjoy absolute freedom; activities like apostasy, adultery, alcohol consumption, and usury would be prohibited. Despite these restrictions, it was posited that such a society would enable individuals to thrive within clearly defined limits because human actions would be directed towards pleasing God – the ultimate source of individual fulfilment and social harmony – rather than pursuing immediate material satisfaction.[35]

Al-Nabhani and his followers were convinced that it was only a matter of time before the masses would embrace their call for the re-establishment of an Islamic state. As we will see below, however, their idealism, naivety, and profound ignorance of even the most basic political realities ultimately prevented Hizb al-Tahrir from ever gaining traction.

## Into obscurity

We do not know with certainty when al-Nabhani became an Islamist in the traditional sense of the word. He was an active participant in one of Haifa's Islamic societies, the Preservation Association (jam'iyyat al-i'tisam), in the 1940s. Even so, when a visiting Muslim Brotherhood delegation from Cairo visited the association some time between 1941 and 1948 and proposed merging the organizations, al-Nabhani vehemently

---

34  Al-Din Nabhani, *Mafahim Hizb al-Tahrir*, 64.
35  Commins, 'Taqī al-Dīn al-Nabhānī and the Islamic Liberation Party', 198, 203.

refused. Besides, upon his return to Jerusalem from Syrian exile in 1948, al-Nabhani did not associate himself with religious functionaries but with Western-educated Palestinian intellectuals – lawyers, journalists, and former associates of Hajj Amin al-Husseini – and much indicates that al-Nabhani was in contact with the Syrian pan-Arab Baath Party as well.[36] The Baath Party and al-Nabhani did differ in important respects, as the former accepted Islam as only one ideological strand, albeit rich and influential, while the latter contended that Arab nationalism could rehabilitate itself only through religion. Nevertheless, there is also evidence that he initially sympathized with the revolutionary aspirations of the pan-Arab socialists. When Jordanian Baathists, inspired by Husni al-Za'im's 1949 coup in Syria, contemplated a similar move against Jordanian King Abdullah I bin al-Hussein, al-Nabhani was tasked with facilitating communication between them and al-Za'im in May 1949. Notably, Jordanian Colonel Abdallah Tal, a key conspirator in the coup and governor of Jerusalem, is cited as one of al-Nabhani's closest associates in this period.[37]

Indeed, his 1950 monograph, *Saving Palestine*, was decidedly nationalist in orientation. In it, al-Nabhani portrayed the Arab masses – not the Muslims – as a unified nation and the driving force for change. The liberation of Palestine was thus an *Arab* affair. Although he later developed an interpretation of Islam as a comprehensive system of life and politics, his belief in revolutionary change through spiritual transformation – a feature closely resembling the ideas of Syrian Arab nationalist philosopher Michel Aflaq – nevertheless remained, and it deeply influenced the approach of his life-long project.[38] As Taji-Farouki observes, there was a clear ideological progression from the ideas al-Nabhani presented in 1950 to the vision and strategy of Hizb al-Tahrir.[39]

The failure of the 1949 Jordanian coup plot may have precipitated a growing disillusionment with Arab nationalism, and al-Nabhani had already begun distancing himself from the Baathists by the early 1950s. In the first parliamentary elections in the West Bank following Jordanian annexation, for example, al-Nabhani refused to associate himself with the Baathists and ran – unsuccessfully – as an independent candidate. By early 1952, al-Nabhani had begun initiating discussions with other religious

---

36   Taji-Farouki, *A Fundamental Quest*, 4.
37   Ibid., 2–3.
38   Høigilt, 'Prophets in Their Own Country?', 509.
39   Taji-Farouki, *A Fundamental Quest*, 4–5.

functionaries on the necessity of establishing an Islamic political party. Over the ensuing months, they convened intermittently in Jerusalem and Hebron, where they held informal religious discussions during which a group identity crystallized.[40] The first indigenous Palestinian Islamist organization, Hizb al-Tahrir, was formed by the end of the year. Hizb al-Tahrir differed from the Muslim Brotherhood from its inception. For Ahmad Yassin and the Islamic Complex, the solution was a network of social services spreading Islamic values from below to construct a revivalist foundation in society. An Islamic state would then naturally follow once preconditions were in place. Hizb al-Tahrir, on the other hand, worked to establish an Islamic state first, which would then impose its vision and jurisdiction on society from the top down.[41] The organic development of the Islamic state meant that the Palestinian Muslim Brotherhood could pursue a strategic opaqueness enabling the movement to circumvent any critique of its programme by leftist or nationalist forces. It could make sweeping promises about the virtues of the Islamic state without having to provide any details of what such a society would look like. Nor did they have to explain how one would transition from theoretical concepts to practical implementation. Al-Nabhani, on the other hand, outlined the features of the Islamic state in detail, and he even provided a draft constitution in his writings.[42] Little was left to the imagination, and the articles defined, for example, the ruling institutions, the administrative and economic system, the role of women, the education policy, and foreign policy. While some articles in the draft constitution offered broad stipulations, such as guaranteeing employment for all citizens (§149), others specified intricate details, like how sharecropping would be practised on lands planted with trees (§131).

This meant that Hizb al-Tahrir never enjoyed the tactical flexibility of the Muslim Brotherhood, which avoided direct confrontation with the Hashemite Kingdom. When the founders of Hizb al-Tahrir submitted a formal application to the Jordanian Interior Ministry on November 17, 1952, for permission to establish a political party, it was denied because the proposed platform challenged the very legitimacy of the Jordanian

40    Amnon Cohen, *Political Parties in the West Bank under the Jordanian Regime, 1949–1967* (Ithaca, NY: Cornell University Press, 1982), 209.

41    Commins, 'Taqī al-Din al-Nabhānī and the Islamic Liberation Party', 211.

42    See, for example, al-Din Nabhani, *al-Dawla al-islamiyya*, 253–98.

regime. Al-Nabhani and his colleagues then decided to exploit a loophole in the Ottoman Associations Law, still effective in the West Bank, which stated that an association could be formed if the highest authority in the area was notified, or if such an intention was published in the local press.[43] They informed the governor of Jerusalem of their intentions, announced their position in the newspaper *al-Sarih*, and even informed the minister of the interior that their original application for a political party was, in fact, a mistake on their part and asked for it to be ignored. 'This move did not amuse the authorities', Taji-Farouki observes, and al-Nabhani and the other founding members of Hizb al-Tahrir were swiftly arrested.[44]

Although Jordanian authorities never officially recognized Hizb al-Tahrir, they ceased persecuting al-Nabhani and his colleagues. Party members thus began preaching about the necessity of re-establishing the Islamic state from pulpits, actively distributed leaflets, and organized study circles where followers engaged deeply with al-Nabhani's writings. These study circles, the backbone and most distinct feature of the party, operated through a clearly defined hierarchical system. Each circle was typically composed of five members, which was led by a religious functionary. This leader was, in turn, a member of another study group consisting of his peers, and which was led by an even more experienced member. This chain extended upwards until it reached al-Nabhani, the pinnacle of the organizational structure. The primary goal of Hizb al-Tahrir was thus, Milton-Edwards observes, the indoctrination of as many followers as possible.[45]

Hizb al-Tahrir was able to attract a certain following among Palestinians in the early 1950s. Teachers affiliated with the party gained visible support in the camps surrounding Jericho and its activities in Hebron were similarly successful. Party branches were not merely established in Jerusalem, Qalqiliya, Tulkarem, and Nablus, but also outside Palestine, including Lebanon and Kuwait. Hizb al-Tahrir was therefore marked by a clear sense of optimism by early 1953, and some members even believed that they would be ready to topple the Jordanian regime with three months of preparations. Their optimism was unfounded, however,

---

43   Cohen, *Political Parties in the West Bank*, 209–10.
44   Taji-Farouki, *A Fundamental Quest*, 7.
45   Beverley Milton-Edwards, *Islamic Politics in Palestine* (London: I. B. Tauris, 1999), 66.

and the leadership expressed their disappointment about the rate with which its support among Palestinians was growing by the end of the year.[46] In addition, new obstacles arose from their progress. Undeterred by the need to postpone the toppling of the Jordanian regime, followers of al-Nabhani ran in the Jordanian general elections in 1954 and openly campaigned in Jenin, Nablus, Hebron, Tulkarem, and Qalqiliya. Although the party suffered overall defeat in the elections, it used the opportunity to spread its ideas among the Palestinian public. Meanwhile, Ahmad al-Dawr won a seat as an independent candidate from the Tulkarem-Qalqiliya area. His parliamentary duties in Amman unfortunately removed him from his local community, and rather than strengthening Hizb al-Tahrir, his electoral victory undermined the party's influence and presence in the northern West Bank instead.[47]

The success that Hizb al-Tahrir enjoyed also brought renewed repression by local authorities. Authorities first clamped down on the party's activities in Hebron. Hizb al-Tahrir tried to circumvent further repression by avoiding delivering sermons with subversive content in the local mosques, and the party leadership began dispatching cadres from other districts to preach and spread the message, as they were less known to local authorities there. By September 1953, several Hebronite party members had been treated so harshly by the authorities that they chose to emigrate to neighbouring countries, and a decline in party activities was already discernible. Its activities in Nablus – described as 'particularly impressive' – were by June 1954 similarly curbed by government surveillance, which forced the Hizb al-Tahrir cadres to adopt a lower profile. This effectively limited its open contact with the local population.[48]

Even worse, in late 1954, Jordanian authorities banned mosque preaching or teaching without the written permission of the chief judge or his representatives. The Jordanian Preaching and Instruction law of 1955 further hampered the preaching of Hizb al-Tahrir as the government now surveyed the pulpits more closely and began imposing its control to avoid the spread of subversive political propaganda. Although they continued to distribute leaflets and organize study circles, the mosque presence of Hizb al-Tahrir – one of the most important recruitment spheres for the

---

46  Taji-Farouki, *A Fundamental Quest*, 9.
47  Cohen, *Political Parties in the West Bank*, 211.
48  Taji-Farouki, *A Fundamental Quest*, 9–10.

party – largely ended. While several party members used their positions as schoolteachers to convey their ideas to pupils, schools were from mid-1955 explicitly forbidden to include political material in their lessons.[49] Last, al-Nabhani and other high-ranking party members were either expelled or fled abroad, which severely limited party communication and further limited the effectiveness of their call. Al-Nabhani was prevented from re-entering Jordan after a visit to Damascus, and went on to head the party from Beirut before he died in exile in 1977.[50]

Hizb al-Tahrir did not merely lack tactical flexibility. Because a correct understanding of Islam alone could bring forth earthly redemption, al-Nabhani developed a dogmatic insistence on the need for both intellectual and ideological purity within the ranks of his party. This insistence applied not only to the ideas spread by the party activists but also to their methods.[51] '[Al-Nabhani's] authority was absolute, regarding decisions of both the party's ideology and its day-to-day management', and the party leadership meticulously tracked the activities of its branches, either through detailed reports or by dispatching supervisors to conduct investigations.[52] Internal dissent was not resolved through dialogue, mediation, and consensus-building, but by expulsions. In 1958, al-Nabhani expelled several local party leaders for disagreeing with him, and Hizb al-Tahrir quickly devolved into a small sect of followers studying the intricate details of the future Islamic state.[53]

Despite the numerous setbacks, al-Nabhani and other leading party figures maintained their optimism, and they devised new strategies to circumvent government repression, reach the public with their call, and, in the end, seize political power. Although it was clear to them that the Islamic state would not be established in three months, some of the party strategists believed they would need no more than fifteen years to succeed. One strategy involved recruiting members from the Jordanian army and police force. From the mid-1950s, Hizb al-Tahrir thus appointed a dedicated official to liaise with military personnel. Needless to say, the armed forces remained loyal to the king and the outcome of this initiative

49   Cohen, *Political Parties in the West Bank*, 212, 215, 217.

50   Milton-Edwards, *Islamic Politics in Palestine*, 70.

51   Noman Hanif, 'Hizb Ut Tahrir: Islam's Ideological Vanguard', *British Journal of Middle Eastern Studies* 39, no. 2 (August 2012): 208.

52   Cohen, *Political Parties in the West Bank*, 221.

53   Ibid., 212.

was at best modest.[54] Another strategy involved openly criticizing the ruling elites in the Arab world and positioning itself as the champion of the people. This strategy, implemented at the pinnacle of Gamal Abdel Nasser's popularity and prestige, failed as well. Party sources also attributed their failures to the popularity of Abdel Karim Qasim, the Iraqi military officer who led the 1958 coup d'état against King Faisal II, and they regretfully noted that the policies of King Hussein resonated well with the Jordanian population. Hizb al-Tahrir was, in effect, no match for the new revolutionary states in the region, the Arab charismatic rulers, and the single-party regimes.[55] Because society no longer responded to the efforts of Hizb al-Tahrir, and because it remained weak in both numerical and political strength, the party leadership then attempted to court patronage from societal elites. Though they dispatched delegates to Syria and Iraq, this strategy was also abandoned after a couple of years.[56]

Hizb al-Tahrir was, in a sense, both the victim of circumstance and its own dogged naivety. Its refusal to soften its most dogmatic stances – even when circumstances demanded strategic pragmatism – meant that it antagonized most, if not all, authorities in places where it organized its activities. With an inherent inability to ground its analysis in reality and with its only answer being to re-establish past political and administrative structures, it also failed to fulfil a political role, and to have a meaningful impact, in the everyday lives of the Palestinians. Hizb al-Tahrir did have some supporters left among the Palestinians, but its ranks were depleted in the West Bank due to the hostile political atmosphere. Al-Nabhani's followers either left voluntarily or were expelled by the Jordanian authorities.[57] In cities where it was active, such as Nablus and Jerusalem, it stood little chance against secular-nationalist and leftist forces. Even in more conservative cities like Hebron, it failed to make significant inroads, partly due to stiff competition from the Muslim Brotherhood. The leadership thus sealed the fate of the party when it ordered a halt to activities one year after the Six-Day War because, as they cited, victory was temporarily blocked by the Israeli occupiers.[58]

---

54  Ibid., 217, 219.
55  Taji-Farouki, *A Fundamental Quest*, 20–1.
56  Ibid., 25.
57  Milton-Edwards, *Islamic Politics in Palestine*, 90–1; Cohen, *Political Parties in the West Bank*, 220.
58  Cohen, *Political Parties in the West Bank*, 217.

The primary reason for its limited appeal among Palestinians, however, was the fact that its name, the Liberation Party, was a misnomer. Hizb al-Tahrir never was a liberation movement aspiring to end Israeli occupation. That was, after all, the main grievance and concern for the Palestinians. Its complete opposition to the establishment of a Palestinian state – because it would further fragment the Muslim nation – was thus naturally unpopular.

It was similarly not an option for Palestinians to postpone their liberation in wait for the establishment of an Islamic state in some distant and uncertain future, as the followers of al-Nabhani advocated. Other Palestinian movements and organizations – whether nationalist, leftist, or Islamist – faced state repression; they too had political, ideological, and strategic shortcomings. Yet they were able to survive despite external pressure because of the Palestinian popular support they enjoyed. This support stemmed from the immediate, practical solutions these movements and organizations offered in response to the Palestinian plight, which resonated deeply with those living under occupation. Hizb al-Tahrir, in contrast, could only face isolation and irrelevance under similar circumstances.

Indeed, if the history of Hizb al-Tahrir tells us anything about Palestinian Islamism, then it is, as Hroub observes, that the successful construction of an Islamist identity depends on the stance adopted on the Palestinian cause.[59] Palestinian Salafis, for example, have never enjoyed a popular appeal in the Occupied Territories because they isolated themselves from society, withdrew from Palestinian politics, and focused less on the liberation of Palestine and more on the transnational unity of the umma. Their one-sided focus on the minutiae of practising faith effectively led to a marginal role in Palestinian society.[60]

Although the Palestinian Muslim Brotherhood was able to carve out a presence for itself in the Occupied Territories from the 1970s through the construction of a welfare infrastructure and a network of social services, it was not immune to this dynamic. Because the Palestinian nationalist guerrilla movements were immobilized by the 1980s and the Brotherhood refused to take up arms against the Israeli occupation, an inescapable void

---

59    Khaled Hroub, 'Salafi Formations in Palestine and the Limits of a De-Palestinised Milieu', *Holy Land Studies* 7, no. 2 (November 2008): 157.

60    Björn Brenner, *Gaza under Hamas: From Islamic Democracy to Islamist Governance* (London: I. B. Tauris, 2016), 69–70.

surfaced. If you were a Palestinian in Gaza in the mid-1980s, there was no viable organizational vehicle for engaging in Palestinian armed struggle. A segment of the Brotherhood young guard became increasingly disgruntled by the perceived passivity of the Palestinian Islamic movement. As the Israeli occupation was approaching its twenty-year anniversary, they were no longer content with proselytizing and working for the establishment of an Islamic state. It was not Hizb al-Tahrir, then, that would challenge the hegemony of the Brotherhood, but a group of Palestinian students who had begun to question the quietist line of Ahmad Yassin. For them, the Palestinian Islamist movement should not merely participate in but lead the armed struggle for the liberation of their homeland. This is the topic of the next chapter.

# 3

# Rise of the Vanguard

On December 11, 1987, a communiqué was spread in the villages, refugee camps, and cities of Gaza and the West Bank: 'Today, they obsessively scream: Save us from this hell . . . Today, they realize that they are losing and that they will never be able to survive among us . . . Today, they are fully aware that we have nothing to lose and that we love martyrdom more than they love life.' The communiqué proceeded by urging the Palestinian people to 'pull the trigger, roll up your sleeves, prepare yourselves moment by moment to meet the Lord', and to 'defy your depraved world [and] to spit a thousand times on life under occupation.'[1] The call to arms was signed 'The Islamic Jihad Movement in Palestine'.

Although the movement had operated under various names before the First Intifada erupted, such as the Sons of the Islamic Uprising in Palestine, Sons of the Quran Movement, and Sons of al-Aqsa, the declaration of Palestinian Islamic Jihad (PIJ) was, in many ways, the worst-kept secret in the Occupied Palestinian Territories.[2] Founded in the Gaza

---

1    Palestinian Islamic Jihad communiqué, December 11, 1987.
2    Abu Imad al-Rifa'i, *Harakat al-jihad al-islami fi Filastin: Bidayat al-mashru' al-jihadi wa samatihi* (Beirut: Palestinian Islamic Jihad, 2001), 11–12.

Strip by a group of Palestinian students in 1981, the movement raised the slogan 'Islam, Jihad, and Palestine': Islam as the starting point, jihad as the means, and Palestine as the goal of liberation. PIJ soon developed into a small but cohesive network of military cells consisting of no more than a hundred fighters carrying out armed operations against Israeli targets from 1984.[3] What was PIJ, why was it founded, and what did the movement signify in the evolution of Palestinian Islamism?[4]

This chapter investigates the rise of PIJ. It analyses the variables contributing to the distinct ideological formation process of its founding fathers and the political debates in which they participated throughout the 1970s. We will see that violence was highly controversial in the 1980s. We will also see that the PIJ founding fathers did not just aspire to engage in armed struggle against the Israeli occupation, but also to go to the cinema.

## Embracing modernity and tradition

There, in Egypt, we met as a believing and intellectual group of young Palestinian men, with the roots of rich cultural and political experiences. We discovered each other at evening gatherings as most of us read Shakespeare, Dostoyevsky, Chekhov, Sartre, T. S. Eliot, and others. – Fathi al-Shiqaqi.[5]

Before the 1948 Palestine war, the grandfather of Fathi Ibrahim Abdel Aziz al-Shiqaqi was the imam of the small village of Zarnuqa in the Ramla district. As a little boy, al-Shiqaqi's father, Ibrahim, would come to the mosque to read, pray, and listen to his stories and sermons.[6] Although a Palestinian village, Zarnuqa was considered 'friendly' by Jewish armed

---

3    Beverley Milton-Edwards, *Islamic Politics in Palestine* (London: I. B. Tauris, 1999), 120; Ziad Abu-Amr, *Islamic Fundamentalism in the West Bank and Gaza* (Bloomington: Indiana University Press, 1994), 99.

4    This chapter is based on chapters 1–3 in Erik Skare, *A History of Palestinian Islamic Jihad: Faith, Awareness, and Revolution in the MIddle East* (Cambridge: Cambridge University Press, 2021).

5    Fathi al-Shiqaqi, 'al-Jihad: al-Qissa al-haqiqiyya', in Rif'at Sayyid Ahmad, ed., *Rihlat al-damm alladhi hazam al-sayf: al-A'mal al-kamila li-l-shahid al-duktur Fathi al-Shiqaqi* (Cairo: Markaz Yafa li-l-dirasat wa-l-abhath, 1996), 1139.

6    Christoph Reuter, *My Life Is a Weapon: A Modern History of Suicide Bombing* (Princeton, NJ: Princeton University Press, 2004), 96.

forces when the war erupted, probably due to its economic dependence on wages from cultivating Jewish-owned orange groves. In May 1948, for example, its *mukhtar* (mayor) went to the Qatra police station, announcing that Zarnuqa, in addition to the Palestinian villages of Mughar, Bash-Shit, and Qubayba, wanted to surrender. Besides, Zarnuqa's most powerful clan, Shurbaji, proposed that the village should hand over its weapons to the Jewish paramilitary organization Haganah for protection.

Its population was expelled on May 27, 1948, however, and the houses of Zarnuqa were demolished in June. Initially camping near Majdal, Zarnuqa's population did attempt to return to reap their agricultural fields, 'with hunger rampant' among them, but they were expelled by Jewish troops once more.[7] Their flight only ended in Gazan Rafah, settling as refugees with an uncertain future. It was there, under Egyptian administration, that Fathi al-Shiqaqi was born a refugee in 1951.[8]

Al-Shiqaqi's political project, Palestinian Islamic Jihad, did not commence in the Occupied Palestinian Territories. Instead, it emanated from Palestinian student circles in Egypt in the mid-1970s, where al-Shiqaqi was central. His peers there were Ramadan Shallah, who succeeded him as secretary-general in PIJ after al-Shiqaqi was assassinated by Mossad in 1995. Muhammad al-Hindi, future deputy leader of PIJ, was also there with Nafidh Azzam, a future member of its political bureau. There, in the Egyptian city al-Zagazig, located in the eastern part of the Nile delta, they organized study circles in al-Shiqaqi's apartment, where they read, interpreted, and fiercely debated politics, religion, and literature.

Their intellectual pursuit extended beyond Islamist classics such as the letters of Hassan al-Banna and the fiery tracts of Sayyid Qutb. It also encompassed Western classics by William Shakespeare, Fyodor Dostoyevsky, and Anton Chekhov. They read the Arabic classics of Naguib Mahfouz, Badr Shakir al-Sayyab, and Salah Abdel Sabour. They read Sophocles and Mahmud Darwish, Jamal al-Din al-Afghani and Albert Hourani, and they read Muhammad Abduh and Jean-Paul Sartre. As Shallah recalled this period:

---

7    Benny Morris, *The Birth of the Palestinian Refugee Problem Revisited* (Cambridge: Cambridge University Press, 2004), 95, 258–9, 444; Benny Morris, *1948 and After: Israel and the Palestinians* (Oxford: Clarendon Press, 1990), 82n4.

8    Text in this and the preceding paragraph is taken from Skare, *A History of Palestinian Islamic Jihad*, 14.

[We read] about the resistance against colonialism in Algeria, Abdelha-
mid Ben Badis, Omar Mukhtar in Libya, Senussi in Tunisia, Izz al-Din
al-Qassam in Palestine, al-Mahdi in Sudan, al-Kawakibi and al-Afghani.
[We did so] all the way up to the contemporary Islamic movement with
the emergence of an independent state in the Arab and Islamic homeland based on secular grounds, and then the position of the Islamic
movement. It was here I got acquainted with the writings of Mawdudi,
Sayyid Qutb, Sheikh al-Ghazali, Sheikh al-Qaradawi, and others, and I
began to realize that there was another view of the world than what we
learned in our schools and homes.[9]

One could describe the list of literature as eclectic, but it is more precise
to describe their intellectual enterprise as open-minded and driven by
genuine curiosity. This curiosity was partly spurred by the lively debates
in Cairo, one of the major cultural centres in the Middle East, and on
Egyptian campuses. Involving nationalists, leftists, communists, and
Islamist students of various colours, the Palestinian students engaged
with youthful audacity in fierce discussion and polemics. When the
communist student bloc announced its newspaper, *The Steeds*, al-Shiqaqi
and his friends issued a competing newspaper, *The Horsemen*. Interviews
and written sources thus indicate that the founding fathers of PIJ were
attempting to make sense of the world and the way forward. As one co-
founder of PIJ described this period: 'We tried to understand the world,
the Arab world, to find a way.'[10]

The Palestinian students were also driven by a collective sense of
crisis caused by the Six-Day War in 1967. Al-Shiqaqi, for example, did
not immediately embrace Islamism. On the contrary, he was an ardent
Nasserist in his teens and actively promoted secular pan-Arabism among
his friends and at school. Left in shock from the Arab defeat, his ideological world crumbled as he was unable to find an explanation in Nasserist
thought and ideology:

---

9   Ghassan Charbel, 'Ziyara li-dhakirat al-amin al-amm li-harakat 'al-jihad
al-islami fi Filastin' 4. Shallah: Talabtuhu bi-tashkil tanzim wa hin kashaf al-sirr
baya'tuhu bay'at 'al-jihad' al-Shiqaqi an hassan nasrallah: sayakun khumayni al-
Arab idha 'ash', *al-Hayat*, January 10, 2003.
10   PIJ co-founder, interview with Erik Skare, August 6, 2018.

The actual explanations of [Nasserism] did not provide the reasons for the defeat, while the Islamic idea, on the other hand, became far more convincing with its deep questions such as 'Who are we? Why were we defeated? And why now? Why have we triumphed before and why do we lose now?'

Turning to religion, however, did not mean leaving his sympathy for the Palestinian guerrilla movements behind, nor did it entail abandoning his belief in direct action, political work, or creating what he believed was a new and better world. Although he joined the Muslim Brotherhood in 1968 after he became acquainted with Ahmad Yassin as a sixteen-year-old, al-Shiqaqi never felt at home there. In contrast to the quietist Brotherhood, politics was never a dirty word for him and armed struggle not something to be avoided.[11] Through immersion in history, past anti-colonial struggles, Islamic sciences, and the focus on the Palestinian cause, the Palestinian students began to crystallize a distinct activist approach focusing on action to obtain qualitative change:

> We had realized at the time that the Muslim Brotherhood did not have an intellectual study of the [current] development and that there were intellectual and dynamic flaws in the movement that would leave the Brotherhood – and perhaps the whole Islamic movement – to a stand-still . . . Rather, maintaining the organization was more important than taking the right position, which isolated them from the masses . . . [We believed] that the Islamic movement must be the locomotive for this change – to move the body of the *umma* as a whole.[12]

The Arab defeat was in other words a profoundly destabilizing event that undermined inter-generational continuity. There was the passive old guard of the Muslim Brotherhood, on the one hand, and young, action-oriented Palestinian students, on the other. As inherited orientations suddenly appeared irrelevant, and in the search for new meaning, al-Shiqaqi began to dismiss the Brotherhood old guard as a 'generation of hesitation and distress'.[13] In his eyes, if there was anything characterizing

---

11    Skare, *A History of Palestinian Islamic Jihad*, 213–14.

12    Muhammad Muru, *Fathi al-Shiqaqi: Sawt al-Mustad'afin fi muwajahat mashru' al-haymana al-Gharbi* (Cairo: Markaz Yafa li-l-dirasat wa-l-abhath, 1997), 2.

13    Loren D. Lybarger, *Identity and Religion in Palestine: The Struggle Between*

the preceding generation, it was their impotence and lack of strategy and analysis. It was up to al-Shiqaqi and his companions – the 'generation of awareness and revolution' – to light the torch anew. The study circles in Egypt formed new meanings and associations as a distinct identity and group dynamic crystallized.[14]

Abdallah al-Shami, a founding member of PIJ, reflected on the grievances of the student group in this period: 'The Islamists at that stage proclaimed education, ignored jihad in the path of God, and denounced the illegality of our project.'[15] One of the PIJ leaders in the West Bank, the late Yusuf Arif al-Hajj Muhammad, similarly noted that 'the negative attitude that the Islamic movements and groups on the Palestinian scene took to armed jihad against the occupation' was one of the main variables pushing the Palestinian students to create PIJ.[16]

Their critique of Hizb al-Tahrir echoed similar sentiments. As discussed in chapter 2, despite advocating for jihad, its founder, Taqi al-Din al-Nabhani, believed that the Muslim world's decline stemmed primarily from the dissolution of the caliphate; he maintained a firm stance against engaging in armed conflict without a caliph's leadership. Hizb al-Tahrir thus rejected armed struggle and proselytizing, instead aspiring to construct an Islamic state from the top-down. The postponement of Palestinian liberation made Shallah ask:

> Considering the theoretical, educational, and moral preparations [of the Islamic Complex and Hizb al-Tahrir], no one denies its importance, but the question is, until when?! How many years do we have to wait preparing, while the enemy stretches, expands, and grows its power, perils, and ambitions every day?[17]

---

*Islamism and Secularism in the Occupied Territories* (Princeton, NJ: Princeton University Press, 2007), 17–18; Fathi al-Shiqaqi, 'al-Qadiya al-Filastiniyya: Hiya al-qadiya al-markaziyya li-l-haraka al-islamiyya . . . limadha?', in Ahmad, *Rihlat al-damm alladhi hazam al-Sayf,* 65.

14   Anwar Abu Taha, *Harakat al-jihad al-islami fi Filastin: Nash'atan wa min-hajan* (Beirut: Palestinian Islamic Jihad, 2001), 16.

15   Al-Quds Brigades, 'Dhikra 'al-Shiqaqi' fi dhakirat 'al-shami', saraya.ps, January 7, 2015.

16   Yusuf Arif al-Hajj Muhammad, *al-Masira al-jihadiyya li-harakat al-jihad al-islami fi Filastin* (Gaza: Muhjat al-Quds, 2011), 37.

17   Ramadan Shallah, *Haqa'iq wa mawafiq* (Damascus: Mu'assasat al-Aqsa al-thaqafiyya, 2007), 24.

There were also clear pull factors that accelerated the formation of PIJ: the Iranian revolution in 1979 mesmerized the Palestinian students, who saw a people topple one of the main allies of the United States and Israel in the region. With the Iranian masses rising up against the Shah and advancing, everything at that point seemed possible. As al-Shiqaqi declared: 'The superpowers can . . . be beaten and overturned if we are freed from the dependence on them and possess a free will – one that is believing, active, and energetic.'[18]

Witnessing a people 'recovering lost rights by their own hands', the Iranian revolution cemented the Palestinian students' belief that the Brotherhood's approach was misguided as they connected Ayatollah Ruhollah Khomeini's political line with their own.[19] Just as Khomeini dismissed quietist Shiites who rejected political work while awaiting the Mahdi to establish the rule of Islam and fill the land with justice,[20] so did al-Shiqaqi and his companions dismiss the quietist Brotherhood and Hizb al-Tahrir for postponing the struggle to an uncertain future while awaiting for society to return to Islamic values or for the establishment of the caliphate.[21]

The ideological formation process of PIJ fused orthodox Islamist ideology, modernist political traditions, Palestinian nationalism, and anticolonial thought. The fact that so many of the PIJ founding fathers were former secular-nationalists also left a distinct mark on its developing ideology with a largely secular, if not materialist, analysis. Al-Shiqaqi, for example, always seemed more infatuated with history and historical analysis than religious exegesis, and the Arab Nahda movement of the nineteenth century was more relevant for him than the first five centuries of Islam (known as the Islamic golden age).[22] Al-Shiqaqi essentially perceived economic impetus and not religious metaphysical forces as the major driving force of colonialism. 'The West must maintain its growth

18    Fathi al-Shiqaqi, 'al-Thawra al-islamiyya fi Iran wa-l-thawra al-Filastiniyya', in Ahmad, *Rihlat al-damm alladhi hazam al-sayf*, 558.

19    Shallah, *Haqa'iq wa mawafiq*, 80.

20    The Mahdi, a messianic figure in Islamic eschatology, is believed to have disappeared 873–4 CE, entering a state of occultation, only to return at the end of times to restore justice and equity on Earth.

21    Fathi al-Shiqaqi, *al-Khumayni: al-Hall al-islami wa-l-badil* (Cairo: al-mukhtar al-islami, 1979), 37.

22    Skare, *Palestinian Islamic Jihad*, 2.

rates and economic and social prosperity,' Fathi al-Shiqaqi wrote about the Afghan–Soviet War, 'which means keeping the North rich and the South poor. The goods of this earth are sufficient for all humankind to live in real prosperity . . . and not with this dreadful disparity between the lives of the person in the North and the hunger of the person in the South.'[23] Until his last days, al-Shiqaqi stressed colonialism as the main force behind the sluggish development and suffering in the Third World, and he maintained throughout his writings that 'this is the history of the superpowers' relationship with the oppressed peoples.'[24]

The impasse of the Palestinians did not commence with the establishment of the State of Israel in 1948, according to al-Shiqaqi. Instead, it began with the advent of Western colonialism and its war against the Muslim world.[25] Although he perceived colonialism as inherently violent, al-Shiqaqi also saw it – like Yassin and al-Nabhani – as a forced process of deculturalization spreading westernization and fragmentation through the use of European preachers, missionaries, schools, newspapers, and Arab expeditions to Paris and London to emulate European administrative systems.[26] As the Ottoman Empire collapsed in 1924, al-Shiqaqi perceived the resultant division of the Islamic world into isolated Arab nation-states as a pivotal colonialist accomplishment and a key factor in Western regional dominance – with Arab nationalism and socialism in response replacing a predominant Islamic identity.[27] Both, al-Shiqaqi believed, failed miserably in their attempt to expel the colonial domination of the West.[28]

The establishment of the State of Israel mattered because PIJ perceived it as a 'central part of this [colonial] project' and as an ally of 'imperialist colonialism against the wealth of the peoples, and of the western attack on Islam and its homeland.'[29] The State of Israel was only established,

---

23    Fathi al-Shiqaqi, 'Afghanistan: Judhur al-sira: al-Thawra. al-Mustaqbal. Hal huwa inbi'ath salibi jadid?', in Ahmad, *Rihlat al-damm alladhi hazam al-sayf*, 144.

24    Ibid., 142.

25    Al-Shiqaqi, 'al-Tarikh limadha?'.

26    Al-Shiqaqi, *al-Khumayni*, 30–1.

27    Al-Shiqaqi, 'Markaziyyat Filastin wa-l-mashru' al-islami al-mu'asir', in Ahmad, *Rihlat al-damm alladhi hazam al-sayf*, 431.

28    Al-Shiqaqi, 'al-Qadiya al-Filastiniyya', 178–9.

29    Ibid., 174; al-Shiqaqi, 'Markaziyyat Filastin wa-l-mashru' al-islami al-mu'asir', 450.

then, in line with the interests of colonialism as the Israeli project ensured Western hegemony through which the subordination and dependency of the oppressed was established and sustained. Because of Israel's nature as a colonial entity in the region, al-Shiqaqi concluded that all Arabs and Muslims would persist in their state of dependence on the intellectual, political, economic, and military levels as long as Israel exists.[30]

The internal discussions in the Islamic movement on whether one should confront Westernization and dependency or the Israeli occupation first was, according to al-Shiqaqi, a false binary.[31] In fact, the destruction of the State of Israel was the first step towards ending colonial rule in the region, thereby significantly undermining Western colonialism globally. Recognizing any part of Israel, or giving up any inch of Palestine, was consequently unlawful, and a two-state solution an oxymoron, as long as one of the two states constituted the very precondition for the Global South's continued subjugation.[32] That meant that Israel did not just present a threat for the Palestinians and Muslims but also to

> all the oppressed in the world. Israel's close relationship with the forces of international arrogance and its assistance to the racist governments and dictatorial regimes in Africa and elsewhere affirms the danger it constitutes against the future of the oppressed in the world as well as Muslims.[33]

That is not to say that PIJ developed into a secular movement. On the contrary, although al-Shiqaqi relied on a largely secular analysis of the conflict and its history, much of PIJ's public discourse was characteristically religious, with explicit references to holy texts to legitimize its own normative claims. When the movement attempted to ignite the flames of Palestinian revolution in 1987, for example, they declared (with a clear reference to the Muslim Brotherhood):

---

30   Skare, *A History of Palestinian Islamic Jihad*, 42.
31   Al-Shiqaqi, 'Markaziyyat Filastin wa-l-mashru' al-islami al-mu'asir', 431.
32   Skare, *A History of Palestinian Islamic Jihad*, 42–3.
33   Al-Shiqaqi, 'Markaziyyat Filastin wa-l-mashru' al-islami al-mu'asir', 454.

You must be aware that you have two options, and there is no third: You can either obey God and His messenger, and continue your blessed intifada until it bears fruit and you are victorious, or you can obey the generals of the [Israeli] enemy and its leaders, remain silent and calm 'and you will then become losers' [surat al-'imran: 149].[34]

Besides, when the movement urged the people to continue struggling despite Palestinian losses, they similarly referred to Sumaya bin Khattab (c. 550–615 CE), the first member of the Islamic nation to fall as a woman martyr: 'Remember, O compassionate and grieving father, that you, your son, and your wealth is the property of God.'[35] Religion clearly mattered for the ideological formation process of PIJ, and one of the movement's general principles is that it adheres to Islam as creed ('aqida), code (shari'a), and system of life in order to analyse and understand the nature of the conflict.[36]

In fact, just as there was a historical dimension to the Israeli–Palestinian conflict (the role of colonialism and its driving forces), the PIJ founders declared that the Palestinian cause had a religious one, as well. Palestine was the first qibla of the Muslims and it was there, where the al-Aqsa Mosque was built, that Prophet Muhammad departed to the seventh heaven with Archangel Gabriel.[37] Palestine was therefore blessed by God himself, given that 'there is no land connected to so many blessed verses [in the Quran] as the land of Palestine.'[38]

Religion highlighted the prominence of Palestine and the central role of the Palestinian cause; it provided insights for understanding the current conflict with the Israeli occupation. Referring to the seventeenth chapter in the Quran, al-Isra', al-Shiqaqi claimed that the current conflict with the Israelis was predestined by God: just as the Israelites had risen

---

34   PIJ communiqué, 'Forward, O March of Sacred Struggle', December 18, 1987.

35   PIJ communiqué, 'O World, Listen for a Moment, and Hear the Cries of Our Children and Mothers', January 29, 1988.

36   Skare, Palestinian Islamic Jihad, 46.

37   Qibla is the direction Muslims face when in prayer. While Muslims originally faced Jerusalem in prayer, this changed to the Kaaba in Mecca approximately one and a half years after the emigration of Prophet Muhammad.

38   Fathi al-Shiqaqi, 'Filastin nuqtat al-sidam ma' al-mashru' al-Gharbi al-isti'mari', in Ahmad, Rihlat al-damm alladhi hazam al-sayf, 709.

in power and arrogance in the time of Prophet Muhammad, they were defeated by true Muslims. Just as the Jews had risen before, they were predestined to do so again.[39]

For al-Shiqaqi, Israel was the obvious manifestation of this predestined second rise ending the Islamic golden age 'as has been evident since the fall of Jerusalem, the establishment of their state, and the continuation of their rise and corruption.'[40] He was equally certain that an Islamic victory was equally inevitable if 'we wake up from our sleep and return to the approach leading to that which is most suitable and gives good tidings to the believers.'[41] As Anwar Abu Taha, member of PIJ's political bureau, concluded, the destruction of Israel and the liberation of Jerusalem would usher in Islam's victory over all religions and its spread throughout the world.[42] Abu Taha confirmed this sentiment when asked by the author:

> The West created Israel, and Israel protects the Arab regimes, while the Arab regimes deal with the West. What is the solution with Israel? Fighting. Here is the West, what is the solution? Conversion [to Islam]. Not Marxism [to end colonialism], but conversion. Do you know the word *taghrib* [Westernization]? What is anti-Westernization? The Islamization of the entire world.[43]

Al-Shiqaqi never bothered to develop his religious analysis at length and only bits and pieces exist in his writings; it should thus be viewed, in part, as the distinct response to a period in which the Gazan Muslim Brotherhood refused to move beyond quietist activism. His references to and particular interpretation of religious texts offered a crucial religious mandate for the Palestinian Islamic movement to engage in armed struggle now, and not later. Elevating the necessity of armed struggle from the political to the theological plane, PIJ did not merely proclaim that armed struggle was an individual duty ordained by God, but that divine revelation assured that the Palestinian Islamic movement would be triumphant as well. In effect, their specific reading of the religious texts

---

39    For a more elaborate analysis of the Quranic dimension, see Skare, *A History of Palestinian Islamic Jihad*, 43–8.

40    Al-Shiqaqi, 'Markaziyyat Filastin wa-l-mashru' al-islami al-mu'asir', 441.

41    Ibid., 437.

42    Abu Taha, *Harakat al-jihad al-islami fi Filastin*, 45–6.

43    Anwar Abu Taha, interview with Erik Skare, March 19, 2018.

functioned as an iron gauntlet flung at the traditional Islamic movement, with PIJ flipping the logic of the Muslim Brothers on its head.[44] Instead of Islamization for liberation, al-Shiqaqi and his companions stressed liberation for Islamization – not just of Palestine, but of the world. In certain respects, this meant that, while Hamas Islamized the Palestinian cause by stressing the need for religious observance and morality in the struggle,[45] PIJ ended up Palestinianizing Islam by not simply stressing the blessed land of Palestine just as the launching pad, but as the very precondition, for the commencement of Islam's global victory.[46]

PIJ was, in other words, the product of a specific historical stage in the course of Palestinian resistance. The Six-Day War and the Arab defeat in 1967 made a number of Palestinians turn to religion in search for an answer. The Iranian revolution in 1979 further bolstered their belief in Islam as the ideological vehicle facilitating the creation of a new world. The political opportunity structure in Gaza was equally important: If you were a Palestinian in Gaza who wanted to join the armed struggle in the 1980s, there was no viable organizational alternative for you to join. The PLO and its factions had become both politically and militarily irrelevant in the Occupied Territories, particularly so after the evacuation from Beirut to Tunis in 1982. Many Palestinians were also dissatisfied with the PLO's adoption of its Ten-Point Programme in 1974 in which it opened the possibility of using other means than violence, negotiations with the State of Israel, and acceptance of only a partial liberation of Palestine. The Muslim Brotherhood was at the same time not a viable alternative because of its passivity, and al-Shiqaqi only joined hesitantly. For the founding fathers of PIJ, that was the point when they began asking the Leninesque question: 'What is to be done?'[47]

Moreover, the PIJ leadership comprised of young Palestinian men with academic degrees in the natural sciences and humanities; their political project was in various ways an attempt to fuse religious tradition and modernity.[48] As one of its earliest members, Taysir al-Khatib, reminisced,

44  Skare, *A History of Palestinian Islamic Jihad*, 45, 47–8.

45  Rashid Khalidi, *Palestinian Identity: The Construction of Modern National Consciousness* (New York: Columbia University Press, 2010), 148–9.

46  Skare, *A History of Palestinian Islamic Jihad*, 220.

47  Muhammad, *al-Masira al-jihadiyya*, 31.

48  Meir Hatina, *Islam and Salvation in Palestine* (Tel Aviv: Moshe Dayan Center for Middle Eastern and Africa Studies, 2001), 27.

they wanted to be true to their religion *and* go to the cinema; they wanted to go to the mosque *without* being cut off from modern thought and ideas; and they wanted to read, debate, and critique *without* being restricted by the narrow orthodoxy of the Muslim Brotherhood.[49] The conflict between PIJ and the Brotherhood was thus just as much a clash of generations as it was political, and it was just as much intellectual as it was theological. The observation made by Dot-Pouillard and Rébillard is an astute one: PIJ was not merely a *political* tendency but also a critique of the Muslim Brotherhood's inability to embrace new ideas.[50]

These differing views on modernity and religious tradition necessarily produced two distinct social practices on the ground once PIJ and Hamas were founded. The activists of the latter continued patrolling the streets of Gaza to combat perceived moral and behavioural impropriety throughout the 1980s, 'primarily directed against women'.[51] Stores selling alcohol were firebombed, cafés and video shops were attacked, and protests were organized against cinemas to prevent the spread of perceived moral corruption and degradation.[52] Although the movement matured politically in the early 1990s and its doctrinaire discourse diminished, upholding community values became a more or less persistent feature of Hamas's political conduct. In the 2010s, for example, there were reports of Hamas's police officers issuing threats to male hairdressers for servicing female clients.[53] PIJ, on the other hand, did not bother to any great extent what clothes one wore or whether unmarried couples held hands in Gaza; the only thing that mattered was the armed struggle against the Israeli occupation. Although PIJ is often viewed as one of the most radical Palestinian groups in the West, this principled position on violence has paradoxically led to its perception among Palestinians as one of the most restrained.

The ideological formation process of the PIJ founding fathers in Egypt was, then, not so much the articulation of a qualitatively new ideology as

---

49    Nicolas Dot-Pouillard and Eugénie Rébillard, 'The Intellectual, the Militant, the Prisoner and the Partisan: The Genesis of the Islamic Jihad Movement in Palestine (1974–1988)', *Muslim World* 103 (2013): 9.

50    Ibid.

51    Sara Roy, 'The Political Economy of Despair: Changing Political and Economic Realities in the Gaza Strip', *Journal of Palestine Studies* 20, no. 3 (1991): 65.

52    Milton-Edwards, *Islamic Politics in Palestine*, 107–8.

53    Human Rights Watch, 'Gaza: Halt Morality Enforcement Campaign', hrw.org, March 2, 2011.

much as it was the innovative re-articulation of old ones. The founding fathers of PIJ merely extended the worldview of the Palestinian Islamic currents through the incorporation of armed struggle, which, *in extenso*, functioned as an antidote to the secular-nationalist PLO currents.[54] Indeed, this synthesis of modernity and tradition is not exclusive to Islamism. The postwar Italian Communist Party, for example, 'combined the tradition of the old socialist movement with the organizational efficiency of Leninism and the moral authority of a secular Catholic Church'. As its leader, Palmiro Togliatti, proclaimed: 'In every household a picture of [Karl] Marx next to the one of Jesus Christ.'[55]

This embrace – alongside a call for armed struggle now, and not later – made the project of PIJ especially appealing to two demographics once al-Shiqaqi and his friends returned to Gaza in 1980. This is where we turn next.

## Strife and discord in the Gaza Strip

Although the Palestinian students had no connection to the assassination of Anwar Sadat on October 6, 1981, they quickly fled the country following a widespread arrest campaign targeting anyone who could be considered an Islamist. The ideological formation process of the PIJ nucleus had matured to such an extent at this point that al-Shiqaqi and his friends knew what the next stage required. There was enormous controversy when they returned to the Gaza Strip and began confronting the Islamic Complex with its passivity. Fierce discussions and polemics rapidly ensued between those who advocated proselytizing and social work, and those who proclaimed that the time had come for the Islamists to confront the Israeli occupation with violence.

The Islamists were not afraid of using unscrupulous tactics to get the upper hand. When al-Shiqaqi attempted to spread the message in the mosques of Gaza, the caretakers cut the electricity to prevent him from speaking.[56] He was thus forced to spread his message in the dark. When

---

54    Skare, *A History of Palestinian Islamic Jihad*, 36.

55    Eric Hobsbawm, *Interesting Times: A Twentieth-Century Life* (New York: Pantheon Books, 2002), 218.

56    Al-Quds Brigades, 'Khabar: al-Qiyadi al-shami li-"l-i'lam al-harbi" al-Shiqaqi sana' mashru' islami thawri shamilt', saraya.ps, October 27, 2013.

the spiritual guide of PIJ, Abdel Aziz Awda, exited the mosque after one of his sermons, he saw that someone had punctured the tires of his car.[57] The Islamic Complex further slandered the PIJ founding fathers to delegitimize their claims; they claimed that al-Shiqaqi, Shallah, and the other students were Shiites in disguise and Iranian lap dogs.[58] '[The members of the PIJ nucleus] were accused of loyalty to Iran,' Anwar Abu Taha writes, 'in an attempt to cover the main issue of the dispute: the position on armed struggle against Israel.'[59] The depiction of PIJ as an Iranian puppet did not, then, develop organically once contact with the Islamic Republic commenced in 1988. Instead, it was a rumour the Brotherhood had spread to discredit an annoying competitor seven years earlier.

The dispute rapidly worsened by 1983, as old friends turned into enemies.[60] Yahya al-Nahal and the first leader of PIJ's military wing, Mahmud al-Khawaja, had been close since childhood. Yet,

> [Al-Khawaja joined PIJ and] I remained with my commitment to the youth in the Islamic Complex. I was one of his strongest opponents, and there was a strong disagreement between us after [the split], and with Mahmud in particular. We were like enemies in the mosques.[61]

While the Islamic Complex had previously used confrontations and low-scale violence to combat PLO elements and perceived vice in the Gaza Strip, they now turned to their Islamist competitors: 'They began to chase us in the mosques and closed the doors to us,' Abdallah al-Shami recalls, 'raised charges and rumors, and attacked our symbols such as Dr Fathi al-Shiqaqi.'[62] Followers of al-Shiqaqi were confronted during prayer when members of the Islamic Complex assaulted them with sticks and chains in the mosque.[63] Al-Shiqaqi and Awda were also physically assaulted by the young guard in the Brotherhood. Al-Shiqaqi managed to escape without

---

57    Riyad Salih Hashish, *Rihlat haya bayn al-bilad wa-l-shahada* (Gaza: al-kalima li-l-nashr wa-l-tawzi', 2018), 174–5.
58    Shallah, *Haqa'iq wa mawafiq*, 71.
59    Abu Taha, *Harakat al-jihad al-islami fi Filastin*, 21.
60    Milton-Edwards, *Islamic Politics in Palestine*, 119–20.
61    Hashish, *Rihlat haya bayn al-bilad wa-l-shahada*, 165–6.
62    Al-Quds Brigades, 'Dhikra 'al-Shiqaqi' fi dhakirat 'al-shami'.
63    Hashish, *Rihlat haya bayn al-bilad wa-l-shahada*, 171.

serious injuries.[64] Awda, on the other hand, who lectured at the Islamic University of Gaza, was hospitalized in 1983 by Brotherhood supporters who controlled campus.[65] The disputes were, at best, troublesome for this group of inexperienced Palestinian students.

Much indicates it was a lost cause for al-Shiqaqi and his companions in persuading the Muslim Brotherhood to alter its approach; confrontation was inevitable. One reason was the dogmatic line that the Brotherhood in Gaza had adopted and its strict hierarchical structure, offering few channels for dialogue and expressions of internal dissent. Its inflexibility caused frustration within its own membership base and particularly so within its young guard.[66] 'I remember that I and some brothers visited Yassin in the mosque of the Islamic Complex,' al-Shiqaqi reminisced, '... in an attempt to defuse the conflict ... and [I] showed my readiness to solve our principles if we could express our views freely.'[67] Yassin only accepted conditionally, however, according to al-Shiqaqi's account: the PIJ founding fathers could present their views directly to the Brotherhood leaders if they had concerns, but they were not allowed to spread discord among its bases. This was independently confirmed by one of the PIJ founders I interviewed: he stated that the main push factor causing al-Shiqaqi to give up reconciliation was the inability of the Palestinian Muslim Brotherhood to tolerate internal differences.[68] A hundred flowers did *not* bloom in Gaza.[69]

The fact that the Brotherhood felt threatened by the PIJ project did little to salvage the deteriorating relationship. According to al-Shiqaqi, Yassin believed that the PIJ project would 'pull the rug from under their feet' and that PIJ was meant to replace the Brotherhood in the Occupied Territories.[70] His worries were not without merit. When assessing the

64    Al-Quds Brigades, 'Khabar: al-Qiyadi al-shami li-"l-i'lam al-harbi" al-shiqaqi sana' mashru' islami thawri shamil', saraya.ps, October 27, 2013.

65    Jean-Pierre Filiu, *Gaza: A History* (Oxford: Oxford University Press, 2014), 158.

66    Tareq Baconi, *Hamas Contained: The Rise and Pacification of Palestinian Resistance* (Stanford, CA: Stanford University Press, 2018), 18.

67    Muhammad al-Sarsawi and Adnan Ali, *D. Fathi al-Shiqaqi al-shahid wa-l-shahid* (n.p., 1996), 19.

68    PIJ co-founder, interview with Erik Skare, August 6, 2018.

69    *Britannica*, 'Hundred Flowers Campaign', December 29, 2023, britannica.com.

70    Al-Sarsawi and Ali, *D. Fathi al-Shiqaqi al-shahid wa-l-shahid*, 19.

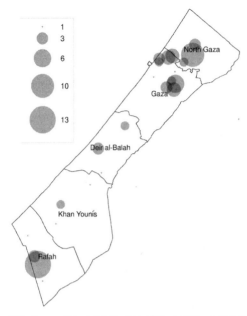

**Figure 3.1.** Geographical distribution of Gazan PIJ martyrs, 1985–99

geographical distribution of PIJ and al-Qassam martyrs from 1985/1988 to 1999 (Figures 3.1 and 3.2), it is evident that the former began recruiting militants from the same areas as Hamas did. Al-Khawaja was represent-ative in that he was a member of the Islamic Complex's young guard before he was swayed by al-Shiqaqi's political message.[71] The focal points of the PIJ nucleus's recruitment efforts in the 1980s were to the south and the north of Gaza: Rafah, Gaza City, and North Gaza. Although the al-Qassam brigades had a smaller presence in Deir al-Balah and Rafah before the Second Intifada compared to PIJ, its recruitment efforts in the north seem to have been in competition with its little sister.

That is not to say that the founding fathers and early members of PIJ were blameless for the growing tensions in Gaza. Al-Shiqaqi was known for fiery rhetoric and did not fear making enemies. He had already severed his ties to the Egyptian wing of the Muslim Brotherhood due to his uncompromising stances, and his booklet *Khomeini: The Islamic*

---

71   Hashish, *Rihlat haya bayn al-bilad wa-l-shahada*, 168.

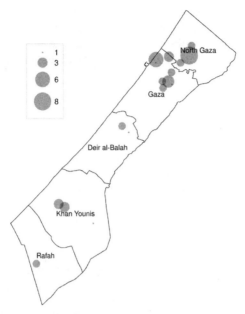

**Figure 3.2.** Geographical distribution of Gazan al-Qassam martyrs, 1988–99

*Solution and Alternative* had landed him twice in Egyptian jail as a student.[72] Others who joined the PIJ project were equally confrontational:

> Mahmud [al-Khawaja] was severely narrow-minded pertaining to the jihadist idea, which came forth through a terrifying zeal in observing it. This narrow-mindedness repulsed me and made me stay away from him, fearing that I would get in trouble with people and the other Islamic movements.[73]

It is, then, hardly unexpected that a fistfight nearly broke out between him and Muhammad Sham'a, a key founder of Hamas, following a heated debate between the two in one of Gaza's mosques.[74]

Al-Shiqaqi, Shallah, Awda, and the other students concluded that they were at an impasse: Palestinian nationalists without Islam and Islamists

---

72   Skare, *A History of Palestinian Islamic Jihad*, 23–4.

73   Hashish, *Rihlat haya bayn al-bilad wa-l-shahada*, 174.

74   Ibid., 168.

without Palestine. While the PLO ignored religion, the Brotherhood ignored the liberation of the homeland. Unable to convince the leaders and followers of the Brotherhood, they set out to form their own project, to create an Islamic vanguard to liberate Palestine through the barrel of a gun.

## Student and prisoner

Awda and al-Shiqaqi continued to use the mosques of Gaza to spread their message. The most important mosques for the PIJ project were, as noted, in the north and south of Gaza: the al-Salam Mosque in Rafah, the Izz al-Din al-Qassam Mosque in Beit Lahiya, the al-Rahman Mosque in al-Shuja'iyya, and the Hassan al-Banna Mosque in Beach Camp.[75] There, they organized seminars, meetings, religious lessons, and study circles in much the same way al-Shiqaqi and his friends had done in al-Zagazig.[76]

Violent encounters with the Brotherhood nevertheless compelled the PIJ founding fathers to meet in the homes of sympathizers during the initial years of their project. One of the most frequent meeting places was al-Khawaja's childhood home. Their reference to his home – the house of al-Arqam (*dar al-arqam*) – is indicative of the troubles they faced during this period,[77] for the home of Arqam bin Abi al-Arqam served as a crucial sanctuary and safe haven for Prophet Muhammad for prayer, preaching, education, and training during a period of increased persecution in Mecca.[78]

Whom al-Shiqaqi and his compatriots recruited in the earliest phase of PIJ was largely the result of the founding fathers' sociological makeup, in addition to unintended consequences of Israeli repression; the first PIJ recruits were essentially Palestinian students or PLO fighters serving time in Israeli prisons. The recruitment of Palestinian students, for example, was partly driven by dynamics specific to PIJ. Awda and Shallah lectured

---

75    Milton-Edwards, *Islamic Politics in Palestine*, 120; Hatina, *Islam and Salvation in Palestine*, 29; Muhammad, *al-Masira al-jihadiyya*, 46–7.

76    Al-Quds Brigades, 'Fathi al-Shiqaqi . . . Thawra tajub al-watan . . . wa fikra tardad tawajjuhan', saraya.ps, October 25, 2015.

77    Al-Quds Brigades, 'Suwwar . . . al-shahid al-qa'id mahmud al-khawaja: Haqqan annahu rajul la yatakarrar', saraya.ps, November 22, 2015.

78    Skare, *A History of Palestinian Islamic Jihad*, 62.

Islamic law and economics, respectively, at the University of Gaza. Taysir al-Khatib and Abdallah al-Shami, on the other hand, lectured on Arabic language or on history at the high schools of Gaza.[79]

The recruitment of students was also facilitated by the changing structural conditions in the Occupied Territories. The overall rise in education levels by the late 1970s meant that new Palestinian demographics obtained access to higher education; PIJ's student recruits largely came from refugee camps, small villages, and low-income families. These were environments deeply rooted in religious tradition, and higher education catalysed an enhanced Palestinian national awareness.[80] Access to higher education did nevertheless not equal social mobility. 'While university enrolment reached 13,500 in 1984–85,' Sayigh writes, '. . . only 20 percent of the 1,000 graduates and 10,500 school-leavers entering the local job market each year could find employment.'[81] Direct personal ties to Gazan students and high school pupils, in combination with the developing class character of the Gazan student body, enabled the PIJ leaders to tap into a young and particularly discontented Palestinian demographic in the 1980s, one which was especially susceptible to the call for armed struggle now and not later.

This is reflected in the class background of the PIJ martyrs who were killed between 1985 and 1999. Almost 30 per cent of them held – or, at least, had commenced – a university-level education, while an additional 42 per cent of them pursued, or had completed, a secondary level of education.

That did not mean that the PIJ martyrs became teachers, professors, functionaries, or judges. Instead, they were students, labourers, or unemployed – almost 75 per cent combined. Although two of them were governmental employees, the overall trend was blue-collar work. PIJ thus

---

79    Palestinian Islamic Jihad, *Masirat harakat al-jihad al-islami fi Filastin* (Beirut: PIJ, 1989), 17; 'Ab'ad da'wat Abbas li-l-hiwar ma' Hamas', *al-Jazeera*, June 16, 2008; Dot-Pouillard and Rébillard, 'The Intellectual, the Militant, the Prisoner and the Partisan', 8.

80    Reuven Paz, 'The Development of Palestinian Islamic Groups', in Barry Rubin, ed., *Revolutionaries and Reformers: Contemporary Islamist Movements in the Middle East* (New York: SUNY Press, 2003), 23.

81    Skare, *A History of Palestinian Islamic Jihad*, 67; Yezid Sayigh, *Armed Struggle and the Search for State: The Palestinian National Movement, 1949–1993* (Oxford: Oxford University Press, 1997), 608.

**Table 3.1.** Education level of PIJ martyrs, 1985–99

| Level of Education | Number (%) |
|---|---|
| Elementary school | 4 (4.49%) |
| Intermediate school | 15 (16.85%) |
| Secondary school | 38 (42.70%) |
| University | 25 (28.09%) |
| Vocational diploma | 7 (7.87%) |
| **Total** | **89** |

evolved into a relatively well-educated working-class movement. The PIJ leader Khadr Habib was typical of PIJ's social profile, as he obtained a university degree in business administration before he began working in construction.[82]

**Table 3.2.** 10 most common occupations, PIJ, 1985–99

| Occupation | Number |
|---|---|
| Labourer | 28 |
| Student | 13 |
| Unemployed | 9 |
| Carpenter | 3 |
| Electrician | 3 |
| Farmer | 3 |
| Tailor | 3 |
| Governmental employee | 2 |
| Pupil | 2 |
| Salesman | 2 |

Although no one specific dominant field of study prevails among the PIJ students (with specializations broadly distributed across various disciplines), there was a predominantly secular character among the earliest student recruits, given that religious fields such as Islamic law and the

82   Markaz Ru'ya li-l-Tanmiya al-Siyasiyya, 'Khadr Habib', Vision Centre for Political Development, April 18, 2023, vision-pd.org.

principles of religion comprised only one-third, approximately, of preferred academic pursuits. The PIJ base and the leadership thus enjoyed
similar educational profiles, as neither of the two aspired to become
religious scholars, but instead engineers, economists, and paediatricians.

**Table 3.3.** Most common known
education specializations, PIJ, 1985–99

| Specialization | Number |
| --- | --- |
| Principles of religion | 3 |
| Science and technology | 2 |
| Chemistry | 1 |
| Engineering | 1 |
| Geography | 1 |
| Interior design | 1 |
| Islamic law | 1 |
| Islamic studies | 1 |
| Medicine | 1 |
| Secular law | 1 |

PIJ was also able to recruit from the West Bank in this period. One of
the most important agents for these recruitment efforts was al-Shiqaqi,
who worked as a paediatrician at the Augusta Victoria Hospital in
Jerusalem. The recruitment was also facilitated by PIJ students in Gaza
who travelled to the West Bank to pursue higher education. Hani Abid,
for example, moved to Nablus for his master's degree and was a driving
force behind PIJ's student group at al-Najah University.[83] Still, the geographical distribution of the movement's martyrs between 1980 and 1999
(Figure 3.3) clearly indicates that PIJ was predominantly a Gaza-centred
movement with the majority of its members and militants originating
from the Strip. It was only when the Second Intifada erupted in 2000 that
PIJ obtained a greater presence in the north-east of Palestine.

PIJ's recruitment from the second pool, the PLO fighters, was inadvertently facilitated by Israel's own actions. The founding fathers of
PIJ began spreading statements, issuing fiery Islamist journals, and
disseminating calls for violence against Israeli targets, so it was not too

83   Skare, *A History of Palestinian Islamic Jihad*, 77.

surprising, perhaps, that al-Shiqaqi was arrested by Israeli authorities in August 1983 along with twenty-five other PIJ members.[84] While the PIJ nucleus was a student movement with no experience engaging in violence in its initial phase, direct lines of communication were suddenly established in the prison courtyards between the PIJ leadership and a group of Palestinians who had years of experience engaging in sabotage and armed operations.

Exactly when al-Shiqaqi recruited the PLO fighters remains unclear. However, we know that several incarcerated secular-nationalist militants joined the PIJ project between 1983 and 1986. Among these recruits were Misbah al-Suri, a member of the Palestine Liberation Front (PLF), Sami al-Shaykh Khalil from Fatah, and Muhammad Sa'id al-Jamal of the Palestinian Popular Struggle Front (PPSF). Ziyad al-Nakhala was arrested on May 29, 1971, for his armed involvement with the Arab Liberation Forces and was recruited by PIJ in prison.[85] After having worked as the deputy of al-Shiqaqi and Shallah for twenty-six years, al-Nakhala became the secretary-general of PIJ in 2018.[86]

Similarly, in 1986, Issam Brahma made the decision to join PIJ, which was significant given that he belonged to a Fatah family and had been a lifelong member. Upon his release from prison in 1990, it was Barahma who established the PIJ cell in Jenin, which became a permanent stronghold for the movement in the West Bank.[87] Other notable figures who joined PIJ during this period included Sayyid Baraka and Ahmad Muhanna. Muhanna's story is especially compelling, as he was a former officer in the Palestine Liberation Army (PLA), the armed wing of the PLO, who embraced Islamism in Israeli prisons.[88] The case of Abdel

---

84    Palestinian Islamic Jihad, *Masirat harakat al-jihad al-islami fi Filastin*, 17.

85    'al-Sira al-dhatiyya li-l-amin al-amm al-muntakhab li-harakat al-jihad al-islami al-ustadh al-nakhala', *Filastin al-Yawm*, September 27, 2018, paltoday. ps; al-Quds Brigades, 'al-Shahid al-Qa'id Misbah al-Suri: Khaddab bi-dammihi Judran sijn Ghazza al-markazi', saraya.ps, October 6, 2011.

86    For a more elaborate analysis of PIJ's recruitment efforts of the PLO fighters in prison, see Skare, *A History of Palestinian Islamic Jihad*, 70–6.

87    Al-Quds Brigades, 'al-Shahid al-qa'id 'Issam Musa Brahma': Awwal qa'id 'Askari li-l-jihad al-islami bi-l-diffa al-muhtalla', saraya.ps, June 29, 2011.

88    Rif'at Sayyid Ahmad, 'Rihlat al-damm alladhi hazam al-sayf', in Ahmad, *Rihlat al-damm alladhi hazam al-sayf*, 59; Milton-Edwards, *Islamic Politics in Palestine*, 120; Hatina, *Islam and Salvation in Palestine*, 33.

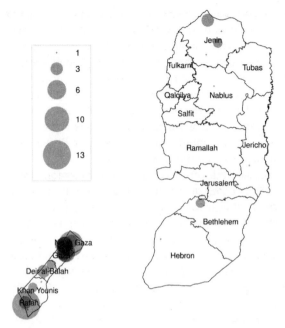

**Figure 3.3.** Geographical distribution of PIJ martyrs, 1985–99

Rahman al-Qiq is similar. He transitioned to PIJ from the Popular Front for the Liberation of Palestine (PFLP), as did Imad al-Saftawi, the son of a 'staunch Fatah man, Assad Saftawi'.[89] This period reflected a larger trend away from Palestinian secular-nationalist organizations as agents of armed resistance.

The question is to what extent the wave of former secular-nationalist militants who joined PIJ in prison represented a *religious* shift in the Occupied Palestinian Territories. Palestinian nationalism was never of a republican type divorced from religion. Fatah, for example, was from its inception a conservative movement sensitive to religious feelings, and religiously laden concepts such as 'jihad', 'mujahidin', or 'fida'iyyin' featured heavily in Fatah's declarations and manifestos. Its leader, Yasser Arafat, often relied on references from the Quran and, occasionally, also provided oral teachings from the hadith. Fatah's youth movement was

---

89 Filiu, *Gaza*, 190.

organized in separate structures for boys and for girls in the 1970s, and its student movement organized events with religious content to commemorate dates on the Islamic calendar.[90]

Fatah never employed the term 'secular' in its public discourse, and Arafat openly dismissed the DFLP's idea of a 'secular democratic state in Palestine'. Several prominent Fatah members like Khalil al-Wazir and Salah Khalaf were sympathetic to the Islamist groups as former members of the Muslim Brotherhood, and other Fatah cadres such as Munir Shafiq, Hamdi Tamimi, and Muhammad Bhays theorized the relationship between Palestinianism and Islam.[91]

Indeed, although scholars tend to write the history of decolonization in the Muslim world as one of secular-nationalist liberation, much indicates that the secular nature of this process is heavily exaggerated. Abdel Nasser routinely pointed to the affinities between Islam and socialism, and the ideologues of ben Bella promoted a synthesis of Islam and socialism. Even Algeria's National Liberation Front invoked Islam to mobilize the pious majority and initially promised a post-colonial state based on the 'principles of Islam'.[92] Most Arab nationalist groups were often less secular than commonly assumed, and little indicates the Palestinian national movement was any different.

Abu Samir Musa, leader of PIJ in southern Lebanon, for example, stated that he joined the Democratic Front for the Liberation of Palestine (DFLP) in his youth and then the PLA. Still, he stressed that he never adopted Marxism or considered himself a communist. Instead, Musa joined because he 'believed in the option of resistance . . . to liberate Palestine' and perceived the PLO as the most viable vehicle to do so.[93] His trajectory parallels that of Abdel Aziz al-Minawi, who was a military chief in the PFLP although he never defined himself as a 'complete Marxist'.[94]

---

90    Hillel Frisch, 'Has the Israeli-Palestinian Conflict Become Islamic? Fatah, Islam, and the al-Aqsa Martyrs' Brigades', *Terrorism and Political Violence* 17, no. 3 (October 2005): 394–6.

91    Abu-Amr, *Islamic Fundamentalism*, xv.

92    David Motadel, 'Islamic Revolutionaries and the End of Empire', in Martin Thomas and Andrew S. Thompson, eds, *The Oxford Handbook of the Ends of Empire* (Oxford: Oxford University Press, 2018), 556, 564, 570.

93    Abu Samir Musa, interview with Erik Skare, Rashidiyya, March 21, 2018.

94    Dot-Pouillard and Rébillard, 'The Intellectual, the Militant, the Prisoner and the Partisan', 14.

One of the PIJ founders similarly noted in an interview with this author that he had met, and become close to, al-Shiqaqi in Egypt in the 1970s as a member of Fatah. Still, he stressed:

> It is important to remember that the jump from Fatah to the Islamic orientation was not a very big one because Fatah at that time was very conservative, and many of its founders and later members had been part of the Muslim Brotherhood.[95]

As the armed Palestinian factions focused on practice without theoretical underpinnings, it was not so much ideology or religious convictions that divided the groups as much as it was strategic questions on *how* Palestine should be liberated, *who* should liberate Palestine, and *how much* of it could be liberated.[96] A significant segment of PLO fighters joined the movement because of the adherence to a specific strategy of liberation rather than the adherence to any secularist positions. They were thus happy to leave once an armed Islamist alternative appeared on the Palestinian scene which combined their religious beliefs with the emphasis on armed struggle.

The turn to an Islamist liberation theology was equally apparent in the Palestinian diaspora. A number of Fatah Maoists in Lebanon, for example, turned to Islamism. Munir Shafiq, a Palestinian Christian Marxist who later converted to Islam in the 1980s, stands as perhaps the most prominent example of this trend. For some, conversion was driven by the death of Mao Zedong in 1976 and the fall of the 'Gang of Four'. For the majority, conversion was fuelled by the same grievances and inspirations as for the PIJ founding fathers: They were aggrieved by the PLO Ten-Point Programme in 1974 and mesmerized by the Iranian Revolution in 1979. Their conversion similarly entailed an open-minded approach to religion and an uncompromising stand on armed struggle. Islam did not interfere in details of everyday life; instead, it provided overarching and general principles to follow. It was also an 'ontological re-framing' through which Islam was utilized by them to act as better Marxists; they claimed that they as Islamists were more in line with the Muslim masses

---

95   PIJ co-founder, interview with Erik Skare, August 6, 2018.
96   Frode Løvlie, 'Questioning the Secular-Religious Cleavage in Palestinian Politics: Comparing Fatah and Hamas', *Politics and Religion* 7, no. 1 (March 2014): 103.

and with their material needs. This transformation largely mirrored that of the PIJ founding fathers as they re-articulated anticolonial tropes, the lessons of other liberation struggles, and an Arab-Islamic identity. Historical necessity by God's will meant that they did not have to bother about 'ripe' circumstances and 'adequate' means for revolutionary acts, which, for more than a century, had divided Marxist theoreticians.[97]

The pull factor on former secular-nationalist militants was strong partly because the initial framework of PIJ was so similar to that of Fatah. The PIJ founding fathers returned from Egypt in 1980 and rallied students at the Islamic University of Gaza, proclaiming that one could not wait for the caliphate or the return of Palestinian society to Islamic values. Twenty years earlier, Arafat had done the same when he rallied students at the University of Cairo, proclaiming that one could not wait for pan-Arab unity.[98] In fact, the founders of Fatah – such as Salah Khalaf and Khalil al-Wazir (Abu Jihad) – had themselves been members of the Muslim Brotherhood.[99] They too harboured grievances similar to al-Shiqaqis's. Abu Samir's emphasis on armed struggle underlines that the main contradiction between the secular-nationalist movements and the Islamists in the 1980s was the choice between armed resistance and quietist proselytization. Both 1960s Fatah and 1980s PIJ proposed immediate action on the path of liberation without any detours, which necessarily swayed militants aggrieved by the PLO's increasing number of compromises.

## Forcing Hamas into existence

The former secular-nationalist-turned-Islamist militants were quickly put to use in PIJ. On May 21, 1985, as part of the prisoner exchange deal known as the Jibril Agreement, the Israeli government released 1,150 Palestinian prisoners. In return, the Popular Front for the Liberation of

---

97   For a comprehensive analysis and exploration of the Fatah Maoists' shift to Islamism, which informs this paragraph, see Manfred Sing, 'Brothers in Arms: How Palestinian Maoists Turned Jihadists', *Die Welt des Islams* 51, no. 1 (2011): 1–44.

98   Skare, *A History of Palestinian Islamic Jihad*, 214.

99   Wendy Pearlman, *Violence, Nonviolence, and the Palestinian National Movement* (Cambridge: Cambridge University Press, 2014), 64.

Palestine – General Command (PFLP-GC) released three Israelis who had been captured during the First Lebanon War. Several of the released prisoners were militants who had sworn allegiance to PIJ in prison and who now started carefully constructing its military apparatus; it was al-Nakhala whom al-Shiqaqi appointed to establish the military wing of PIJ.[100] Known today as the Quds Brigades, the military wing was initially called the Sword of Islam Brigades before changing its name to Islamic Mujahid Forces, abbreviated as Qassam. It was not before the outbreak of the Second Intifada in 2000 that its current name was officially adopted.

Other fighters set up training camps. Al-Suri's group, for example, trained approximately fifty PIJ cadres in the use of various types of light weaponry in al-Sarsuriyya, in eastern Gaza City.[101] This must have been a valuable resource, given that most of the PIJ founders were students who had never touched a rifle. Others travelled to Algeria, Libya, and Yemen to train in PLO camps – presumably facilitated by the personal networks of PIJ fighters with secular-nationalist backgrounds.[102]

Most importantly, they carried out several operations against Israeli targets as a wave of spectacular attacks commenced in Gaza. They bombed Israeli banks in Gaza, stabbed Israeli settlers, and engaged in armed confrontations against the Israeli soldiers in the Strip. The cell of Misbah al-Suri assassinated the Israeli army captain Ron Tal in September 1986, and then executed an Israeli soldier in a failed kidnapping attempt.[103] The Islamic Jihad Brigades, which some refer to as PIJ's Lebanese wing in the 1980s, also carried out attacks. The most important was the Gate of Moors operation in 1986, when its militants threw three hand grenades at Israeli soldiers during a graduation ceremony, injuring seventy and killing the father of one conscript.[104] After enjoying relative calm in the Gaza Strip in the 1970s, Israeli settlers and soldiers were now ambushed

---

100    'al-Yawm, al-sira al-dhatiyya li-l-amin al-amm al-muntakhab li-harakat al-jihad al-Islami al-Ustadh al-Nakhala', *Filastin al-Yawm*.

101    Al-Quds Brigades, 'al-Shahid al-Qa'id Muhammad Sa'id al-Jamal: Dhikhra butulat ta'abba al-nisyan', saraya.ps, October 6, 2011.

102    Anwar Abu Taha, interview with Erik Skare, March 19, 2018.

103    David McDowall, *Palestine and Israel: The Uprising and Beyond* (Berkeley: University of California Press, 1989), 109; al-Quds Brigades, 'Abu sarhad yarwi li-l-ilam al-harbi adaq tafasil amaliyyat al-hurub al-mu'jiza li-l-Marra al-ula . . . suwwar', saraya.ps, October 3, 2013.

104    Sing, 'Brothers in Arms', 3.

with every means at disposal to the Palestinian Islamists, from knives to guns and explosives.

It is unfair to suggest that PIJ conditioned the creation of Hamas, although it catalysed the transformation of the Brotherhood. The spectacular attacks by Palestinian Islamists beginning in 1984 caused a significant headache for the leaders of the Islamic Complex. While they had maintained that the liberation of Palestine was a task too great for the Palestinians alone, the young guard who remained with the Centre were electrified by the violence.[105] Yassin feared, as noted earlier, that the PIJ founders intended to replace them as the main Palestinian Islamic movement, and the recruitment of the most zealous Brotherhood youths spurred tense internal discussions on whether social change or armed struggle should be accorded priority.[106] Both schools of thought have their adherents within Hamas today – moderates and hardliners – and the organization's evolution has largely been decided by their interplay.

Tamimi argues that the Israelis' arrest of Yassin and his colleagues in 1984 on charges of acquiring arms is indicative, as it coincided with the year PIJ began using violence against Israeli targets.[107] This arrest should, however, not be given too much weight when analysing the Brotherhood's transformation into Hamas, given its history of intra-Palestinian violence. In the mid-1980s, there were growing tensions between the adherents of Ahmad Yassin and PLO elements in Gaza. The arms were presumably intended for self-defence rather than targeting an external enemy.[108] As we will see in the next chapter, the main aim of Majd, the security apparatus established by the Islamic Complex in 1985, was executing Palestinian collaborators rather than Israeli settlers or soldiers.[109]

Episodes of Gazan violence – several executed by PIJ cells – had become an increasingly common phenomenon by 1987; they were coupled by a growing number of Palestinian demonstrations and civil unrest. Though one usually refers to the Israeli agricultural vehicle killing four Palestinians

---

105    Azzam Tamimi, *Hamas: Unwritten Chapters* (London: Hurst, 2009), 44.

106    Khaled Hroub, *Hamas: Political Thought and Practice* (Washington, DC: Institute for Palestine Studies, 2000), 33.

107    Tamimi, *Hamas*, 45–6.

108    Jean-Pierre Filiu, 'The Origins of Hamas: Militant Legacy or Israeli Tool?', *Journal of Palestine Studies* 41, no. 3 (June 2012): 186.

109    The name *Majd* was an acronym for Munazzamat al-Jihad wa-l-Da'wa, Organization for Jihad and Proselytizing.

as the cause of the First Intifada, there were clear economic and social structures fuelling its eruption on December 8, 1987. Access to higher education, coupled with limited employment opportunities, has already been cited as a key driver behind PIJ's recruitment of young Gazans in the early 1980s. Indeed, as the Israeli economy was increasingly absorbing Palestinian labour, there was a significant decline in industrial, agricultural, construction, and service jobs available to the Palestinian workforce. This dependence made the Palestinian household economy vulnerable to fluctuations in the Israeli economy, and the 1980s oil glut, which caused a drop in oil revenues, sharply reduced opportunities for work in the Arab petro-monarchies. Palestinian migrant workers in the Gulf rapidly declined from an annual average of 17,900 between 1974 and 1981 to just 4,900 from 1982 onward.[110] Consequently, only a small spark was required to ignite the Palestinian streets.

There are disagreements on how the Brotherhood perceived the outbreak of the First Intifada in December 1987. Tamimi, for example, states that the uprising was a 'gift from heaven' for the Brotherhood.[111] Løvlie, on the other hand, notes that the intifada was first perceived as a challenge and not as an opportunity.[112] This view is echoed by Mishal and Sela, who argue that the leaders were taken by surprise and presented with a dilemma 'in view of their previous official abstention from armed struggle against the Israeli occupation'.[113] Most of the traditional Brotherhood leaders advocated maintaining their quietist strategy instead of joining the protests. They remained convinced that Islamization conditioned liberation; the old guard also remembered Egyptian repression between 1948 and 1967. If the Brotherhood adopted the military line and *if* the intifada failed, the Islamic Complex and its infrastructure of social welfare could be at stake. Everything the Brotherhood had built up in Gaza over the previous twenty years could crumble to dust.[114]

Regardless of the doubts harboured, or the internal dissent they were facing, the Brotherhood leaders agreed on December 9 that this was the

---

110    Sayigh, *Armed Struggle and the Search for State*, 607–8.

111    Tamimi, *Hamas*, 53.

112    Frode Løvlie, 'The Institutional Trajectory of Hamas: From Radicalism to Pragmatism – and Back Again?' (PhD thesis, University of Bergen, 2015), 115.

113    Shaul Mishal and Avraham Sela, *The Palestinian Hamas: Vision, Violence, and Coexistence* (New York: Columbia University Press, 2006), 35.

114    Løvlie, 'The Institutional Trajectory of Hamas', 116.

right moment to 'translate their new conviction into practice' and prioritize a full confrontation with the Israeli occupation.[115] Those present on that fateful evening were none other than Ahmad Yassin, his protégé Abdel Aziz al-Rantisi, Salah Shahada, Muhammad Sham'a, Isa al-Nashar, Abdel Fattah Dukhan, and Ibrahim al-Yazouri. The fact that the new organization would be a proxy of the Brotherhood suggests that the creation of Hamas was a compromise between the Brotherhood young guard desiring direct action and its old guard fearing for their civilian organizational structure. In making Hamas formally independent of the Muslim Brotherhood, their hope was that the Islamic Complex would remain immune from Israeli reprisals.[116]

In hindsight, the Brotherhood veterans had little chance of winning over the young guard. With both structural and partisan pressure points forcing them towards a more confrontational style, the emergence of Hamas was not so much an organic development within the Muslim Brotherhood as much as it was forced into existence by events. As Mishal and Sela aptly note, the Islamic Complex's decision to engage in armed struggle was largely a matter of survival.[117] Join the intifada and risk annihilation, or persist with a slow, yet certain, suicide.

The formation of Hamas and its entry into the armed Palestinian struggle improved its relationship with PIJ. In 1992, Hamas and PIJ signed the Charter of Brotherhood and Cooperation, which formally ended hostilities by stipulating a shared adherence to Islamic principles with regard to the Palestinian cause, the impermissibility of using violence to resolve disputes, and the creation of a coordination committee.[118] Collaboration increased between Hamas and PIJ following adoption of the charter and both groups began sharing technical knowledge and provided mutual assistance.[119] In 1994, for example, Hamas prepared a suicide operation for PIJ, and provided the car bomb used in it.[120]

So why did Hamas and PIJ not merge in the 1990s? Personal chemistry presumably mattered. So did intra-Palestinian competition, which

115   Hroub, Hamas, 39.
116   Mishal and Sela, The Palestinian Hamas, 35.
117   Ibid.
118   Abu Taha, Harakat al-jihad al-islami fi Filastin, 53–4.
119   Milton-Edwards, Islamic Politics in Palestine, 172.
120   Skare, A History of Palestinian Islamic Jihad, 159.

persisted over the next thirty years. The arrogance of the Muslim Brotherhood had alienated the early leaders and members of PIJ. This arrogance did not end with the formation of Hamas, which asserted itself as a distinct, mass Palestinian Islamic movement and claimed an exclusive capability to liberate Palestine. This elitist stance likely hindered Hamas's ability to go beyond local cooperation and coordination efforts.[121] For Hamas, Palestinian Islamist unity meant effectively dissolving its competitor through the complete absorption of PIJ. PIJ conversely viewed Hamas as a smug opportunist, harvesting the fruits of its own military efforts dating back to 1984.[122]

Ideology also played a role.[123] From the early 1990s, PIJ and Hamas interpreted ideological notions differently in order to justify their respective practices. One already-mentioned example was PIJ's lack of interest in upholding community values or proselytizing, two features that became deeply ingrained in Hamas's political behaviour. Another example is the notion of 'interest' (*maslaha*): the judicial principle of preventing harm as preferable to bringing about benefits; it emphasizes the duty to preserve the public's welfare.[124] Hamas, for example, pragmatized its core attitudes from the 1990s because its grass-roots nature made it far more open to public needs.[125] PIJ, on the other hand, proclaimed that only armed resistance could liberate the Occupied Palestinian Territories; it was the movement's duty to persist because the benefits of armed resistance outweighed the potential harm and damage it could inflict on the Palestinian public. PIJ explicitly rejected what it termed Hamas's 'jurisprudence of interest' (*fiqh al-maslaha*), which Hamas used as a normative justification for maximizing its gains within the political system.[126] As Abu Taha summarized when he was asked about the issue, essentially, 'Hamas is a political movement dealing with the military field; PIJ is a military movement dealing with the political field.'[127]

---

121   Hatina, *Islam and Salvation in Palestine*, 108.

122   Hroub, *Hamas*, 127–8.

123   This paragraph uses text from Skare, *A History of Palestinian Islamic Jihad*, 215.

124   Hatina, *Islam and Salvation in Palestine*, 107, 197.

125   Menachem Klein, 'Competing Brothers: The Web of Hamas–PLO Relations', *Terrorism and Political Violence* 8, no. 2 (June 1996): 128.

126   Muhammad, *al-Masira al-jihadiyya*, 193.

127   Anwar Abu Taha, interview with Erik Skare, March 19, 2018.

PIJ thus continued to enjoy a justification for continuing existence in the 1990s despite the emergence of Hamas. This justification was largely maintained by the theological diversification of Palestinian Islamism in the 1980s. While Hamas Islamized the Palestinian cause, PIJ Palestinianized Islam. Instead of bothering with community values, PIJ prioritized armed struggle; and its curiosity-driven ideological formation process – with its innovative re-articulation of already-existing Palestinian ideologies – essentially meant that PIJ carved out an intermediate position for itself between the PLO and Hamas. This was a position that PIJ and al-Shiqaqi were eager to exploit. When the latter was asked in 1994 about the title of PIJ's next journal, al-Shiqaqi responded that the journal of Hamas was called *Muslim Palestine*, whereas the journal of the PLO was called *Revolutionary Palestine*. PIJ would be content, then, merely naming its journal *Palestine*. Al-Shiqaqi smiled and added that *Palestine* would be 'the resulting message of both' and would therefore outbid what both the PLO and Hamas represented.[128]

---

128     Hroub, 'Between Islam and Nationalism', *Journal of Palestine Studies* 31, no. 3 (2002): 108.

# 4

## Peace, Blood, and Twisted Metal

On October 26, 1995, a man returned to his hotel room carrying a Libyan passport under the name Ibrahim Ali Abdallah Chaouch. Ten months had passed since two PIJ militants had detonated their explosive vests at the Beit Lid road junction, killing twenty-two Israelis and injuring more than sixty. Yahya Ayash, Hamas's chief bomb maker, had prepared the explosives, and he was, at that point, responsible for at least seven other bombings. Returning to Damascus after a short visit to Libya, Chaouch made a stop in Valletta, Malta, where he had the chance to relax and – on this particular day – do a bit of shopping. In front of the Diplomat Hotel, two men approached him from behind on a motorbike. As they neared, one of them pulled out a concealed semi-automatic pistol and shot him six times in the head. Fathi al-Shiqaqi, the founder and first leader of PIJ, dropped dead to the ground as the Mossad agents sped away from the scene.

This chapter examines the Oslo Accords and the Islamist opposition's rejection of the peace process. Beginning in 1993, Hamas and PIJ carried out a number of suicide bombings to thwart the negotiations. We will see that there was a logic to this violence. Although there was a clear ideological and religious component to their campaign, targeting Israelis in the 1990s was driven equally, if not more so, by intra-Palestinian competition and the fear of being politically isolated. As hardliners and moderates competed for power, violence became a source of political capital and authority. There was from the beginning not one Hamas, but many.

## From Majd to the Qassam Brigades

> Why do we remain silent about these traitors, who watch us and report our names to the [Israeli] intelligence, so the army comes and arrests us and forces us to hide or cover our faces? They are the ones who ought to be afraid and to hide. – Yahya Sinwar[1]

Yahya Ibrahim Hassan Sinwar was born in the slum of Khan Younis refugee camp on October 29, 1967. Like Ahmad Yassin and Fathi al-Shiqaqi, he was a refugee. His family was originally from the Palestinian town of Majdal on the southern coastal plain between Gaza City and Ramla. In 1948, at the onset of the 1948 Palestine War, the town had approximately 10,000 inhabitants, all of them Christians and Muslims. The majority were forced to flee, however, when Jewish forces conquered the city on November 4, 1948, with only 2,700 of Majdal's original residents remaining. The Israeli Southern Command then began forcing out those who remained: 500 more Palestinians were deported in December 1948 before the rest were expelled to Gaza one year later, which 'shock[ed] some left-wing Israelis as this was done during "a time of peace".[2] Today, Majdal is better known as Ashkelon.

Sinwar's account suggests an ordinary Gazan childhood. According to his autobiographical novel, Sinwar often woke up at dawn to enjoy the sound of his grandfather's prayers, as he recited *al-Fatiha*, the Quran's opening chapter. They often went to the mosque together, where Sinwar

---

1  Yahya Sinwar, *al-Shawk wa-l-qaranful* (n.p., 2004), 214.

2  Nur Masalha, *The Palestine Nakba: Decolonizing History, Narrating the Subaltern, Reclaiming Memory* (London: Zed Books, 2012), 115–16; Ilan Pappé, *The Ethnic Cleansing of Palestine* (Oxford: Oneworld Publications, 2008), 194.

tried as best he could to imitate the prayers of the grownups. Although religion was clearly present, Gazan religious practice in the 1960s was yet to be institutionalized as it became twenty years later with the emergence of Islamism as a political force in Palestinian society. The conservatism of Sinwar's family was instead indicative of Gazan customs and traditions, and his mother warned her sons to preserve their family's honour by not initiating relationships with the girls of the camp.

Despite the warnings of anxious parents, adolescence in Gaza was like everywhere else; the youth there fell in love as they do elsewhere. At the street corners of the camps, boys would wait for girls walking by, hoping for a glance back and for love to develop. The more audacious boys would throw fleeting words to grab the girls' attention. 'The people of the camp are like everyone else,' Sinwar reminisced. 'Despite their suffering and misery, they love deeply and are passionate, and they live life as all people do.'[3]

The Six-Day War in 1967 did not just introduce an Israeli occupation into the life of Sinwar. It also introduced the Palestinian guerrilla movement, which entered the Palestinian camps of Gaza. With its heyday between 1969 and 1971, 'we began seeing men masked with keffiyehs carrying their weapons – from English [mandate] rifles to Carl Gustav guns, or carrying hand grenades – as they patrolled the alleyways of the camp, especially when evening approached'.[4] The games Sinwar and his friends played in the alleyways of Khan Younis reflected these developments: Instead of cowboy against Indian, they played Palestinian guerrilla against Israeli soldier. Inevitably, perhaps, the game ended with the victory of the guerrilla, who killed his Israeli enemy.[5]

If there is a red thread throughout the account of Sinwar, a leitmotif, it is not the Palestinian guerrilla (the Knight), but the collaborator (the Quisling, the Benedict Arnold). Although he describes a number of successful sabotage missions and armed operations, many others were thwarted by the Israelis. Sinwar recalls one evening when he was playing outside his home. Suddenly, he saw a group of armed Palestinians dragging a man out by his ear as a crowd gathered around. It occurred a couple of days after a group of Palestinian guerrillas was ambushed by

---

3   Sinwar, *al-Shawk wa-l-qaranful*, 61.
4   Ibid., 25.
5   Ibid., 14.

Israeli soldiers and shot in the back. The group's leader, Abu Hatim, had a bamboo stick with which he began hitting the man until he confessed to reporting the guerrillas to Israeli intelligence for a small sum of money.

> Abu Hatim took his rifle from his shoulder and aimed it at the head of the spy. My mother placed her hand in front of my eyes, and I tried to remove it to see what was happening. I heard the sound of gunshots and the people shouting 'Death to the traitors. Death to the collaborators.'[6]

Whether this is an authentic eyewitness account from his childhood or whether it serves as a broader depiction of life in 1960s Gaza remains unclear. It nonetheless demonstrates how collusion with the Israeli occupation was a matter of life and death, something that affected everyone. It is equally evident that experiences with collaborators, either direct or indirect, had a profound impact on Sinwar. As long as they existed, and as long as they could continue in peace, Sinwar argued, the Palestinians would find themselves under the iron heel of the Israeli occupation.

It was, consequently, Sinwar – then a Brotherhood activist in his twenties and a student of Arabic at the Islamic University of Gaza – who approached Ahmad Yassin in the mid-1980s and contended there was a need for an internal intelligence agency to deal with fifth columnists in Palestinian society. The agency was called Majd ('glory' in Arabic), an abbreviation of the name Organization for Jihad and Proselytizing.[7] With the help of several Brotherhood cadres, Sinwar began targeting anyone under suspicion of working with the Israelis. As Sinwar himself recalled Gaza in the mid-1980s:

> The hunt for collaborators began spreading through the streets of the homeland where groups from all factions began tracking them down, arresting them or kidnapping them . . . Then, some of these groups would kill these collaborators and throw their corpses on garbage dumps or in public squares to spread fear and create deterrence. Occasionally, a collaborator was brought to a public square where people gathered. He was tied to an electricity pole and flogged, or his hand or leg was cut off. Sometimes he was shot.[8]

---

6   Ibid., 32.
7   Al-Zaydawi, 'Yahya al-Sinwar: Rajul alladhi tukhshah Isra'il hayyan wa maytan', *Maydan*, October 11, 2023.
8   Sinwar, *al Shawk wa-l-qaranful*, 218.

Credible details about Sinwar's activities in this period are sparse, and those that exist are either saturated with his own bravado or the sensationalism of tabloid newspapers. He is reported to have killed several supposed collaborators with his own hands, and, allegedly, made his own brother bury one of them alive.[9] Numerous sources portray Sinwar as a zealot – an ascetic, highly disciplined and unfazed by violence.[10] These descriptions could easily be dismissed as caricatures, and this author has been unable to find references to his supposed moniker 'the butcher of Khan Younis' in Palestinian sources from this period.[11]

Still, the brutality Sinwar displayed towards his perceived enemies repelled even co-militants within his own movement; they were cadres who did not harbour pacifist convictions and who themselves had a history of violence. The senior Hamas member Muhammad Abu Tayr is a case in point; he spent time with Sinwar in prison after the latter was sentenced to four life sentences in 1988 for the murder of twelve Palestinians. Abu Tayr notes how the latter's treatment of alleged collaborators in prison sent shudders down his spine. If someone was under the suspicion of collaborating with the Israelis in or outside prison, Sinwar put out cigarettes on their skins, burnt them with hot plates, or broke their legs. In prison, as elsewhere, Sinwar pulled nails first and asked questions later. 'To illustrate the wrongdoings of the security practices in Ashkelon and other prisons, there was the brother Abu Ibrahim, [Yahya] Sinwar, . . . I love him dearly and endorse him in everything . . .,' Abu Tayr writes, '[But] by God, if I were exposed to what some were exposed to in the [prison interrogation] corners, I would have written a thousand pages of confession.'[12] Sinwar admitted himself that red lines were crossed and injustice committed, but there are few signs of remorse.[13]

---

9    Frank Gardner, 'Yahya Sinwar: Who Is the Hamas Leader in Gaza?', BBC News, November 21, 2023.

10    For references to the moniker in Western secondary sources, see, for example, Peter Beaumont, 'Election of New Hamas Gaza Strip Leader Increases Fears of Confrontation', *Guardian*, February 13, 2017.

11    Mkhaimar Abusada, 'The Strongest Man in Gaza: Inside the Mind of Hamas Leader Yahya Sinwar', *Haaretz*, January 17, 2024.

12    Muhammad Abu Tayr, *Sayyidi Umar: Dhikriyat al-shaykh Muhammad Abu Tayr fi al-muqawama wa thalatha wa thalathin 'aman min al-i'tiqal* (Beirut: Markaz al-zaytuna li-l-dirasat wa-l-istisharat, 2017), 238, 241.

13    Sinwar, *al-Shawk wa-l-qaranful*, 218.

The modus operandi of proto-Hamas in the mid-1980s was, in other words, a continuation of the Brotherhood line insofar as violence was an intra-Palestinian remedy aimed at 'purifying the society from the corrupt elements poisoned by Israeli intelligence'.[14] Majd did, as such, also target Palestinian drug dealers and other 'deviants', as a lapse in security was perceived to be inherently connected to a lapse in morals.[15] The Hamas leader Ibrahim al-Maqadma even used 'moral collaborator' as a category for those who spread perceived vice and corruption in Palestinian society by introducing 'nudity, adultery, bribery, drug and alcohol trafficking, as well as music bands'.[16] Yahya Sinwar thus matters because he so clearly embodies the transitional period during which Brotherhood violence was first systematized through the construction of a nascent organizational infrastructure, which was then redirected against an external enemy, the Israeli occupation.

As he spent the next two decades in Israeli prison, Sinwar was not a part of this redirection – formalized with the establishment of Hamas's military wing, the Izz al-Din al-Qassam Brigades, in early 1991. This was the task of Imad Aql.[17] Born in 1971, Aql grew up in northern Gaza, in Jabalya refugee camp, as the youngest in his family. According to his older brother, Adil, he did not care much about politics or religion and appeared more interested in geography than in Islamic revolution. Aggrieved by the arrests and killings of his relatives in the First Intifada, however, Imad and his brother joined Hamas. The decision ultimately led

---

14    'Dabit majmu'at al-shuhada' ', *al-Markaz al-Filastini al-Ilami*, February 19, 2010, palestine-info.com.

15    Yezid Sayigh, *'We Serve the People': Hamas Policing in Gaza* (Washington, DC: Brandeis University, Crown Center for Middle East Studies, 2011), 46.

16    Ibrahim al-Maqadma, *Ma'alim fi al-tariq li-tahrir Filastin*, 2nd ed. (n.p., 2002), 285.

17    There are disagreements with regard to who founded the Izz al-Din al-Qassam Brigades in the early 1990s, presumably due to uncertainties caused by its clandestine nature. While some refer to Imad Aql as its founder in early 1991 ('Dabit majmu'at al-shuhada' '), others refer to his namesake, Walid Aql, in central Gaza in late 1991 (Mishal and Sela, *The Palestinian Hamas*, 64) or Yasir al-Namruti from Khan Younis, who worked with Sinwar in Majd before targeting Israelis from 1992 (al-Qassam Brigades, 'Yasir al-Namruti'). Because of the Brigades' early nature, it is more precise to describe them all as co-founders of more or less connected military cells across the Occupied Palestinian Territories.

to Imad's arrest on September 23, 1988.[18] Like so many before him, it was in prison that Imad became acquainted with the Palestinian factions and guerrillas; he was no longer a mere member but a soldier in the service of Hamas when he came out.

It was not a given that Aql would call himself a 'Qassami' when he was released from prison. He could just as well have identified as an 'Azzami'. Like PIJ, the military apparatus of Hamas operated under different names during its earliest period. There were internal differences about what they should name the militia and, accordingly, what historical references and emotional responses the name should conjure. The Gazan militants expressed a strong preference for the name Martyr Izz al-Din al-Qassam Brigades, while their West Bank counterparts contended that Abdallah Azzam Brigades would be more fitting.[19] Azzam was, after all, from the northern West Bank village al-Sila al-Harithiyya. The fact that the former won out underlines the Gaza Strip's historical dominance in militant Palestinian Islamism.

Such conjuration mattered for Hamas precisely because it feared that the Palestinian population would share PIJ's perception of the Islamic Resistance Movement as a latecomer to the armed struggle. It had to strengthen its insurgent credentials by underplaying the preferential treatment it had received from Israeli occupation authorities before the First Intifada and its historical reluctance to taking up arms. Tracing its lineage to Izz al-Din al-Qassam in the 1930s was part of that revisionism, as was highlighting the contingent of fighters sent by the Egyptian Muslim Brotherhood to fight in the 1948 Palestine War. Ahmad Yassin even claimed that Fatah began with the Brotherhood.[20] Yet, as Løvlie points out, the role of the Brotherhood soldiers of 1948 is highly exaggerated, and although Khalil al-Wazir and Salah Khalaf (Abu Jihad and Abu Iyad) were initially members of the Brotherhood, they left precisely because of its nonconfrontational stance. The reference to Hamas's 'unbroken tradition of resistance' thus relies heavily on selective memory.[21] As

18    Robert Fisk, 'Hamas Mourns Its Greatest Martyr', *Independent: News*, November 29, 1993.

19    Sarri Samur, 'Fashal al-thuwar al-Afghan ahraj wa ad'af al-tayar al-salafi fi Hamas', *al-Jazeera*, September 10, 2019.

20    'al-Shaykh Ahmad Yasin: Shahid ala asr al-intifada', episode 3, *al-Jazeera*, May 1, 1999.

21    Frode Løvlie, 'The Institutional Trajectory of Hamas: From Radicalism to Pragmatism – and Back Again?' (PhD thesis, University of Bergen, 2015), 114.

al-Maqadma admitted, the passivity of the Brotherhood was a significant embarrassment, and particularly so for its young guard.[22]

The men Aql and his compatriots recruited to the Qassam Brigades in the early 1990s were – as discussed in the preceding chapter – from approximately the same areas as those recruited to PIJ. They were from Rafah, Jabalya, al-Shujaiyya, and Beach Camp. Like the PIJ militants of the 1980s and 1990s, the Qassam militants were also relatively well educated (Table 4.1). Only a minority had dropped out of school during the primary stages of their education. The clear majority were either pursuing an academic degree or had already graduated. Almost 80 per cent were either university students or had at least finished secondary school. Similarly, the Qassam militants were either students or blue-collar workers (Table 4.2).[23] They were construction workers, painters, tailors, mechanics, or farmers.[24] What all militants in PIJ or the al-Qassam Brigades had in common was the sociological makeup and the belief in the feasibility of armed struggle to end Israeli occupation.

**Table 4.1.** Education level of al-Qassam martyrs, 1988–99

| Level of Education | Number (%) |
| --- | --- |
| Elementary school | 4 (4.04%) |
| Intermediate school | 13 (13.13%) |
| Secondary school | 34 (34.34%) |
| University | 42 (42.42%) |
| Vocational diploma | 6 (6.06%) |
| **Total** | **99** |

---

22   Al-Maqadma, *Ma'alim fi al-tariq li-tahrir Filastin*, 268.

23   The ten most common occupations among al-Qassam Brigades members account for three-quarters of the total. Lower-ranked jobs reflect the types of occupations listed in the table and include plasterer, repair man, stonecutter, car painter, tile worker, and tanner. Specialized positions included one teacher, one imam, and one physiotherapist.

24   A total of 111 Hamas militants were killed in this period. Twelve lacked information about education level and are omitted from Table 4.1. Table 4.2 accounts for one-third of the total. The other occupations reflect the table and include plasterer, repairman, stone-cutter, and the like. Of specialized labour, there was one teacher, one imam, and one physiotherapist.

**Table 4.2.** 10 most common occupations, PIJ, 1985–99

| Occupation | Number |
|---|---|
| Student | 9 (17.65%) |
| Salesman | 5 (9.80%) |
| Construction worker | 4 (7.84%) |
| Painter | 4 (7.84%) |
| Tailor | 4 (7.84%) |
| Mechanic | 3 (5.88%) |
| Carpenter | 2 (3.92%) |
| Driver | 2 (3.92%) |
| Farmer | 2 (3.92%) |
| Pupil | 2 (3.92%) |
| **Total** | **37 (72.55%)** |

Who joined the Qassam Brigades or PIJ thus depended on other variables than the socio-economic background of the militants. For many, it was mere coincidence. For some, it was simply determined by whom they first became acquainted with in prison. For others, like a number of PIJ militants in the northern West Bank, pre-existing social ties and kinship were the determining factor. They joined PIJ because a family member or a neighbour had done so.[25] Personal loyalty also mattered. Although an early proponent of Islamist militancy, Sinwar was reportedly close to Ahmad Yassin and unwavering in his loyalty. This contrasted with the first leader of PIJ's military wing, Mahmud al-Khawaja, who jumped the Brotherhood ship as soon as al-Shiqaqi returned to Gaza in 1981.

The early violence of the Qassam Brigades was also similar to that of PIJ. It was exploratory and spontaneous, amateurish, and – given the inexperience of its militants – largely unsuccessful. The operations consisted mostly of stabbings and shootings, sometimes also the use of explosives (with hand grenades bought on the black market or manufactured at home). Sometimes the violence was determined by what was available.

25 Erik Skare, *A History of Palestinian Islamic Jihad: Faith, Awareness, and Revolution in the Middle East* (Cambridge: Cambridge University Press, 2021), 79–80.

Hamdan Husayn al-Najar from al-Qassam Brigades used a stone to bash in a settler's head in Hebron.[26]

The organizational infrastructure of both Islamist militias were essentially undeveloped and unsophisticated in the late 1980s and early 1990s, with their leaders largely incapable of providing militants with arms.[27] It is therefore illustrative that the slogans of PIJ throughout the 1980s appeared to be the product of local and individual initiatives without central planning and coordination with the leadership.[28] Often, if the militants wanted to join the armed struggle, they had to rely on their own acumen and creativity. Several of the PIJ militants in the mid-1980s sold their wives' jewellery to buy weapons, and senior PIJ member Abdallah al-Shami recalled how the military possibilities open to them were 'limited and nonexistent'.[29] Sinwar himself recalled how 'the territories were completely void of weapons' in the early year of Palestinian Islamist insurgency, '[and] people did not know how to use [them] even if they found them'.[30]

Aql's legacy was not the violence he and his men carried out against Israeli targets. He was killed far too early in the history of the Qassam Brigades – on November 24, 1993 – after a collaborator revealed his hiding spot to Israeli occupation forces. His true legacy was instead the student he mentored, Muhammad Deif, the future commander of the Qassam Brigades.[31] Deif also grew up in Khan Younis refugee camp, a couple of metres from Sinwar, and the two played together as children. Like Aql, Deif was arrested during the First Intifada when he was still a chemistry student at the Islamic University of Gaza. Following his

---

26    Bilal Shalash, 'al-Qassam fi shahr (Kanun al-thani– janayir)', n.d., document in author's possession. See appendix for note on active citation.

27    Shaul Mishal and Avraham Sela, *The Palestinian Hamas: Vision, Violence, and Coexistence* (New York: Columbia University Press, 2006), 57; Skare, *A History of Palestinian Islamic Jihad*, 92–3; Erik Skare, 'Insulated Eruptions of Discontent: Palestinian Protests in the Absence of Trusted Organisations', *Contemporary Levant* 7, no. 2 (July 2022): 106–17.

28    Adnan Abu Amer, 'Harakat al-jihad al-islami: Al-Nash'a wa-l-Tatawwur wa-l-mawaqif al-siyasiyya', Adnan Abu Amer blog, January 16, 2018.

29    Al-Quds Brigades, 'Khabar: al-Qiyadi al-shami li-"l-i'lam al-harbi" al-Shiqaqi sana' mashru' islami thawri shamil', saraya.ps, October 27, 2013.

30    Sinwar, *al-Shawk wa-l-qaranful*, 229.

31    Muhammad Deif was the nom de guerre of Muhammad Diab Ibrahim al-Masri.

release from prison in 1991, he, alongside Aql, co-founded the Qassam Brigades in northern Gaza.[32] Under the leadership of Aql, Deif got his first experience with planning armed operations, streamlining logistics, securing safe houses, and slowly – piece by piece – constructing the cells of a future military body. Like Aql before him, Deif earned the moniker of 'the Phantom'.[33]

## Oslo Between Hardliners and Moderates

The Islamist opposition reacted with dismay when it learned about the prospects of a peace agreement between Israel and the PLO. As al-Shiqaqi asked in 1992: 'What is the meaning of an olive branch in the mouth of the gun killing our children and our people?'[34] In response, Hamas and PIJ organized protests, demonstrations, and, not least, a series of suicide bombings from 1993 – a tactic previously unknown in the occupied Palestinian territories. Together with Yahya Ayash, an electrical engineer from Birzeit University and Hamas's chief bomb maker in the 1990s, Deif helped plan, prepare, and organize these attacks. In direct or indirect cooperation with PIJ, Deif and Ayash manufactured car bombs or suicide vests to target Israeli buses, bus stations, traffic junctions, and shopping streets. By executing harrowing attacks in Israel, both Islamist movements hoped to keep the fire of the intifada burning and thwart the peace process by weakening the credibility of Yasser Arafat as a negotiation partner.[35]

The most lethal suicide bombing of the 1990s was carried out by PIJ on January 22, 1995, with the help of Ayash, who prepared the explosives. At approximately 9:30 a.m., the bus stop at the HaSharon Junction – also known as the Beit Lid Junction – was bustling with Israeli soldiers and reservists waiting to return to their military posts after weekend leave.

---

32  Nidal al-Mughrabi and Maayan Lubell, 'Deep Underground, Mohammed Deif Shapes Hamas War with Israel', Reuters, August 14, 2014.

33  Sinwar, *al-Shawk wa-l-qaranful*, 255; Nicolas Pelham, 'Hamas's Deadly "Phantom": The Man behind the Attacks', *Economist*, October 20, 2023.

34  Fathi al-Shiqaqi, 'al-Intifada ba'd Madrid', in Rif'at Sayyid Ahmad, ed., *Rihlat al-damm alladhi hazam al-sayf: al-A'mal al-kamila li-l-shahid al-duktur Fathi al-Shiqaqi* (Cairo: Markaz Yafa li-l-dirasat wa-l-abhath, 1996), 544.

35  Mishal and Sela, *The Palestinian Hamas*, 67.

Disguised in Israeli military attire, a Palestinian infiltrated the crowd and then detonated the explosives concealed on his body. As a crowd rushed to the scene to help and to evacuate those injured from the first blast, another one detonated his suicide vest at the same spot.[36] Nineteen Israelis were killed in the attack and more than sixty were injured.

Israeli Prime Minister Yitzhak Rabin signed the red paper, a kill order for al-Shiqaqi, the following day. Al-Shiqaqi met his fate nine months later, on October 26, when two Mossad agents assassinated him in Malta as he was returning to Damascus. Whereas al-Khawaja, the leader of PIJ's military wing, Qassam, had already been assassinated on June 22, it took another three months before the Israelis reached the one constructing the explosives. Having enlisted a Palestinian collaborator whose nephew was close to Ayash, Israel's internal security service, the Shin Bet, managed to supply the engineer with a new phone. They claimed the phone would be used to eavesdrop on Ayash, but the Shin Bet handlers did not disclose that it also contained an explosive charge. As his father called on January 5, 1996, Ayash picked up the phone and told him how much he loved him and missed him. Then the line went dead.[37] Deif, now at the top of the Qassam Brigades, never used a mobile phone again.[38]

The causes for the Islamists' opposition to Oslo differed, and what aspect Hamas and PIJ emphasized to justify their rejection depended on who spoke on behalf of the movements and whether they did so in a period of calm or of heightened tensions. For some Palestinian Islamists, the rejection was intrinsic; they held absolute religious and ideological convictions. Evidenced by references in the holy texts, they viewed Palestine as blessed land. Both Hamas and PIJ referred to Palestine as the land of the night journey to which the prophet Muhammad travelled on the back of the Buraq before he ascended to the seventh heaven to meet God and greet the prophets. All of the land belonged to the *waqf*, an Islamic endowment in Islamic jurisprudence given to all future generations of Muslims. 'The battle is not for a piece of land, although the land is its stage. Nor is it for colonialism, although colonialism is apparent in some of its stages,' Ibrahim al-Maqadma wrote.

---

36   Skare, *A History of Palestinian Islamic Jihad*, 126.

37   Ronen Bergman, *Rise and Kill First: The Secret Story of Israel's Targeted Assassinations* (New York: Random House, 2018), 444.

38   Pelham, 'Hamas's Deadly "Phantom"'.

It is not a national or ethnic conflict . . . nor is it a class conflict . . . it is not a conflict between the oasis of democracy in the Middle East, as the Americans and Westerns claim, and the backward Arabs who refuse the development and progress offered to them by the Jews!!

Instead, 'the conflict between us and the Jews, Christians, and polytheists is eternal and will continue until God inherits the Earth and everything on it'.[39] Palestine was, in other words, impermissible to partition no matter the costs or benefits.

Absolute ideological stances were undoubtedly fuelled by historical grievances from the *nakba*. A vast majority of the founding fathers of both Hamas and PIJ were either forced, or born, into refugeehood. Ahmad Yassin was displaced from his native village of al-Jura in 1948 when he was twelve years old. Al-Shiqaqi was born a refugee in Rafah in 1951 and then deported to Lebanon in 1988 when he was thirty-seven. How could they possibly recognize the legitimacy of a state project that had displaced them from their original homes and had taken everything away from them? How could they possibly accept a Palestinian state on a fifth of the land that they had never agreed to forsake in the first place?

In any case, the Islamist opposition harboured few illusions about the reality which the peace negotiations would produce in the Occupied Palestinian Territories. Al-Shiqaqi dryly noted that the Oslo Accords were merely a solution to free Israel from its political and ethical obligations as an occupying force, while Yassin dismissed it as 'an unfair and bad agreement' fragmenting Palestinian unity.[40] In the view of Hamas and PIJ, the PLO had sold out the Palestinians instead of liberating them, and especially those who had sacrificed so much during the Intifada.[41] Oslo brought *istislam* (capitulation) instead of *salam* (peace).[42] Few

---

39    Al-Maqadma, *Ma'alim fi al-tariq li-tahrir Filastin*, 73, 76.

40    Fathi al-Shiqaqi, 'al-Ittifaq hall al-mashakil allati yu'ani minha al-kayan al-sahyuni mundhu ihtilal 1967 hatta alan', in Ahmad, *Rihlat al-damm alladhi hazam al-sayf*, 912; 'al-Shaykh Ahmad Yasin: Shahid ala asr al-intifada', episode 8, *al-Jazeera*, June 5, 1999.

41    Beverley Milton-Edwards and Stephen Farrell, *Hamas: The Islamic Resistance Movement* (Cambridge: Polity Press, 2010), 70.

42    François Burgat, *Face to Face with Political Islam* (London: I. B. Tauris, 2003), 53.

summarized this particular sentiment better than Hamas senior member Muhammad Abu Tayr:

> [The Oslo Agreement] was a project to liquidate the Palestinian cause. If it had not been, then Israel would not have accepted it . . . It does not propose a political solution, but rather a security project to serve the occupation and an economic project to distract the Palestinian people and inundate them with projects that circumvent their national cause. Oslo is what aborted the blessed First Intifada, and turned those return-ing . . . into exploiters at the expense of blood and martyrs . . . Oslo came to stop the Islamic advance, which had taken hold in the Palestinian arena and to rescue the PLO – and specifically Fatah – from disappear-ance and extinction.[43]

In turn, although ideology, religion, and historical grievances played their part in the Palestinian Islamists' rejection of the peace process and overall worldview, so did extrinsic factors. Context-specific variables such as intra-Palestinian competition and the prospect of narrowing Islamist opportunities were, perhaps, the most important. The Oslo Agreement effectively cancelled the First Intifada, the platform paving the way for the rise of Hamas and PIJ as political and military forces.[44] By 1992, polls revealed that Hamas was in a position to repeatedly defeat Fatah in elections,[45] while PIJ attacks had grown annually from 1987 to a peak in 1993.[46] The establishment of the Palestinian National Authority (PA), Gunning argues, shifted the power balance between Fatah and Hamas, as the former secured an unprecedented level of resources and institu-tional backing which starkly contrasted with that available to Hamas. The Islamist opposition thus feared that a successful peace process would marginalize them politically. In the absence of a viable political platform to counterbalance its rival, Islamists saw suicide bombings as a guaranteed way of undermining the position of Fatah.[47] The violence of Hamas – and,

---

43   Abu Tayr, *Sayyidi Umar*, 217–18.
44   Mishal and Sela, *The Palestinian Hamas*, 67.
45   Jeroen Gunning, *Hamas in Politics: Democracy, Religion, Violence* (London: Hurst, 2009), 42.
46   Skare, *A History of Palestinian Islamic Jihad*, 121.
47   Gunning, *Hamas in Politics*, 43, 46.

for that matter, PIJ – was never strictly ideological despite the prevalence of doctrinaire jargon.[48]

Intra-Islamist competition mattered as well. The size and capabilities of PIJ had grown rapidly with the eruption of the First Intifada in 1987. Although Hamas is the predominant Palestinian Islamist movement today, this was not equally evident in the late 1980s and early 1990s.[49] While Hamas carried out sixty-six attacks in the first three years after its establishment, PIJ carried out fifty-four in the same period.[50] As Sara Roy hypothesized in 1991, while the retaliatory violence against Israeli civilians by Hamas was partly driven by its competition with nationalist factions such as Fatah, it could equally be a response to the growing influence of PIJ.[51] It is doubtful Hamas would be indifferent to such a development within the Palestinian Islamic movement. When facing turmoil in the mid-1990s due to financial mismanagement, persons connected to PIJ expressed regret for not exploiting the First Intifada to make it the dominant movement among the Palestinian Islamists.[52]

The prospect of a peace process also altered the relationship between the Palestinian Islamist factions and the leftist ones. While the Muslim Brotherhood and the Popular Front for the Liberation of Palestine (PFLP) had engaged in intra-Palestinian violence in the 1980s, they began collaborating from the early 1990s in their rejection of Oslo. The short-lived Ten Resistance Organizations (TRO) in 1991 gave way to the formation of the Alliance of Palestinian Forces (APF) in 1993. Indeed, both Islamist and leftist factions sought to benefit from their collaboration beyond thwarting a settlement. Hamas, in particular, hoped that aligning with the PFLP and the Democratic Front for the Liberation of Palestine (DFLP) would address concerns about their nationalist, as opposed to religious, commitment. The leftist factions, on the other hand, hoped to exploit

---

48    Khaled Hroub, *Hamas: Political Thought and Practice* (Washington, DC: Institute for Palestine Studies, 2000), 43.

49    Skare, *A History of Palestinian Islamic Jihad*, 160.

50    Mishal and Sela, *The Palestinian Hamas*, 57, 209n6.

51    Sara Roy, 'The Political Economy of Despair: Changing Political and Economic Realities in the Gaza Strip', *Journal of Palestine Studies* 20, no. 3 (1991): 65.

52    *United States of America v. Sami Amin al-Arian, Ramadan Abdullah Shallah, Bashir Musa Mohammad Nafi, Sameeh Hammoudeh, Muhammad Tasir Hassan al-Khatib, Abd al-Aziz Awda, Ghassan Zayed Ballut, Hatim Naji Fariz*, Case No. 8:03-CR-77-T-30TBM (M.D. Fla. 2004), at 19.

Hamas's and PIJ's growing popular support and their generous patrons.[53] Yet, partly because the alliance was premised on common grievances rather than a shared vision of the organization of Palestinian society and resistance, and partly because of their recent history of internecine fighting, suspicion and a lack of trust characterized the relationship between the Islamists and the leftists, especially in the case of Hamas.[54] Although the overt conflict of the 1980s was now a thing of the past, Palestinian Islamist–leftist tensions remained.

These observations on the Islamist opposition to Oslo presume that Hamas and PIJ functioned as united fronts with one unequivocal political line in the 1990s. Yet, Hamas had undergone important structural changes since the publication of its first communique in December 1987, changes that were mainly caused by Israeli repression and counterinsurgency. Yahya Sinwar was not the only Hamas cadre who was arrested by the Israeli occupation authorities in the late 1980s. The kidnapping and execution of the Israeli sergeants Avi Sasportas and Ilan Saadon in Feburary and May 1989 both facilitated Hamas's ascent to military prominence and initiated a mass arrest campaign against the Islamist factions.[55] With 1,500 Hamas members rounded up in the West Bank and Gaza, the Israelis came close to annihilating the movement in 1989.[56]

Hamas had, from the onset, operated with an 'inside' leadership who lived in the Occupied Palestinian Territories and an 'outside' leadership residing in the diaspora. Ahmad Yassin, Abdel Aziz al-Rantisi, Ismail Abu Shanab, and their colleagues represented the interior. Musa Abu Marzuq, Khalid Mishal, and their colleagues represented the exterior. While the latter was initially confined to offering financial support and guidance, in addition to logistical arrangements, the decapitation of the movement prompted an organizational reconfiguration to ensure that Hamas would not collapse from another devastating blow: the outside, far from the reach of the occupation, took control of the inside.[57] As a part of this reconfiguration, Hamas was split into three branches: one political wing, one military wing, and one social wing providing welfare

---

53   Anders Strindberg, 'The Damascus-Based Alliance of Palestinian Forces: A Primer', *Journal of Palestine Studies* 29, no. 3 (2000): 61.

54   Hroub, *Hamas*, 123.

55   Azzam Tamimi, *Hamas: Unwritten Chapters* (London: Hurst, 2009), 57.

56   Ibid., 58–9.

57   Ibid., 60.

services to the Palestinian population. Although they were all part of Hamas, adhered to the same core objectives, and were committed to, and restrained by, the same rules and regulations, the wings nonetheless enjoyed a considerable autonomy.

Hamas's dynamic of violence in the 1990s was strongly affected by its reorganization and the rise of the outside leadership. One variable was the class background of Abu Marzuq and his colleagues. As young technocrats with higher education in the liberal professions, they subscribed to a form of Islamism advocating the imposition of religion from above. This differed from the inside leadership, which preferred working with ordinary processes of communal activity such as proselytizing and engaging in social work. Another variable was the internal competition for authority. Because it controlled the funding of the Qassam Brigades, the outside leadership often intensified military efforts when it feared being marginalized by the political manoeuvring of the inside leaders.[58] When Ahmad Yassin and his colleagues considered the possibility of integrating with, and piggybacking on, the newly established (in 1996) PA, Hamas's suicide bombings effectively ended the tentative rapprochement between the internal leadership and Arafat.[59]

Although Hamas's restructuring was intended to safeguard the movement from Israeli counter-insurgency, it also introduced blurred hierarchical links and a fragmentation of authority between political-religious leaders and military activists.[60] The Palestinian Islamist leaderships were simply incapable, at times, of restraining their militants, the fervent young guard, on the ground.[61] The political leadership did not always know about planned attacks because of the compartmentalization of Hamas, and Ahmad Yassin admitted that often only members of the Qassam Brigades knew about their cell's existence.[62] It consequently did not matter that his deputy, Ismail Abu Shanab, was strongly against

---

58    Mishal and Sela, *The Palestinian Hamas*, 166.

59    Gunning, *Hamas in Politics*, 113; Baruch Kimmerling and Joel S. Migdal, *The Palestinian People: A History* (Cambridge, MA: Harvard University Press, 2003), 369.

60    Mishal and Sela, *The Palestinian Hamas*, 56–7.

61    Wendy Kristianasen, 'Challenge and Counterchallenge: Hamas's Response to Oslo', *Journal of Palestine Studies* 28, no. 3 (1999): 22.

62    'al-Shaykh Ahmad Yasin: Shahid ala asr al-intifada', episode 6, *al-Jazeera*, May 22, 1999.

the use of suicide bombings as long as key commanders in the Qassam Brigades did not share his views.[63] 'While [Hamas's] consultative council decided when to escalate or cease fire,' Baconi writes, '[the Qassam Brigades] followed its own tactical considerations, designing and executing operations autonomously and clandestinely.'[64] Sometimes, militants even refused following direct orders from their leaders: When al-Shiqaqi's successor, Ramadan Shallah, ordered his PIJ militants to evacuate the camp before the Battle of Jenin in April 2002 to avoid the onslaught, they simply refused.[65] When the dust had settled, after eleven days of carnage, all PIJ militants had been either killed or arrested, which significantly weakened the movement in the northern West Bank.

A disconnection developed between hardliners and moderates in Hamas, and between parts of its political wing and the military wing. There was no longer just one Hamas, but many. For every Ismail Abu Shanab proposing a ceasefire, there was a Muhammad Deif preparing an insurgency. For every Ahmed Yousef pulling Hamas towards an Islamic-democratic platform, there was a Nizar Rayan pushing the movement towards one that instead was Salafist, anti-Shiite, and sectarian. While important elements in the political wing attempted to develop a viable political project, the raison d'être of its military wing was fighting an external enemy. While the behaviour of the latter was dictated by 'operational efficiency and secrecy', the former vied for 'popularity, legitimacy, and visibility.'[66] As the outside leadership neither suffered from the hardship of occupation nor Israeli counter-insurgencies, they could afford to adopt a hardliner position on violence and ceasefires.[67] The 1990s witnessed the continuous manoeuvring of the Qassam Brigades and the political wing vis-à-vis each other – sometimes in tandem and at others independently and at odds with each other.

---

63    Wolf Blitzer, 'Who Was Ismail Abu Shanab?', CNN, August 21, 2003.

64    Tareq Baconi, *Hamas Contained: The Rise and Pacification of Palestinian Resistance* (Stanford, CA: Stanford University Press, 2018), 35.

65    Thabit Mardawi, *Namut fi al-watan . . . wa lan nughadir. Malhamat jinin bi-shahadat al-asir al-mujahid Thabit Mardawi* (Gaza: al-markaz al-Filastini li-l-tawasul al-hadari, 2006), 134.

66    Jeroen Gunning, 'Peace with Hamas? The Transforming Potential of Political Participation', *International Affairs* 80, no. 2 (March 2004): 236.

67    Sara Roy, *Hamas and Civil Society in Gaza: Engaging the Islamist Social Sector* (Princeton, NJ: Princeton University Press, 2011), 30.

1. Hassan al-Banna (front row, centre) visiting the Muslim Brotherhood branch in Gaza City, March 19, 1948. Also pictured: Gazan Brotherhood leaders Zafer al-Shawa (back row, left) and Omar Sawan (front row, second from left) (source: al-Zaytouna Centre for Studies and Consultation).

2. Muslim Brotherhood scouts in Gaza before the 1948 Palestine War (source: al-Zaytouna Centre for Studies and Consultation).

3. Ismail Abdel Aziz al-Khalidi, co-founder of the Muslim Brotherhood in the Gaza Strip (source: al-Zaytouna Centre for Studies and Consultation).

4. Members of the Tawhid Association, with Zafir al-Shawa (encircled), 1949 (source: al-Zaytouna Centre for Studies and Consultation).

5. Ahmad Yassin (standing) as a teacher, late 1950s (source: al-Zaytouna Centre for Studies and Consultation).

6. Ahmad Yassin (second from right, back row) on excursion with Muslim Brotherhood to one of Gaza's beaches, late 1950s/early 1960s (source: al-Zaytouna Centre for Studies and Consultation).

7. Ahmad Yassin (far right) in an orange grove in Beit Hanoun, 1961 (source: al-Zaytouna Centre for Studies and Consultation).

8. Taqi al-Din al-Nabhani, founder of Hizb al-Tahrir.

9. Fathi al-Shiqaqi, co-founder and first PIJ secretary-general (source: Palestinian Islamic Jihad/rabdullah.com).

10. Co-founders of PIJ as students in Egypt, 1970s. From left: Fathi al-Shiqaqi, Ramadan Shallah, unknown, and Nafidh Azzam (source: Palestinian Islamic Jihad/rabdullah.com).

11. Fathi al-Shiqaqi (right) and Ramadan Shallah (left) in exile after the former's deportation to Lebanon (source: Palestinian Islamic Jihad/rabdullah.com).

12. Last known photograph of Fathi al-Shiqaqi (centre) from visit to Libya, 1995, with Muammar Gaddafi standing in front (source: Palestinian Islamic Jihad/rabdullah.com).

13. Abdel Aziz al-Rantisi as a young
student, 1980s (source: *Filastin
al-Muslima*, July 1989, p. 23).

14. Hamas activist, late 1980s (source:
*Filastin al-Muslima*, November 1989,
front page).

15. Hamas demonstration in commemoration of the assassination of Hassan al-Banna, 1989 (source: *Filastin al-Muslima*, April 1990, p. 2).

16. Imad Aql, co-founder of Hamas's Izz al-Din al-Qassam Brigades and Muhammad Deif's mentor (source: al-Qassam Brigades).

17. Poster advocating for the release of the imprisoned Ahmad Yassin. 'Towering behind bars, you guard our spirit. Resisting defeat within us.' (source: *Filastin al-Muslima*, June 1995, p. 63).

18. Muhammad Deif holding the passport of kidnapped Israeli soldier Nachshon Wachsman, 1994 (source: al-Qassam Brigades).

19. Muhammad Deif (source: Israel Defense Forces handout).

20. Leader of the al-Qassam Brigades, Salah Shahada, posing with three suicide bombers (source: al-Qassam Brigades).

21. Yahya Ayash, chief bomb maker of Hamas, mid-1990s (source: al-Qassam Brigades).

22. Mahmoud Saqr al-Zatma, chief PIJ bomb maker, manufacturing an explosive device during the Second Intifada (source: Palestinian Islamic Jihad/al-Quds Brigades).

23. Yahya Sinwar (right) at the Islamic University of Gaza, November 15, 1980, with Dr Ma'mun Abu Amir (left) (courtesy of Dr Ahmad Ma'mun).

24. Hamas graffiti from the First Intifada featuring the words *Quran* and *jihad* on either side of the map of Palestine (source: *Filastin al-Muslima*, July 1989, p. 2).

25. Ramadan Shallah receiving his doctorate in economics from Durham University in 1990 (source: Palestinian Islamic Jihad/rabdullah.com).

26. Ziyad al-Nakhala (second from left) and Ramadan Shallah (centre, with hands raised) at the funeral of Fathi al-Shiqaqi (source: Palestinian Islamic Jihad/rabdullah.com).

Overcoming these internal contradictions depended largely on the leadership's prestige and authority. By stressing the long-term nature of the conflict and the need for patience in the Palestinian struggle, Ahmad Yassin and his colleagues could distinguish between a permanent and temporary settlement and between a short-term policy delaying its ultimate goals and a long-term strategy based on a steadfast commitment to an Islamic doctrine.[68] Essentially, the theological concept of patience afforded Hamas crucial flexibility on the ground, which enabled the movement to justify deviations from rigid dogma without causing the movement to splinter. As Mishal observes, Hamas's strategy of temporary settlement enabled Hamas to acquiesce in the Oslo Agreement without recognizing Israel, to endorse the establishment of a Palestinian state in the West Bank and Gaza without giving up on its maximalist territorial aspirations, and to restrain violence without giving up armed struggle: 'Political activity here and now was thus justified in terms of the hereafter. Acceptance of a political settlement in the short run was interpreted as being complementary, not contradictory, to long-term desires.'[69]

The moderate/hardliner dichotomy is not without its nuances, however. For example, Salih al-Aruri, the Hamas deputy who was killed in an Israeli airstrike in Beirut in January 2024, was an ardent proponent of armed struggle and a central figure in arming militants in the West Bank in the early 2020s. Yet he was also one of the greatest advocates for reconciliation with the PA in the West Bank and organizing new Palestinian democratic elections. Al-Aruri was reportedly close to Fatah strongman Jibril Rajoub despite the political divide.[70] Although senior members in Hamas and PIJ could be radical on one question, they could be equally moderate in another. Others saw their perspectives change over time. Mahmud al-Zahar, for example, is today viewed as one of the least compromising personalities in Hamas, partly because of his refusal to accept the PLO's past agreements with Israel and because of his repeated references to Fatah as 'traitors and collaborators'.[71] In the 1990s, however, he was viewed as a dove, and al-Zahar received death threats from the Qassam Brigades

---

68    Mishal and Sela, *The Palestinian Hamas*, 64, 151.

69    Mishal, 'The Pragmatic Dimension of the Palestinian Hamas', 576.

70    Mohammed al-Kassim, 'Saleh al-Arouri Killing Deals Blow to Hamas but Conflict May Still Widen', *Jerusalem Post*, January 5, 2024.

71    'A Hamas Hardliner', *Economist*, January 31, 2008.

for discussing the possibility of a peace agreement with Israel.[72] Only when the Israelis tried to assassinate him in 2003 by dropping a ton of explosives on his house – killing his twenty-year-old son and maiming his daughter – did al-Zahar develop into one of Hamas's most ardent hardliners.

The organizational restructuring and emerging internal contradictions were, as such, symptomatic of the formative challenges Palestinian Islamism experienced in this period. PIJ had to restructure its organization after its leadership was deported to Lebanon in 1987 and 1988. Now, the PIJ founding fathers were not just far from the grip of the occupation, but also from its membership base. Exile forced the movement to undergo a process of bureaucratization with the establishment of a formal leadership taking decisions on behalf of the inside. The formalization of organizational structures was certainly driven by al-Shiqaqi's genuine fear of being sidelined by the inside. It was also implemented to streamline its military efforts. As PIJ was a loose cell network in the 1980s, al-Shiqaqi now implemented vertical power structures to keep the wheels turning. Al-Shiqaqi, the structural architect, delegated the responsibility of naming the military wing to al-Khawaja, its leader. The official name he chose for PIJ's military wing was the Islamic Mujahid Forces, abbreviated to Qassam.[73]

Israeli repression and counterinsurgency also mattered for the power balance between the inside and outside leaderships and between hardliners and moderates. When the PA commenced its security cooperation with Israeli authorities as a part of the Oslo Agreement, it confirmed the worst fears of both Hamas and PIJ. Suddenly, Arafat's newly established security agencies began targeting their members and militants, which effectively pushed the Islamists into a corner. The internal leadership of PIJ were quickly put behind bars between September 1993 and September 1994. Mahmud al-Zatma, the chief bomb maker of PIJ, was also incarcerated and tortured. The PIJ field commanders Amar al-A'raj and Ayman al-Razayna were then assassinated by the intelligence services of the PA in 1996.[74] The first leader and founder of the movement, al-Shiqaqi, was, as noted, assassinated in Malta, October 26, 1995.

---

72   Mishal and Sela, *The Palestinian Hamas*, 71.
73   Skare, *A History of Palestinian Islamic Jihad*, 114–15.
74   Ibid., 122.

The lack of coordination between Palestinian security and police agencies, in addition to little – if any – judicial oversight, augmented the intensity and brutality of the PA's clampdown on the Islamist opposition. Indeed, Arafat's neo-patrimonial leadership produced an inflated, opaque, and multi-headed security structure in the Occupied Territories with no unified command.[75] As PIJ's secretary-general, Ramadan Shallah, complained in 1996:

> Arafat has so many intelligence services in the self-rule areas that if you open your window, Preventive Security peeps in; if you open your door, the Presidential Security Service comes in; if you go out to your garden, you bump into Military intelligence, and if you go out to the street, you come across General Intelligence.[76]

Hamas and PIJ were profoundly impacted by the counter-insurgency of the 1990s, which effectively curbed their ability to carry out armed operations and suicide bombings against Israeli targets. While both Hamas's and PIJ's capabilities had grown from the late 1980s to a peak around 1993–94, their attacks suddenly dropped as plots were thwarted and prisons saw an influx of Islamist militants, members, and sympathizers.[77] By 1999, the military infrastructure of both Hamas and PIJ had largely been dismantled in the Occupied Territories: 'The prisons of Junayd, Nablus, Jericho, Beituniya, al-Dhahiriya, Bethlehem, and others bear witness to this difficult period faced by those in Hamas' military wing,' writes the former Qassam Brigades commander Husam Badran. 'The mujahidin – pursued and hunted by the occupation – had to hide from the Palestinian security apparatus, which made their situation even more difficult.'[78] The senior PIJ member in the West Bank, Yusuf Arif Al-Hajj Muhammad, mirrored the account of Badran when he described the situation for PIJ in this period: 'In these seven lean years [1993–2000], the Islamic resistance suffered distress, and . . . the possibilities of guerrilla

---

75  Lia, *A Police Force Without A State*, 307–9.
76  Quoted in ibid., 307.
77  Data in Figure 4.1 are from Palestinian Islamic Jihad, 'Jadwal tafsili bi-amaliyyat harakat al-jihad al-islami mundhu nash'atha hatta (2006/2)', document in author's possession; Hamas data are from the Global Terrorism Database, start.umd.edu.
78  Husam Badran, *Katibat al-shimal: al-Sabiqun ila al-janna* (n.p.: al-maktab al-i'lami li-kata'ib al-shahid Izz al-Din al-Qassam, 2010), 16–17.

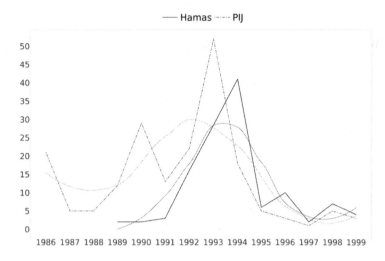

**Figure 4.1.** Number of Hamas and PIJ attacks, 1986–99, with moving average

work were . . . weak, as the eyes [of collaborators] were opened in the neighborhoods, in the alleys, and sometimes even inside of the houses.'[79]

The de facto annihilation of the Qassam Brigades mattered because it effectively altered the dynamic between the outside and inside leaderships in Hamas. It did not matter that the coffers of Hamas remained in the hands of the outside leadership because they no longer had anyone to support in the Occupied Territories. The militants in the Occupied Territories were either dead or in prison. With a military wing incapable of launching new attacks, and with disillusioned activists defecting from the political wing because the leadership had failed to achieve any meaningful political change, Hamas began shifting emphasis away from political-military action to socio-cultural reform in the mid-1990s. By 1997, it became increasingly evident that Hamas was no longer consistently advocating for political or military action against the occupation, but was instead shifting its focus to social work and proselytizing.[80] Searching for 'accommodation and consensus within the status quo', Hamas attempted

---

79    Yusuf Arif al-Hajj Muhammad, *al-Masira al-jihadiyya li-harakat al-jihad al-islami fi Filastin* (Gaza: Muhjat al-Quds, 2011), 70.

80    Sara Roy, 'Hamas and the Transformation(s) of Political Islam in Palestine', *Current History* 102, no. 660 (2003): 15.

to survive by returning to its roots and providing social services to an increasingly needy population.[81]

The shift to social services in the mid-1990s also illustrates how Hamas had developed an organizational structure far better equipped to deal with counterinsurgency than its sister-movement, PIJ. The latter – a movement that never developed a statist infrastructure of social welfare or semi-legal political institutions – was unable to pursue alternatives to political violence to alleviate Israeli pressure. By 1999, PIJ was caught in a state of asphyxiation and was effectively pushed onto the sidelines as an effective military force. As al-Hajj Muhammad dryly noted, the situation for PIJ was so dire that many believed that its military wing, Qassam, had been dissolved.[82]

## Controlling the state

Most research has focused on Hamas's and PIJ's violent reaction following the commencement of the peace process – discussing the two Palestinian Islamist movements as spoilers or semi-spoilers.[83] The Islamist opposition's literary production spurred by paradigmatic shifts in the 1990s, and its contribution to Palestinian political thought, have largely been ignored, even though the prospects of Palestinian self-rule confronted Hamas and PIJ with fundamental questions about social organization, political governance, and the legality of democracy.[84]

The urgency of these questions is illustrated by the booklet *The Palestinian Democratic Transformation*, authored in 1999 by the senior West Bank member of Hamas, Jamal Mansur, and the published lecture

---

81  Roy, *Hamas and Civil Society in Gaza*, 86–7.

82  Muhammad, *al-Massira al-jihadiyya*, 73.

83  Mishal and Sela, *The Palestinian Hamas*; Dipak K. Gupta and Kusum Mundra, 'Suicide Bombing as a Strategic Weapon: An Empirical Investigation of Hamas and Islami Jihad', *Terrorism and Political Violence* 17, no. 4 (December 2005): 579–98; Gunning, *Hamas in Politics*; Wendy Pearlman, 'Spoiling Inside and Out: Internal Political Contestation and the Middle East Peace Process', *International Security* 33, no. 3 (2008–9): 79–109; Milton-Edwards and Farrell, *Hamas*.

84  This section is based on, and uses text from, Erik Skare, 'Controlling the State in the Political Theory of Hamas and Palestinian Islamic Jihad', *Religions* 12, no. 11 (November 2021): 1–12.

'Fundamentalism and Secularism', delivered by al-Shiqaqi in 1995. These two texts were not, in fact, a polemical entry against the peace process or the two-state solution. Instead, they conveyed a profound concern with the authoritarian turn of the PA and the prospects for a future democratic Palestinian society. What both Mansur and al-Shiqaqi offered was a discussion of the just organization of society and the threats of authoritarianism.

We do not know with certainty, of course, what or who influenced al-Shiqaqi's political thinking about the state and the organization of a just society. His visions for civil society largely resembled those of the Tunisian Islamist Rachid al-Ghannouchi,[85] and al-Shiqaqi also discussed the writings of Iranian politician Abolhassan Banisadr about the 'non-authoritarian idea' in Islam and the elimination of centralized power.[86] It is nevertheless implausible that intra-Palestinian political developments did not inform the lecture that al-Shiqaqi gave in al-Yarmuk refugee camp in Damascus in which he discussed secularism, fundamentalism, and the just organization of society – concepts he further elaborated upon in an interview one month later.[87] The PA had already started to clamp down on PIJ when al-Shiqaqi spoke about these issues, and several members of its political bureau, such as Muhammad al-Hindi, Abdallah al-Shami, and Nafidh Azzam, were, as noted, incarcerated in this period.[88]

According to al-Shiqaqi, there was a natural balance of power in past Islamic society with a series of checks and balances to limit the powers of the state. As the source of legislation was the Quran and the Sunna, he claimed, in addition to the consensus of religious scholars, the powers of the state were effectively curbed.[89] If the ruler wanted to impose a jurisprudential system, with all powers in the hands of the state, he would be unable to do so without the scholars' consent. 'The institution of the scholars was able to protect society from the tyranny of the state and to preserve its cohesive fabric'. Thus, 'we had a true civil society for fourteen

---

85    Skare, *A History of Palestinian Islamic Jihad*, 206–7.

86    Fathi al-Shiqaqi, 'Iran al-thawra wa-l-dawla', in Ahmad, *Rihlat al-damm alladhi hazam al-sayf*, 190–9.

87    Fathi al-Shiqaqi, 'al-Harakat al-islamiyya wa tatawwurat al-qadiya al-Filastiniyya', in Ahmad, *Rihlat al-damm alladhi hazam al-sayf*, 1212–23.

88    Skare, *A History of Palestinian Islamic Jihad*, 122.

89    Fathi al-Shiqaqi, 'al-Usuliyya wa-l-ilmaniyya', in Ahmad, *Rihlat al-damm alladhi hazam al-sayf*, 591.

centuries, which was independent from the state and with education, health, *waqf*, and mosque in its hands. Even with the corruption and moral collapse of the state, with its justice or injustice, it did not leave a serious impact on society.[90]

For al-Shiqaqi, colonially imposed secularism – the separation of religion and state – proved disastrous because, in his view, religious scholars were essential to counterbalancing the state's monopoly of power. It was not a step towards liberation from religious tyranny, then, but rather a recipe for political tyranny, as secularism abolished the division of political power and authority. Suddenly, all powers lay in the hands of the state. 'At a time when the secularists wanted to separate religion and state, and to establish civil institutions, they . . . struck the most important civil institution, which was completely subjected to the state after being dismantled, and its internal strength fragmented.'[91]

A society where the state had all power was certainly worrisome for al-Shiqaqi:

> The state is repressive by nature, or a tool of repression against the government classes as defined by Lenin. It is the most dangerous instrument of power created by human society, so Islam worked to sort out a mode of human society depriving this state of its power and domination, and thus making it weaker than, and accountable to, society even if the most powerful caliphs and sultans controlled it.[92]

Yet because al-Shiqaqi saw the conflict between the state and civil society as the main contradiction in society, in which the state invariably sought to dominate the latter, he arrived at the opposite conclusion from Lenin – the latter arguing that the working class had to consolidate its power in the form of the dictatorship of the proletariat for the transformation of society into a classless one. Instead, because he believed that the state was repressive by nature and had to progressively turn despotic, a just society was one with an inherently weak state kept in check by a strong civil society counterbalancing it. Essentially, the state had to be deprived of its power and its tools of domination, thus making it accountable to

---

90   Ibid., 592.
91   Ibid., 591.
92   Ibid.

civil society. Abu Taha corroborated this notion of the state's nature to turn repressive, notably applying a Weberian instead of a Leninist conception:

> It is in the nature of the state always to become despotic. A strong civil society prevents the state from controlling more power. What is the state? The definition of the state is the monopoly of force; it holds legitimate force. The power of any state, any society, must be distributed. If the economy, such as money, is distributed, then power is distributed – and it is not as if the state has its hands on everything. The state then becomes weaker and a servant for society, and not society as a servant for the state. Today, the university administration [should] serve the students, and not the students who [should] serve the university administration. The state [should] serve the people, and not the people serve the state.[93]

It is highly doubtful, however, that such a power structure ever actually existed in Islamic society, and al-Shiqaqi's political theory reflected contemporary grievances more accurately than historical realities. Indeed, it is unlikely that he arrived at this conclusion from reading history alone, and the democratic 'deficiencies' of the PA must presumably have added to this feeling of state power inevitably turning authoritarian. His experience with authoritarian Arab regimes must have accentuated his perceptions of the state as well. After all, Egyptian authorities imprisoned al-Shiqaqi twice during his studies in Egypt. When asked about the necessity of separating legislative power from the state, for example, al-Shiqaqi referred to Egypt:

> The state controls everything today from legislation to jurisdiction and executive power. There is thus no legislative authority independent from the state preventing the latter from infringement, particularly since unlimited security apparatuses support this state. Take Press Law no. 93 of 1995 in Egypt, for example. The state imposed the law on the Egyptian parliament, despite the comprehensive opposition. The legislation has today become subjected to the state or the executive power, whilst it under Islam was subjected to the class of scholars and judges, and those qualified to appoint or depose a ruler on behalf of the Muslim community (*ahl al-hall wa-l-aqd*).[94]

---

93    Anwar Abu Taha, interview with Erik Skare, March 19, 2018.
94    Al-Shiqaqi, 'al-Harakat al-islamiyya wa tatawwurat al-qadiya al-Filastiniyya', 1218.

Due to the emphasis on the inherent contradiction between state and society, PIJ does not immediately seek the establishment of an Islamic state through which Islamic values are imposed from above. The state should be exempt from religious matters, as it is the main contender for power and threat to Islamic values that the movement attempts to preserve as guidelines for societal development and order. Instead of seeking a strong Islamic state, values are maintained and preserved through civil society from the bottom up. As Abu Taha postulated, the state 'becomes a functional state and not a divine state or a sovereign state; nor a theocratic state, a Marxist state or an Islamic state, no. It becomes a functional state apparatus that serves the people.'[95] The state's role will be confined to that of the executive branch of power. Meanwhile, the institution of scholars will function as the legislative branch, yet according to PIJ's political philosophy, they remain distinct and separate from the core structures of the state.

Hamas, in contrast, had already begun to vacillate in its approach to power when Mansur published his theory of the state and democracy in the booklet *The Palestinian Democratic Transformation* in 1999. The Islamic Resistance Movement's rejection of the Oslo Agreement was not merely ideological; the peace process threatened to weaken the movement, as Fatah could gain the upper hand both politically and economically. It is this context that shaped the political thought of Jamal Mansur, the West Bank Hamas leader, when he theorized the relationship between the state, civil society, and its subjects, and thus the requirements for a democratic transformation in the Occupied Palestinian Territories. Mansur was not just a Hamas cadre but also one of the First Intifada's university-educated representatives of the local leadership, which PLO chairman and President of the Palestinian Authority Yasser Arafat perceived as competitors for national leadership.[96]

Mansur fundamentally differed from al-Shiqaqi on the question of the just organization of society. Not because they disagree about the goal – keeping the state or executive authority in check in a society governed by Islamic law and values – but because the very premise of their analyses differed. While the main threat to al-Shiqaqi's vision of an ideal society is the political tyranny of an all-powerful state, Mansur fears a societal descent into 'chaos'. Similarly to Hobbesian political theory, Mansur

---

95    Anwar Abu Taha, interview with Erik Skare, March 19, 2018.
96    Kimmerling and Migdal, *The Palestinian People*, 367–8.

takes a rather dim view of human nature and operates implicitly with an imagined 'state of nature' in which it is all against all as the premise for his discussion of justice – a state constituted by competing contradictions, interests, and differences at the economic, social, intellectual, and political levels. It is, then, to be expected that all groups will compete against each other for power and control over others, which will 'pave the way for the rule of chaos'.[97] All civilizational progress has consequently come at a cost; and human rights charters, for instance, only appeared 'in the wake of devastating global catastrophes and wars, the human longing for justice and equality, and a desire for dignity after terrible abuses throughout the world over long periods of time'.[98]

Because man is a social animal organizing in competing groups to secure his material or spiritual interests, differences must be carefully managed according to a set of pre-agreed rules to which all subscribe. Contrary to Thomas Hobbes, who theorized the state of nature to justify absolutist rule and to advocate the multitude's unconditional surrender of its own powers, Mansur postulates that political power derives from, and stands responsible to, the people, who are capable of removing those in power if deemed necessary (and morally obligated to do so).[99] 'The demand for democracy has therefore become a form and a method of governance,' Mansur writes, 'and a guarantee of freedoms and safety from tyranny and oppression – of ensuring that the political community is not drawn into societal political violence.'[100] Furthermore,

> elections are considered means of managing conflicts in an open, orderly, and peaceful manner . . . and were thus introduced to prevent these conflicts from breaking out, and to prevent the parties [involved] from resorting to material – and possibly armed and bloody – means [to obtain power].[101]

---

97   Jamal Mansur, *al-Tahawwul al-dimuqrati al-Filastini* (Nablus: Markaz al-buhuth wa-l-dirasat al-Filastiniyya, 1999), 19.

98   Ibid., 20.

99   Ellen Meiksins Wood, *Liberty and Property: A Social History of Western Political Thought from the Renaissance to Enlightenment* (New York: Verso, 2012), 243.

100   Mansur, *al-Tahawwul al-Dimuqrati al-Filastini*, 15, 19.

101   Ibid., 19.

Essentially, '[democratic mechanisms] were able to neutralize the elements of tension and conflict in society and to turn them into a healthy competition that guarantees the rights of all to political participation and the peaceful transfer of power'.[102]

There is little doubt that Mansur's analysis is a political initiative informed by contemporary Palestinian political reality in the 1990s with the incomplete and undeveloped formation of the PA. Mansur describes, for example, the absence of clear Palestinian constitutional reference, which is supposed to control the balance between the pillars of the state – the executive, judicial, and legislative powers – intended to ensure political stability and societal harmony. Instead, 'we notice legal and legislative chaos . . . in the Legislative Council, which cannot find a basis for its various legislations'. Even worse,

> the president accepts, rejects, or freezes whatever laws he wants by virtue of the [existing peace] agreements, the rule of the historical [Palestinian] leadership and the status quo, and the weak role of the legislative council . . . The evidence of this is the deteriorating state of freedoms, human rights, and legal and judicial status [in the Occupied Palestinian Territories] . . . The absence of law and its rule will pave the way for the rule of chaos, the rule of centers of power, and the rule of the security and customary spirit in public life.[103]

This stage in Palestinian state-building, marked by evident democratic deficiencies, is, presumably, why both al-Shiqaqi and Mansur assigned themselves one particular theoretical task in the 1990s: To outline how one can avoid all political power being concentrated in one hand. Yet, as a representative of Hamas's 'internal' reformist leadership addressing 'the realities in our societies under the logic of interests and corruption', Mansur never arrived at al-Shiqaqi's conclusion of defanging the state so that Islamic law and values can be safeguarded from below, but instead operates well within the limits of the political system.[104]

For Mansur, the democratic deficiencies of the Palestinian Authority are not caused by the inherent essence of the state itself which must almost

---

102   Ibid., 95.
103   Ibid., 37–8.
104   Ibid., 24.

instinctively turn despotic. Although he notes that an unhinged executive power will cause chaos, the state itself is nevertheless an instrument capable of managing competing interests and preserving social cohesion if a balance between the centres of power is found:

> In order to ensure the creation of a political entity and a modern state, a commitment to an effective balance and equilibrium between the three authorities must be found, as this is one of the important general concepts, which the world has known for civilization as a basis for a normal rule, but it is the defining boundary that distinguishes the modern state from the clan and the most important guarantee of public liberties.[105]

There is thus a clear, yet cautious, optimism between the lines of Mansur's piece insofar as he believes in the feasibility of reforming the Palestinian political system to unleash its full democratic potential. As he admits, the draft of the Palestinian Basic Law, for example, was a 'reasonably balanced project' which was an acceptable foundation for a political system with 'most of the democratic requirements', and a major step forward is to strengthen it further:[106]

> The constitution is, in this way, considered a contract between the pillars of society or its parts, and it represents the most important principle of social cohesion at the societal or group level. This is because leaving matters to coincidences or good intentions will lead to problems, unrest, and even conflicts. The clearer and more reliable our contractual rules are, the fewer errors there are and the easier the correction process is.[107]

Both al-Shiqaqi and Mansur refer to the judicial authority (the institution of scholars in the case of al-Shiqaqi) as an independent safeguard as 'the principle of the judiciary's independence is one of the foundations for justice, one of the bases for stability, and one of the safeguards preventing tyranny with the domination of the executive power'.[108] While al-Shiqaqi refers to Lenin, Mansur quotes Montesquieu: 'When the legislative and executive powers are united in the same person, or in the same body

---

105    Ibid., 45.
106    Ibid., 37.
107    Ibid., 19.
108    Ibid., 19, 95.

of magistrates, there can be no liberty. Again, there is no liberty, if the judiciary power be not separated from the executive.'[109] In fact, Mansur's use of Montesquieu is even more striking when one considers that he actually adjusts the quote – intentionally or unintentionally – in order to emphasize the danger of the executive power.

There are, consequently, clear differences in the way al-Shiqaqi and Mansur approached the state in the 1990s following the Oslo Accords and the corresponding establishment of the PA. While al-Shiqaqi perceived power with suspicion, stressing the necessity of removing all power from the state because it inevitably would turn despotic, Mansur never intended to overthrow the existing system and assign it to the dustbin of history. Instead, Mansur intended to restore it in its proper role by establishing clear separations between the executive, legislative, and judicial powers. In this way, it is clear that Mansur was far more optimistic with regard to the democratic potential of the PA than al-Shiqaqi was.

Although al-Shiqaqi and Mansur differed in their approach to organizing society to unleash its full potential of justice, they both stressed the necessity and virtue of religion as a fundament for the political system. Moreover, there was little, or no, contradiction between religion as societal foundation and democracy. Al-Shiqaqi, for example, never dismissed the idea of a parliament representing the populace, nor did he dismiss a multi-party system with the rotation of power. As he postulated, 'Islam does not mean this party or that movement.'[110] Al-Shiqaqi explained that the apparent dismissal of 'democracy' by Islamists was an issue of semantics, as 'the problem that some Islamists have with democracy is with the term and not with the principle of consultation and political participation. Nor do they have a problem with the mechanisms, means, systems, institutions, and experiences achieving the purposes and objectives of democracy.'[111]

Mansur also proclaims his support for elections as the only accepted means of transferring power, as man is God's deputy on earth. The people are the source of all political legitimacy. 'If the Islamists are accepted, then they rule. If they lose legitimacy, then they must accept the rule of the

109   Quoted in ibid., 45.
110   Al-Shiqaqi, 'al-Harakat al-islamiyya wa tatawwurat al-qadiya al-Filastiniyya', 1218.
111   Al-Shiqaqi, 'al-Usuliyya wa-l-ilmaniyya', 595.

game and step aside according to the will of the people.'[112] It necessarily follows that Mansur supports the freedom of expression, freedom of beliefs, and the right to organize through which competing groups in society present their ideas in order to 'reach power or to pressure it.'[113]

The issue of democracy is, consequently, an issue of semantics, and – because democracy is an approach and not a creed – Mansur redressed contemporary concepts of democracy with traditional Islamic forms of governance. Elections, for example, become a contemporary form of oath of allegiance, while representative democracy is a form of consultation, 'the cornerstone of Islam's governing mechanism . . . [and a] guarantee of the *umma*'s participation in governance . . . with an explicit mandate from Islamic law.'[114]

Although al-Shiqaqi and Mansur promote and endorse elections, multi-party systems, and a rotation of power, there is nevertheless a certain trepidation in both that the popular will may transgress Islamic values and sideline the religious foundations they both desire for society. Consider the following description by al-Shiqaqi, for example, on participation in democratic elections and its requirements:

> I believe that Islam forms the *umma*'s identity and its civilizational heritage, which cannot be abandoned, and which simultaneously is its reference. With the recognition of this reference, then there is no problem with pluralism. Islam does not mean this party or that movement. All of these Islamic movements and organizations do not equate Islam but are only a part of it. All currents that recognize one reference for the umma is a part of it and has the right to express itself in the appropriate manner. We therefore believe in pluralism and the rotation of power within the framework of all recognizing the reference of the one umma and the constitution on which the umma agrees. After that, if there are a number of independent reasonings and interpretations, even in the understanding of the constitution and religion itself, there is still no problem.[115]

---

112    Mansur, *al-Tahawwul al-dimuqrati al-Filastini*, 96.
113    Ibid., 22.
114    Ibid., 13.
115    Al-Shiqaqi, 'al-Harakat al-islamiyya wa tatawwurat al-qadiya al-Filastiniyya', 1218.

Political pluralism is allowed, and free elections and democracy are man-datory. Yet this can only take place within the consensus that Islam is the common reference guiding the state, with Islamic law constituting the fundamental framework for constitutional structures and legislation. 'It is intended that the Qur'an provides the constitution with the basis and principles on which the constitution is based', and 'the human authority remains governed by the philosophy of Islam in legislation (what is allowed and prohibited).'[116]

True power in future society should, as noted, be in the hands of civil society and the institution of scholars, which are non-elected and not a part of future democratic process – at least not as outlined by the texts of PIJ. When al-Shiqaqi described an ideal past society, it was one in which the state had little influence over society. When he was asked who should have legislative power in future society, al-Shiqaqi said that it should reside in the *umma* and its representatives, and not in the state, in order to preserve Islamic values and law.[117] In addition, the responsibilities of states, such as 'the opportunity to life and health, as well as education', were fixed according to 'Islamic jurisprudence and law'.[118] Although PIJ does not advocate a notion of the complete sovereignty of God's law, one nevertheless sees that man-made laws are to be subordinated to divine law in a fair society aiming for justice.

The same applies to Mansur's conception of just society, as also he stresses the need for religion to have a significant role in governance:

> With the distinctiveness of Islam and its uniqueness and comprehensive-ness in all aspects of life, it is the final religion . . . Being the final religion, it is required that it is superior and has authority to act in all stages of human development as its specific and defining texts are our reference in rule and in life.[119]

As in al-Shiqaqi's writings, religion will form the basis for the state's constitution:

---

116   Ibid.
117   Ibid.
118   Ibid.
119   Mansur, *al-Tahawwul al-dimuqrati al-Filastini*, 13.

For the Qur'an is the constitution in the sense that it is the reference
and supreme legitimacy, and the constitution of an Islamic entity will
never deviate from the requirements of the Qur'an and its legal provi-
sions . . . As for the written constitution, it is a modern necessity and has
legal and structural foundations. It has been accepted in Islam, provided
that the constitution is guided above all by the rules and purposes of
Islamic law.[120]

Democratic freedom could thus, according to al-Shiqaqi and Mansur, go
too far; there was a freedom to choose anarchy. This trepidation effectively
made both of them approach democracy with the notion of 'Yes, but'.
Mansur, for example, stresses the support for democratic means to solve
societal differences. He notes that Islamists' view of democracy 'leads to
the acceptance of pluralism open to all, the right to political participation, and the pursuit of power through peaceful transfer of power'.[121] Yet,
admittedly, this is also based on

our conviction that there is no successful political future for any group
that rejects the culture and religion of the Muslim majority in Muslim
countries . . . We are confident that Islam is the owner of the future in
predominantly Muslim countries, but we are satisfied with the choice of
the people and are all committed to its results.[122]

Because both al-Shiqaqi and Masur postulate that Islam must be the
reference standard of the political system, and because the constitution
and legislation must be based on supposed Islamic values, it is only
within this framework that politics can navigate, negotiate, and implement change. There is little to indicate that the Islamic framework may
be transcended when attempting to limit the powers and influence of
the executive power. In this sense, the future society that al-Shiqaqi
and Mansur outline can then, at best, be described as non-liberal yet
rights-based.

We will never know if Mansur's cautious optimism would have
prevailed over al-Shiqaqi's longstanding pessimism. Nor do we know

---

120    Ibid., 13, 20, 96.
121    Ibid., 96.
122    Ibid., 99.

what political role Mansur would have played within Hamas or on the Palestinian national political scene. Despite being a strictly political figure running welfare programmes and medical clinics in the West Bank, Mansur was assassinated in an Israeli airstrike on July 31, 2001. The Israelis called it a 'preventative measure'.[123]

---

123    'Profile: Hamas Activist Jamal Mansour', BBC News, July 31, 2001.

# 5

# Guns and Governance

'Without . . . your love for martyrdom, the liberation of Gaza could not have been achieved.'[1] Thus spoke Muhammad Deif in September 2005. The Oslo Accords had effectively collapsed, the Second Intifada had erupted and petered out, and the mounting military casualties from defending the Israeli settlements in Gaza compelled Israel to unilaterally dismantle them and redeploy its forces along the border. Viewing the Israeli disengagement as a decisive victory, Hamas decided that it was time to capitalize on its military initiatives by participating in the Palestinian legislative elections. Palestinian Islamic Jihad (PIJ) adamantly declined changing course. Their refusal stemmed not from an opposition to democracy, however, but rather from a commitment to it.

This chapter examines the breakdown of the Oslo Accords and the revitalization of PIJ and the Qassam Brigades from September 2000. It

---

1   Quoted in Robert J. Brym and Bader Araj, 'Suicide Bombing as Strategy and Interaction: The Case of the Second Intifada', *Social Forces* 84, no. 4 (June 2006): 1980.

explores the repercussions of Hamas's unexpected victory in the legislative elections and the serious ideological fissures it set in motion. While Hamas moderates viewed their authority as obliterated by the Qassam Brigades' violent ousting of Fatah, the Qassam militants perceived themselves as glorified janitors of the Gazan blockade. Hamas's governance also expedited the rise and growth of a previously unknown Palestinian Islamist current: Salafi-jihadism. PIJ, the traditional advocates of armed struggle, found themselves in the unexpected role of peacemakers.

## The Children of Oslo

Failure was inscribed into the DNA of the Oslo Accords. One crucial factor was the deliberate strategy of 'constructive opaqueness' where details in the agreement were hazy and critical issues remained conspicuously unaddressed. Jerusalem was too controversial to be immediately addressed. The Palestinian refugees could similarly evoke the conflicting narratives of the 1948 War and the needs of the Palestinians still living in exile. The Israeli settlements and a Palestinian state would have 'revealed the magnitude of the former and how it effectively obstructed the latter'.[2] In fact, the Oslo Accords mentioned neither an independent Palestinian state nor did it indicate the borders of such a Palestinian entity.[3] Because there was no deadline and the agreements were not signed between states, 'each could be reopened and renegotiated ad infinitum'.[4] There would not have been an Oslo agreement had these issues been addressed.

For the Palestinians, the situation on the ground did not improve with the initiation of the peace process. On the contrary, it worsened drastically. Geographically, settlement expansion confiscated 51,000 additional acres of Palestinian land between 1993 and 2000, and the related infrastructure dissected and fragmented the Occupied Territories into enclaves.[5] The

---

2    Oren Barak, 'The Failure of the Israeli-Palestinian Peace Process, 1993–2000, *Journal of Peace Research* 42, no. 6 (2005): 728.

3    Avi Shlaim, 'Reflections on the Israeli–Palestinian Conflict', *Asian Affairs* 42, no. 1 (March 2011): 9.

4    Oren Barak, 'The Failure of the Israeli–Palestinian Peace Process', 730.

5    Sara Roy, 'Why Peace Failed: An Oslo Autopsy', *Current History* 101, no. 651 (January 2002): 9; Jeremy Pressman, 'The Second Intifada: Background and

Israeli settler population increased by at least 117 per cent in Gaza and at least 46 per cent in the West Bank in this period.[6] Economically, Palestinians experienced an increasing and essentially uninterrupted decline between 1992 and 2000 as the average unemployment rate increased from 3 to 28 per cent, which led to higher poverty and child-labour rates.[7] Even worse, 'there was no significant gain in human rights to compensate for the rise in unemployment, poverty and material hardship.'[8] As Pressman observes, while one often refers to Ariel Sharon's visit to the Temple Mount on September 28, 2000, as the event that ignited the Second Intifada, that view overplays the role of individuals and ignores structural factors. What caused the new Palestinian uprising was the fact that the Israeli occupation had deepened instead of abated, and because the reality on the ground fell short of Palestinian expectations created by the peace agreements.[9]

Both Israeli and Palestinian leaders were responsible for pushing the initially peaceful Palestinian protests and demonstrations into a maelstrom of violence. The Israelis believed that the exaggerated use of force would compel Palestinians to accept Israel's terms and conditions and deter them from violence. In the first three weeks of the intifada, Israeli forces fired 1 million rounds. Fifty Palestinians were killed and more than 1,000 were injured in the first five days of fighting. The number of Palestinian casualties effectively constrained the capacity of Palestinian leaders to press for moderation, as Palestinians concluded that laying down rifles had weakened their position in negotiations.[10] As 'the Palestinians found it very difficult to extract Israeli concessions', Kimmerling and Migdal write, 'it was not lost on Palestinian leaders that the one element that could be meted out to exert continuous pressure . . . – violence – had been relinquished from the onset.'[11]

---

Causes of the Israeli-Palestinian Conflict', *Journal of Conflict Studies* 23, no. 2 (2003): 121.

6    Ibid., 120.

7    Roy, 'Why Peace Failed', 9, 12–13.

8    Avi Shlaim, 'Peace Confounded', *Index on Censorship* 30, no. 1 (January 2001): 53.

9    Pressman, 'The Second Intifada', 114.

10    Ibid., 130–1.

11    Baruch Kimmerling and Joel S. Migdal, *The Palestinian People: A History* (Cambridge, MA: Harvard University Press, 2003), 359.

The Second Intifada was a godsend for the Islamist opposition, which had been effectively sidelined from 1993.[12] With the dismantling of its military wing, Hamas had largely reverted its emphasis to social welfare under the pressure of counterinsurgency. PIJ had been flat on the ground with a broken back. 'It can be said that at this stage, the [Qassam] Brigades did not have an existing organizational structure,' former al-Qassam commander Husam Badran reminisced about the late 1990s. 'There was no effective communication and cooperation between the different districts; the relationship with the outside leadership was practically non-existent.'[13] Now, however, the Islamists saw a Palestinian population enraged by the undelivered promises of Oslo. Support for armed resistance doubled from March 1999 to 70 per cent in June 2001. While the popularity of Hamas and PIJ had plummeted to 10 per cent combined in 1996, Palestinian popular support for Hamas and PIJ had risen to 15.5 per cent by April 2000. In early September, six weeks after the collapse of the Camp David talks, support for the Islamist factions had increased further to 19 per cent.[14] This level of popular support remained stable throughout the Second Intifada and averaged 33 per cent combined from January 2001 until January 2006 (10 per cent for PIJ and 23 per cent for Hamas).[15]

Palestinian disillusionment with the peace process, and the corresponding support for armed resistance, mattered for the Islamist factions. The security cooperation between the Palestinian Authority and the Israeli occupation authorities crumbled as Palestinian violence became a currency for claims to political legitimacy. As lawlessness spread throughout the occupied territories in 2000, the PA was simply unable to maintain law and order. The PA's inaction and its unwillingness to confront militants was also influenced by the popular cry for using force to apply pressure on the Israelis.[16] Fatah was pushed to participate in the Second Intifada

---

12    Beverley Milton-Edwards and Stephen Farrell, *Hamas: The Islamic Resistance Movement* (Cambridge: Polity Press, 2010), 104–5.

13    Badran, *Katibat Al-Shimal*, 17.

14    Jamil Hilal, 'Hamas's Rise as Charted in the Polls, 1994–2005', *Journal of Palestine Studies* 35, no. 3 (April 2006): 7.

15    David A. Jaeger et al., 'Can Militants Use Violence to Win Public Support? Evidence from the Second Intifada', *Journal of Conflict Resolution* 59, no. 3 (April 2015): 532.

16    Nasser Abufarha, *The Making of a Human Bomb: An Ethnography of Palestinian Resistance* (Durham, NC: Duke University Press, 2009), 82.

if it was not to be sidelined altogether, and the PA soon began releasing Islamist militants from its prisons.[17] One of them was Salah Shahada, co-founder of the Qassam Brigades, who commenced the work to re-establish Hamas's military wing in the Gaza Strip.[18] Another Islamist militant who was released from prison was Mahmud al-Zatma, PIJ's chief bomb maker, who began orchestrating new campaigns of suicide bombings against Israelis.[19]

Palestinian popular support for violence also mattered because it translated into an influx of new militants, bolstering the ranks of both the Qassam and Quds Brigades, as shown by Figure 5.1. While the military wings of Hamas and PIJ experienced a recruitment level averaging 9 new militants annually between 1994 and 1999, 338 Palestinians joined in 2000 alone (203 to the Qassam Brigades and 136 to the Quds Brigades).[20] Hamas and PIJ essentially turned 'the idea of martyrdom and sacrifice into pop culture'.[21]

Seizing the moment, PIJ strategically redefined its military branch by transitioning from the name Qassam to al-Quds Brigades. This change, as articulated by PIJ's secretary-general, was not only meant to distinguish the group from the Qassam Brigades of Hamas. It also symbolized a 'new birth for the movement' and marked the beginning of a new chapter following the challenges it had faced in the 1990s.[22] The formation of the Quds Brigades and the influx of new members were clearly visible in

---

17    Ibid., 114; Joe Stork, *Erased in a Moment: Suicide Bombing Attacks against Israeli Civilians* (New York: Human Rights Watch, 2002), 112.

18    Bilal Shalash, 'Tahawwulat al-muqawama al-musallaha li-harakat Hamas fi al-diffa al-gharbiyya athna' intifadat al-aqsa min al-markaziyya ila al-shazaya al-mutafajjara', in *Qadiyat Filastin wa mustaqbal al-mashru' al-watani al-Filastini -al-juz' al-awwal: Fi al-hawiya wa-l-muqawama wa-l-qanun al-duwwali* (Doha: Arab Center for Research and Policy Studies, 2015), 418.

19    Erik Skare, *A History of Palestinian Islamic Jihad: Faith, Awareness, and Revolution in the Middle East* (Cambridge: Cambridge University Press, 2021), 176.

20    See appendix for a discussion of the fatality bias in the dataset, as the data only account for those who died. Actual recruitment numbers were presumably higher, although the shift in recruitment numbers from the late 1990s to the early 2000s is reliably depicted.

21    Badran, *Katibat al-shimal*, 90.

22    Ramadan Shallah, *Haqa'iq wa mawafiq* (Damascus: Mu'assasat al-Aqsa al-Thaqafiyya, 2007), 21.

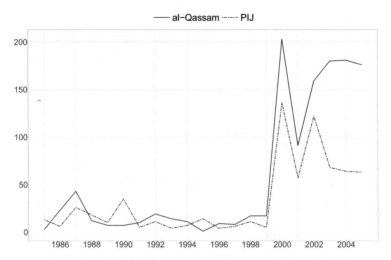

**Figure 5.1.** Militants joining the Qassam Brigades and PIJ, 1986–2004

PIJ's self-representation. While it portrayed itself as an elitist vanguard for the few and dedicated in the late 1990s to justify its limited numbers and military absence, PIJ began referring to itself as a mass movement a couple of years into the Second Intifada.[23]

As the geographical distribution of Islamist militants in Figures 5.2 and 5.3 shows, it was only when the Second Intifada erupted that the Qassam Brigades and PIJ were able to create and sustain significant military activity in the West Bank. Although both armed wings had had a presence there from the early 1990s, it had nevertheless been negligible compared to the Gaza Strip. Still, because the Qassam Brigades and PIJ had to be rebuilt from the ground up, and because of their highly clandestine nature, both had to rely on pre-existing social ties and networks. Most West Bank recruitment during the Second Intifada occurred through personal acquaintance; Islamist entrepreneurs organized their own family members, friends, neighbours, classmates, or those with whom they served time in prison.[24] This created obvious geographical

---

23    Antonella Acinapura, 'A Framing-Sensitive Approach to Militant Groups' Tactics: The Islamic Jihad Movement in Palestine and the Radicalisation of Violence during the Second Intifada', *Critical Studies on Terrorism* 16, no. 1 (January 2023): 136.

24    Badran, *Katibat al-shimal*, 42.

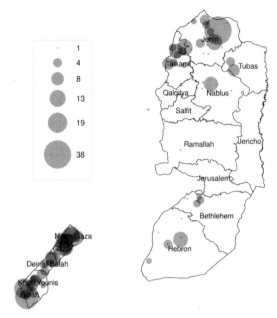

**Figure 5.2.** Geographical distribution of PIJ martyrs, 2000–5

clusters – the main hubs of the Qassam Brigades were Nablus and Hebron during this period, and PIJ's military activity formed a crescent from Tulkarem in the East via Jenin in the North to Tubas in the West. The reliance on pre-existing social networks also led to the formation of specific clusters of kinship where clan affiliation translated into factional ones. The Qawasma clan in Hebron, for example, became synonymous with Hamas.[25] For PIJ, kin dependency was particularly striking in Tulkarem, where education levels were comparably low and few institutions existed to transcend kinship. The martyr biographies of the movement reflect this trend, illustrating the interplay between the militants' familial ties, socioeconomic backgrounds, and educational levels.[26]

Emboldened by Israeli brutality, Palestinian factions adopted a hardline position on violence and the means of struggle. The two first years of the

25   Erik Skare, 'Affluent and Well-Educated? Analyzing the Socioeconomic Backgrounds of Fallen Palestinian Islamist Militants', *Middle East Journal* 76, no. 1 (May 2022): 89.

26   Skare, *A History of Palestinian Islamic Jihad*, 80–1.

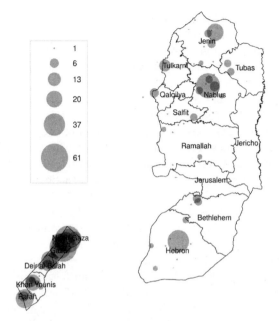

**Figure 5.3.** Geographical distribution of al-Qassam martyrs, 2000–5

intifada were characterized by an intense wave of suicide bombings, which predominantly targeted a civilian population within Israel. Also, secular groups such as Fatah, the Popular Front for the Liberation of Palestine (PFLP), and the Democratic Front for the Liberation of Palestine (DFLP) took active part in this campaign, which killed 2,205 Israelis. While Hamas and PIJ carried out 62 per cent of suicide bombings from October 2000 to June 2002, Fatah was responsible for approximately one-third of the attacks (29 per cent).[27]

By launching a string of suicide bombings, Palestinian factions intended to raise the costs of occupation to insupportable levels.[28] The premise was to apply pressure on Israeli authorities by sowing discontent in the Israeli civilian population: if the Israelis did not like getting blown

---

27    Assaf Moghadam, 'Palestinian Suicide Terrorism in the Second Intifada: Motivations and Organizational Aspects', *Studies in Conflict and Terrorism* 26, no. 2 (March 2003): 78.

28    Nada Matta and René Rojas, 'The Second Intifada: A Dual Strategy Arena', *European Journal of Sociology* 57, no. 1 (April 2016): 79.

to pieces, they should simply call on their government to withdraw from the occupied territories. Whether it was the Qassam or the Quds Brigades, Fatah's Tanzim or al-Aqsa Martyrs' Brigades, all concurred that the success of the intifada hinged on the application of extreme force.[29] Israel would never give up the occupied territories voluntarily.

An increasing number of Hamas's and PIJ's military operations were thus carried out in cooperation with other Palestinian factions as the Second Intifada advanced, although the level of cooperation varied between armed wings. PIJ worked more closely with al-Aqsa Martyrs' Brigades and the Abu Ali Mustafa Brigade of the PFLP than with the Qassam Brigades, for example (see Table 5.1). Factional strength and local presence in a given district certainly influenced the extent of cooperation between groups. The relatively low number of joint PIJ–DFLP attacks was presumably a reflection of the latter's limited prominence. That said, although PIJ and Hamas were far stronger in Gaza, cooperation between their military wings was far more extensive in the West Bank. Conversely, whereas PIJ–PFLP operations were most frequent in southern Gaza, its cooperation with the DFLP was notably higher in the Gazan North. Meanwhile, most of PIJ's operations coordinated with al-Aqsa Martyrs' Brigades took place in the Jenin district.[30] There were thus other drivers influencing intra-factional cooperation besides relative factional strength.

Just as pre-existing social ties within the Palestinian resistance mattered for the recruitment of new fighters, so did they influence insurgent cooperation. Although it was the shared resistance to the occupation that principally united the factions, much indicates that friendships and amiable relations on the ground were key to collaboration – regardless of whether one belonged to an Islamist, nationalist, or leftist faction. PIJ commander Thabit Mardawi, for example, who led a military cell of PIJ, Hamas, and Fatah fighters during the Battle of Jenin in April 2002, reflects in his autobiography how the cooperation with other factions was not determined by top-down strategic decisions in the upper echelons of PIJ,

---

29   Bader Araj and Robert J. Brym, 'Opportunity, Culture and Agency: Influences on Fatah and Hamas Strategic Action during the Second Intifada', *International Sociology* 25, no. 6 (November 2010): 851.

30   The statistics are from PIJ's 'Jadwal tafsili bi-amaliyyat harakat al-jihad al-islami mundhu nasha'tha hatta (2006/2)'. Document in author's possession.

**Table 5.1.** PIJ's cooperation with other armed factions, 2000–6

| | Al-Aqsa Martyrs' Brigades (Fatah) | Abu Ali Mustafa Brigades (PFLP) | Izz al-Din al-Qassam Brigades (Hamas) | Ahmad Abu al-Raysh Brigades (Fatah) | Al-Nasir Saladin Brigades (PRC) | National Resistance Brigades (DFLP) |
|---|---|---|---|---|---|---|
| 2000 | 0 | 0 | 0 | 0 | 0 | 0 |
| 2001 | 1 | 0 | 0 | 0 | 0 | 0 |
| 2002 | 9 | 0 | 3 | 0 | 0 | 0 |
| 2003 | 10 | 1 | 2 | 0 | 0 | 0 |
| 2004 | 33 | 5 | 4 | 6 | 3 | 4 |
| 2005 | 13 | 5 | 0 | 2 | 4 | 0 |
| 2006 | 1 | 1 | 0 | 1 | 1 | 0 |
| **Total** | **67** | **12** | **9** | **9** | **8** | **4** |

but by the fighters' mutual affection on the ground. These were young Palestinian men who had grown up in the camp together, had gone to school together, and had reached adolescence together, although they did not join armed factions together. These ties, he notes, made 'each of them willing to sacrifice and stand by his brother-in-arms until the last moment'.[31]

Similarly, factions often emphasized personal bonds between militants rather than shared ideological commitment when commemorating martyrs killed in joint factional operations, and the biography of Gazan PIJ commander Omar Arafat al-Khatib highlights his *personal* connection with militants from al-Aqsa Martyrs' Brigades as a key factor driving their cooperation.[32] Personal friendships and social ties as a driver of Palestinian partisan cooperation or competition essentially meant that the dynamics of the insurgency could vary from Palestinian district to district in the Second Intifada.

Although PIJ maintained its maximalist aspirations, the suicide bombings concealed how Hamas had begun to waver in its approach to a two-state solution by the early 2000s. Moderates in Hamas had proposed a number of peace offerings (*hudna*) since 1988 if certain conditions were met. Ahmad Yassin, for example, had in November 1993 suggested that an interim yet open-ended peace deal with the Israelis was possible if they withdrew unconditionally from the West Bank, East Jerusalem, and Gaza, dismantled the settlements, and allowed the Palestinians full self-determination.[33] Hamas deputy Ismail Abu Shanab was one of the strongest proponents in the movement for a two-state solution and a peaceful resolution:

---

31   Thabit Mardawi, *Namut fi al-watan. Wa lan nughadir: Malhamat Jinin bi-shahadat al-asir al-mujahid Thabit Mardawi* (Gaza: al-Markaz al-Filastini li-l-Tawasul al-Hadari, 2006), 40.

32   See for example al-Quds Brigades, 'Khabar: Butulat ramadaniyya. "Mustafa Abu Sariyya" wa "Abd al-Karim Na'isa". abtal al-hujum al-naw'iyya al-mazduj ala madinat al-Afula', al-Quds Brigades, August 22, 2010, saraya.ps; al-Quds Brigades, 'al-Shahid al-qa'id Umar al-Khatib', al-Quds Brigades, n.d., saraya.ps

33   Khaled Hroub, *Hamas: Political Thought and Practice* (Washington DC: Institute for Palestine Studies, 2000), 82.

What is the point in speaking rhetoric? Let's be frank, we cannot destroy Israel. The practical solution is for us to have a state alongside Israel . . . When we build a Palestinian state, we will not need these militias; all the needs for attacks will stop. Everything will change into a civil life.[34]

Hamas was thus not *a priori* opposed to negotiations with Israel, but the movement reasoned that such a process had to occur between equal parties. Hamas was similarly not opposed to the Israelis because of their Jewish faith, as Salah Shahada admitted, but because of the occupation.[35] Suicide bombings were, then, an instrument forcing Israel towards equal grounds. 'Throughout the conflict,' Matta and Rojas note, 'Hamas's public declarations insisted that it did not reject a negotiated settlement but instead repudiated the concessionary manner in which the PA conducted peace talks.'[36] Whether the pen was stronger than the sword was irrelevant: He who wielded the sword decided who held the pen. The fact that Israel signed a peace treaty with Egypt a few years after the Yom Kippur War in 1973, and commenced the Oslo process after the First Intifada, strengthened their sense that force was the only language the Israelis understood. PIJ and Hamas were thus largely informed by what they had witnessed in the 1990s when the PLO had given up violence to liberate Palestinian lands.[37] Instead of establishing a sovereign Palestinian state, the PLO gave ever-increasing concessions with nothing to show for them. If the First Intifada was the mother of the Islamist opposition, then Oslo was its father.

Refusing to engage in dialogue with Hamas as a political actor capable of compromise, the Israelis instead approached the movement as an univocally terrorist organization with little or no diplomatic credibility. Despite being ardently against such means, Abu Shanab was assassinated by the Israelis on August 21, 2003, in revenge for Hamas's suicide bombing in Jerusalem two days before. The Israeli approach inadvertently became a self-fulfilling prophecy. Rather than weakening hardliners in Hamas, the targeted killings of its political and military figures effectively underscored

---

34   Quoted in Jeroen Gunning, 'Peace with Hamas? The Transforming Potential of Political Participation', *International Affairs* 80, no. 2 (March 2004): 250.

35   'Salah Shahada. Harakat Hamas shahada tarikhiyya', *al-Jazeera*.

36   Matta and Rojas, 'The Second Intifada', 79.

37   Jeroen Gunning, *Hamas in Politics: Democracy, Religion, Violence* (London: Hurst, 2009), 202–3.

their belief that negotiations with Israel were futile – only through the continued use of extreme force could their aspirations be realized. That is not to suggest that a specific dynamic did not develop. Intra-Palestinian competition, for example, contributed to escalating violence as Hamas, PIJ, and Fatah attempted to outbid each other.[38] Violence was also used as a means of both revenge and deterrence. Israeli targeted killings of Palestinian military and political leaders typically followed Palestinian suicide bombings, and Palestinian suicide bombings followed the assassinations of their leaders and militants, or after Palestinian civilian mass casualties. The Israeli assassinations of Palestinian leaders were seldom guided by rational cost–benefit calculations. They were instead carried out 'by opportunity rather than necessity, and were sometimes motivated by emotion rather than cold reason.'[39] Emotions ran high in Hamas, as well. After a failed assassination attempt against the Hamas co-founder Abdel Aziz al-Rantisi in 2003, Ahmad Yassin proclaimed: 'Israel is targeting Palestinian civilians, so Israeli civilians should be targeted. From now on all Israeli people are targets.'[40]

The Palestinian hardliner approach from 2000 to 2002 largely failed to out-suffer the Israeli public. One reason was the misfortune of bad timing. While Yasser Arafat enjoyed wide international support as the representative of a people under occupation, the terror attacks against the United States on September 11, 2001, saw a change in global public perception. Suddenly, Arafat was ordered by world leaders to stop terrorism, and Israeli Prime Minister Ariel Sharon soon equated the Palestinian factions with al-Qaida.[41] 'Everyone has his own Bin Laden. Arafat is our Bin Laden,'[42] Sharon declared and, 'the fight against terrorism is an international struggle of the free world against the forces of darkness who seek to destroy our liberty and way of life. Together we can defeat these forces of evil.'[43]

---

38    Daniel Byman, 'Curious Victory: Explaining Israel's Suppression of the Second Intifada', *Terrorism and Political Violence* 24, no. 5 (November 2012): 829.

39    Avi Kober, 'Targeted Killing during the Second Intifada: The Quest for Effectiveness', *Journal of Conflict Studies* 27, no. 1 (2007): 79.

40    'Wounded Hamas Leader Vows to Fight Israel', *Sydney Morning Herald*, June 11, 2003.

41    Giora Eiland, 'The IDF in the Second Intifada', *Strategic Assessment* 13, no. 3 (2010): 30.

42    Brian Whitaker, 'Sharon Likens Arafat to Bin Laden', *Guardian*, September 14, 2001.

43    'Sharon: "We Can Defeat Forces of Evil"', CNN, September 12, 2001.

Both Hamas and PIJ distanced themselves from the international terrorism of Usama bin Laden and his deputy, Ayman al-Zawahiri, immediately after September 11. Ahmad Yassin and Ramadan Shallah declared that they were nationalists confining their struggle to occupied Palestine.[44] Both Palestinian Islamist movements attempted to differentiate themselves and their practices from that of al-Qaida. Still, doing so posed a conundrum, as they had to distance themselves from attacks on US civilians while not delegitimizing their own attacks on Israeli ones. One way to reduce cognitive dissonance was by negating the status of Israeli non-combatants as civilians by analysing Israeli society as a militarized outpost with no distinction between civilian and military. 'He who is not a soldier in combat zones is a reservist, whether man or woman . . ', wrote PIJ senior member Abdallah al-Shami in 2000. 'It is, then, a society of war. Its civilians are, moreover, even greater usurpers than its soldiers are. They usurped our homes, houses, and arable land after they displaced our people with the force of arms and with the threat of slaughter and massacre.'[45] Shallah noted that PIJ did not intend to kill Israeli children. They were not of military age, they did not pay taxes, and it was possible they would leave Israel when reaching adolescence.[46]

Still, as a number of attacks during the Second Intifada were retaliations for Israeli state violence against Palestinians, PIJ's justification also adjusted to this reality. The aforementioned PIJ commander Thabit Mardawi, for example, who was responsible for dispatching numerous suicide bombers from Jenin, defended the practice by proclaiming that 'Palestinian civilians are killed, and the response to it is to kill Israeli civilians.'[47] Senior PIJ member in the West Bank Yusuf Arif al-Hajj Muhammad, in contrast, developed an interpretation of *jus in bello* through which the legality of violence depended on the existence or absence of alternative channels of political influence:

---

44  Beverley Milton-Edwards, 'Islamist versus Islamist: Rising Challenge in Gaza', *Terrorism and Political Violence* 26, no. 2 (2014): 262; Ghassan Charbel, 'Ziyara li-dhakirat al-amin al-amm li-harakat al-jihad al-islami fi Filastin 3. Shallah: lam yu'ayyid qatal al-madaniyyin fi 11 aylul wa sha'artu bi-shamata wa-l-shafqa qara' al-Zawahiri hadithi an al-yahud fi al-wasat fa ba'ath ilayy bi-risala itab', *al-Hayat*, January 9, 2003.

45  Abdallah al-Shami, 'Falsafat al-Shahada', *Muhjat al-Quds*, 2000.

46  Charbel, 'Shallah: Lam yu'ayyid qatl al-madaniyyin fi 11 aylul'.

47  Thabit Mardawi, *Namut fi al-watan. Wa lan nughadir. Malhamat Jinin bi-shahadat al-asir al-Mujahid Thabit Mardawi* (Gaza: al-Markaz al-Filastini li-l-tawasul al-dadari, 2006), 144.

The US policy towards the Islamic world incites hatred and intense resentment among Muslims . . . [However,] war comes in various forms, including military confrontation, army against army, people's liberation war against the occupier, and economic warfare . . . Due to the population composition in the United States, which is based on large and small ethnic and religious congregations, there's another form of war within the United States, the war of influence . . . It is natural for Arabs and Muslims to wage a lawful war within the United States against the overwhelming Zionist influence.[48]

September 11, 2001, did not matter because of the mental gymnastics attempted by Hamas and PIJ, however, nor because they were losing an international popularity contest. The attacks mattered because they effectively reshaped Israeli and Palestinian manoeuvrability in the intifada, as Israeli authorities now had a carte blanche in their fight against Palestinian insurgents.[49] While it had condemned the Israelis for their use of targeted killings, the US administration became increasingly sympathetic to Israeli military methods as the Americans themselves now employed the same means in Afghanistan and Iraq.[50] The effect was immediately felt by the Hamas leadership, with Salah Shahada being assassinated in 2002. Ibrahim al-Maqadma and Ismail Abu Shanab were killed in 2003, and Abdel Aziz al-Rantisi, Ahmad Yassin, in addition to the right-hand man of Muhammad Deif, Adnan al-Ghoul, were liquidated in 2004. Muhammad Deif was also targeted in September 2002, when the Israelis bombed his car. Video footage from Hebrew Channel 13 captured a bloodied Deif, sitting visibly disoriented beside the wreckage, while a crowd of Palestinians hastily pulled him away. That was Deif's last appearance in public.

The suicide bombings also failed because the Palestinian factions underestimated the Israeli nation-state building project. Instead of acknowledging the extent to which the Israelis had succeeded in fostering a commonly shared identity, Hamas and PIJ continued stressing the artificial nature of a 'Zionist entity' implanted in Islamic homelands by Western colonial powers. Pointing to the many citizens enjoying dual citizenship, the claim was that they were not actually Israelis. They were

---

48   Yusuf Arif al-Hajj Muhammad, *al-Masira al-jihadiyya li-harakat al-jihad al-islami fi Filastin* (Gaza: Muhjat al-Quds, 2011), 81–2.
49   Eiland, 'The IDF in the Second Intifada', 30.
50   Kober, 'Targeted Killing during the Second Intifada', 79.

instead German, French, or American Jews who would return to where they came from if their living conditions deteriorated sufficiently.[51] The problem was that the suicide bombings produced the opposite results. National identity among Israeli Jews strengthened throughout the Second Intifada as Israeli public opinion was driven to the right, and the Israeli government received overwhelming support.[52] More than 60 per cent of Israelis 'consistently backed targeted assassinations' of Palestinians as a means to stop suicide bombings, and, instead of dividing Israeli society, Palestinian armed factions manufactured an Israeli commitment to military escalation.[53]

The insurgency of Hamas and PIJ was equally unsustainable in confrontation with the Israeli reconquest of the West Bank, the targeted killings, and the construction of a new infrastructure of control and pacification. This was partly due to dynamics specific to their military wings. As there were few viable institutions for the recruitment of nascent insurgents, such as universities, trade unions, or clubs where Palestinians from various backgrounds became acquainted, the Qassam and Quds Brigades relied on a select few to organize the execution of violence through specific geographic clusters. Once the Israeli army assassinated or incarcerated these entrepreneurs and eradicated their cells, there was no organic way for the military networks to sustain their activity or to resurface. After PIJ was de facto removed from Jenin following the killing of Mahmud Tawalba and his cell during the Battle of Jenin in April 2002, the movement's centre of gravity moved to Tulkarem. There, the field commander Lu'ay al-Sa'di continued the movement's suicide bombings in 2003. When he and the members of his cell were killed in 2005, PIJ never managed to replicate the level of violence it had achieved over the previous five years, although it maintained a military presence.[54]

The Qassam Brigades were not exempt from this dynamic. As Badran reasoned, the recruitment efforts of the Qassam Brigades made the Hamas militants doubly vulnerable. First, because social ties made it easy for

51    See, for example, Skare, *Palestinian Islamic Jihad*, 31–3; Hamas has also used the term 'artificial entity' as late as in 2023. See 'Mi'at al-Shuhada' bi-Ghazza wa-l-Qassam tastahdif Tall Abib wa tahbatt muhawalat isti'adat jundi Isra'ili', *al-Jazeera*, December 8, 2023.

52    Brym and Araj, 'Suicide Bombing as Strategy and Interaction', 1981.

53    Matta and Rojas, 'The Second Intifada', 97.

54    Skare, *A History of Palestinian Islamic Jihad*, 174.

the Israeli intelligence to 'analyse, investigate, and connect the dots in the jihadist environment', and, second, because reliance on a few entrepreneurs 'prevent[ed] the integration of new members who wish[ed] to join and [who were] searching for someone to recruit them'.[55] The Gaza Strip – in the absence of Israeli military control on the ground outside Gush Katif and the other settlements – was never under the same pressure as the West Bank. In fear of Israeli military losses, there were fewer incursions and less military pressure.[56]

Hamas and PIJ have always been Gaza-centred movements, and the regional distribution of its martyrs indicates that the West Bank has been far less prominent in their operational history. The Second Intifada stands out as a notable deviation from this pattern. For instance, PIJ maintained a surprisingly stable regional distribution of martyrs with approximately one-fifth coming from the West Bank. While the number of martyrs from the Qassam Brigades rose in absolute numbers during the Second Intifada (from 65 to 207), Table 5.2 demonstrates that there was a relative operational pivot towards Gaza. The fact that both PIJ and the Qassam Brigades had a comparable number of martyrs in the West Bank between 2000 and 2005 (178 and 207), but with differences in their overall regional distribution (44.72 per cent and 35.26 per cent), shows that PIJ was less dependent on the Gazan theatre of war. Significantly, PIJ's ability to sustain its presence in the West Bank after 2007 indicates, first, that the PA security services hit Hamas harder, and, second, that PIJ was able to nurture more organic links to the West Bank than the Qassam Brigades. PIJ's links to the northern West Bank community were deeply rooted and evolved in a way that was integrated within the local social, political, and cultural landscapes. This integration was further bolstered by the status PIJ enjoyed following the Battle of Jenin, during which popular figures like Mahmud Tawalba sacrificed themselves to protect the camp.

It was the Palestinian civilians, not the militants, who faced the intolerable costs of the intifada. Although the Israeli military reconquest of the West Bank in 2002 was driven by Israeli popular anger after years of suicide bombings, the Israeli human rights organization B'Tselem noted that 'the intensity of the pain and anger felt by Israelis made them

---

55   Badran, *Katibat al-shimal*, 42–3.
56   Eiland, 'The IDF in the Second Intifada', 29; Matta and Rojas, 'The Second Intifada', 84.

**Table 5.2.** Regional distribution of Islamist martyrs, 1985–2022

| Time Period | Region | PIJ | al-Qassam Brigades |
|---|---|---|---|
| 1985–99 | Gaza | 75 (81.52%) | 45 (40.91%) |
| | West Bank | 17 (18.48%) | 65 (59.09%) |
| 2000–5 | Gaza | 220 (55.28%) | 380 (64.74%) |
| | West Bank | 178 (44.72%) | 207 (35.26%) |
| 2006–22 | Gaza | 618 (82.95%) | 2,144 (97.59%) |
| | West Bank | 127 (17.05%) | 53 (2.41%) |

forget just who the enemy was. Instead, almost two million innocent civilians were attacked by the most powerful army in the Middle East . . . The entire population in the West Bank suffered as a result.'[57] By 2002, Islamist leaders in Hamas and PIJ privately conceded that the Israelis' heavy-handed repression translated into a loss of popular support for suicide bombings.[58] To avoid a complete disintegration of the Palestinian social fabric, to pre-empt factional infighting, and to prevent alienating a Palestinian civilian population worn out by war, Palestinian Islamist violence was re-calibrated to retain popular support.[59] By June 2003, both Hamas and PIJ agreed to adhere to a unilateral ceasefire 'out of concern for the unity of our Palestinian rank at this dangerous stage'.[60]

Although the June 2003 ceasefire broke down, both Islamist factions began limiting the use of suicide attacks in Israel and instead refocused their attacks on Israeli settlers and soldiers within the 1967 borders of the West Bank. In Gaza, the Murabitun Army[61] was set up by the Qassam Brigades to protect the neighbourhoods from Israeli incursions.[62] By 2004, 'Hamas appeared to renounce unilateral terror

---

57    B'Tselem, *Operation Defensive Shield: Soldiers' Testimonies. Palestinian Testimonies* (Jerusalem: B'Tselem, 2002), 3.

58    Beverley Milton-Edwards and Alistair Crooke, 'Elusive Ingredient: Hamas and the Peace Process', *Journal of Palestine Studies* 33, no. 4 (July 2004): 303.

59    Matta and Rojas, 'The Second Intifada', 102.

60    Muhammad, *al-Masira al-jihadiyya*, 91.

61    The term *Murabit* does not have a direct equivalent in English. Historically, the Murabitun were soldiers serving at the frontier fortifications of the Islamic community.

62    Yezid Sayigh, *'We Serve the People': Hamas Policing in Gaza* (Washington, DC: Brandeis University, Crown Center for Middle East Studies, 2011), 46.

attacks altogether'.[63] Badran, who organized a series of suicide bombings for the Qassam Brigades between 2000 and 2002, acknowledged as much. Despite the legitimacy of striking 'all targets on the enemy's side', he noted that there were a number of advantages to restricting armed activity within the 1967 borders since 'these territories are considered occupied in the view of all parties. The resistance is consequently considered legitimate according to all international laws and covenants.'[64]

The forceful suppression of the Palestinian militant factions and the heavy Palestinian civilian casualties meant that violence as a means of resistance gradually lost its potency. While the failure of the peace process had given the hardliners an opportunity, it was clear by 2005 that their strategy of out-suffering the Israelis had failed in giving the Palestinians their state. With the Qassam and Quds Brigades significantly weakened by years of urban warfare – what Shallah called 'an extermination war' – the moderates saw the chance to implement a pragmatist turn.[65]

## Fissures

> It's a fight between the national project and this small kingdom they want to establish in Gaza, the kingdom of Gaza, between those who are using assassination and killing to achieve their goals, and those who are using the rules of law . . . The coup-seekers, through their madness, have given a golden opportunity to those who want to separate Gaza from the West Bank. – Mahmoud Abbas[66]

> June 14, 2007, [was] a day of triumph for legitimacy. It came through the ballot box, and [it was] a day of liberation from the corruption of the security apparatuses. It was a blessing . . . and, through it, God healed the hearts of the believers. – Muhammad Abu Tayr[67]

---

63  Matta and Rojas, 'The Second Intifada', 102.
64  Badran, *Katibat al-shimal*, 92.
65  Shallah, *Haqa'iq wa mawafiq*, 41.
66  'Abbas Vows to Protect West Bank from Hamas', ABC News, June 20, 2007.
67  Muhammad Abu Tayr, *Sayyidi Umar: Dhikriyat al-shaykh Muhammad Abu Tayr fi al-muqawama wa thalatha wa thalathin 'aman min al-i'tiqal* (Beirut: Markaz al-zaytuna li-l-dirasat wa-l-istisharat, 2017), 363.

We declared from the beginning that both parties, Fatah and Hamas, were responsible for what happened. Regardless of the details, . . . what is important now, after about three months have passed, is to search for a solution rather than revolving in a cycle of condemnation and mutual accusations. It is unreasonable for the Palestinian people to remain hostage to this devastating crisis. – Ramadan Abdallah Shallah[68]

Following the attacks on October 7, several analysts and commentators referred to Hamas's infamous charter adopted in 1988 to explain the movement's current thought and practice.[69] Composed shortly after the founding of Hamas, the charter was intended to present the movement's basic views and ideology to the rest of the world. The charter was unambiguously anti-Semitic and conspiratorial, and the struggle was framed as being explicitly against the Jews who controlled the world media and were behind the French and Russian revolutions. Indeed, 'there was no war that broke out anywhere without their hands behind it' (see the introduction and §22). It was also religiously deterministic and strongly polemical. Palestine was exclusively Islamic land entrusted to Muslims until Judgement Day, and peace conferences were not merely futile but also 'no more than a means of forcing the rule of unbelievers in the land of Muslims' (§11 and §13). The charter similarly reflected the Muslim Brotherhood's long-standing preoccupation with perceived vice and corruption: 'The state of truth has disappeared and the state of evil has been established; as long as Islam does not take its rightful place in the world arena, everything will continue to change for the worse' (§9).

Hamas's 1988 charter was to some extent a reflection of the reactionary inheritance from the Palestinian Muslim Brotherhood. Hamas's identification of friend and foe was 'rather oversimplified' in the first years of its existence.[70] To another extent, it also reflected the fact that the emergence

---

68   Shallah, *Haqa'iq wa mawafiq*, 45.

69   See, for example, Bruce Hoffman, 'Understanding Hamas's Genocidal Ideology', *Atlantic*, October 10, 2023; American Jewish Committee, 'What Hamas Is Hiding', *Global Voice*, October 7, 2023, ajc.org; Menachem Z. Rosensaft, 'Hamas Terrorists Have Genocide in Their Hearts. They Say So Themselves', *Newsweek*, October 12, 2023.

70   Hroub, *Hamas: Political Thought and Practice*, 49.

of Hamas was not an organic development within the Brotherhood; it was a largely reactive move to events outside of its control. The charter was thus hastily composed less than a year after its establishment, and it was reportedly authored by a representative of the Gazan Brotherhood old guard without prior consultation with the rest of Hamas's leadership. Regardless of whether this origin story accurately reflects the events as they occurred or merely serves as a post hoc rationalization, the 1988 charter was frequently cited as a source of embarrassment for a movement that viewed itself as more sophisticated than the reductionist discourse it presented.[71]

The charter thus offers little analytical value today. The doctrinaire discourse of Hamas diminished starting in the mid-1990s, and its leadership has rarely, if ever, referred to it.[72] Similarly, Hamas's social services transitioned from a means of proselytizing and promoting Muslim piety to becoming a tool for community development; they became less ideological and more open and innovative.[73] One reason for Hamas's moderation was the learning curve and maturation of a political movement that suddenly had to deal with the actually existing world and all of its required compromises. Another one was a change in its sociological makeup as a wave of new recruits, previously unaffiliated with the quietist Muslim Brotherhood, joined Hamas. The movement thus enjoyed a far more heterogeneous mass base from the early 1990s whose membership did not require any arduous ideological training.[74] A third reason was the influence of external contacts. Although the outside leadership represented the hardline position in the 1990s, they were also exposed to more heterodox experiences in their encounters with diplomats, international organizations, politicians, and journalists, which influenced both discourse and political thinking. Essentially, Hamas evolved from the 1990s and the movement began distinguishing between Judaism as a religion and Zionism as a political movement. Its enmity against Israel was correspondingly attributed to usurpation rather than religious difference. Hamas softened its approach towards the international community and

---

71   Khaled Hroub, *Hamas: A Beginner's Guide* (London: Pluto Press, 2006), 24, 36.

72   Hroub, *Hamas: Political Thought and Practice*, 44.

73   Sara Roy, *Hamas and Civil Society in Gaza: Engaging the Islamist Social Sector* (Princeton, NJ: Princeton University Press, 2011), 85–7.

74   Gunning, *Hamas in Politics*, 39.

diplomatic resolutions as well, if they were not perceived to contradict the national claims of the Palestinians.[75]

Although Hamas reacted with violence to the establishment of the Palestinian Authority because it threatened to narrow Islamist opportunities, changing political realities in the 1990s led Hamas to vacillate in its approach to governance. It was a clear concern for the movement to avoid political isolation in this period, and while Hamas cooperated with the rejectionist PLO currents against settlement, there were also internal discussions about the possibilities of participating in elections under the Oslo Accords.[76] There were moderates in the movement who favoured integration with, and piggybacking on, the newly established PA instead of maintaining a hardline position.[77] Ahmad Yassin, for example, suggested in 1993 that Hamas should challenge the Oslo institutions from within, which indirectly signalled a recognition of the PA's framework.[78] 'If the council shall have the authority to legislate,' Yassin declared, 'why should we not practice opposition within this council as we do in the streets?'[79]

Hamas's strategy on the ground was thus distinct from that of PIJ as the two movements derived their policies from different ideological and political traditions. PIJ quickly grew suspicious of its sister movement, and of what its position to elections under Oslo actually was. Illustratively, PIJ issued a statement titled 'Is Hamas Serving the Interests of America?' in 1992. Although the explicit aim was to direct a punch against the PLO and the Oslo Agreement in defence of the Intifada, it also presented a clear warning between the lines for Hamas against 'the useless battle for representation and legitimacy'.[80]

Because Hamas inherited the 'policy of stages' from the Muslim Brotherhood, it always enjoyed a greater degree of pragmatism than PIJ,[81] and its ideological resistance to particular frameworks of governance never prevented the movement from participating in such systems if required.[82]

---

75   Hroub, *Hamas*, 50–1.

76   Ibid., 64–5.

77   Kimmerling and Migdal, *The Palestinian People*, 369.

78   Wendy Kristianasen, 'Challenge and Counterchallenge: Hamas's Response to Oslo', *Journal of Palestine Studies* 28, no. 3 (1999): 23.

79   Quoted in Hroub, *Hamas*, 65.

80   Skare, *A History of Palestinian Islamic Jihad*, 121.

81   Kristianasen, 'Challenge and Counterchallenge', 22–3.

82   Beverley Milton-Edwards, 'Prepared for Power: Hamas, Governance and Conflict', *Civil Wars* 7, no. 4 (December 2005): 313.

Although formally boycotting the general elections of 1996, Hamas decided to encourage Islamists to run as independents. Meanwhile, it called on its own followers to vote for Islamic candidates, and even to vote for Fatah candidates who were known for their cordial relationship with the Islamic opposition. Hamas thus chose 'participation through unofficial presence' in the 1990s.[83] The boycott of 1996 was never ideologically premised. It was based on a realist conviction that the elections were implemented under conditions favouring Fatah.[84]

Much had changed from the 1990s once the dust of the Second Intifada had settled. The peace process had failed, the political and charismatic authority of Yasser Arafat had disappeared, and Israel had formally withdrawn from the Gaza Strip in 2005. Hamas's role in the Second Intifada had also boosted its standing, and the movement believed that it was entitled a role in governance.[85] The second round of the Palestinian municipal elections further encouraged Hamas members in the Gaza Strip when the movement won seven out of ten municipal councils.[86] The decision to participate in the Palestinian legislative elections was therefore closely connected to the movement's experience with, and analysis of, the Palestinian resistance: 'For Hamas, resistance naturally encompassed a political element, and the political arena was an extension of military policies, particularly after the failure of armed struggle to achieve its goals.'[87] Electoral participation was not premised on the concessions of the PLO, then, but instead intended to liberate the PA from Fatah's clutches and use its institutions to strengthen the Palestinian resistance.[88] Governance and resistance were two sides of the same coin.

Changes on the meso level also enabled electoral participation by altering the moderate/hardliner balance within the movement. Although moderates such as Ahmad Yassin and Ismail Abu Shanab were assassinated in the Second Intifada, so were hardliners like Salah Shahada, Ibrahim al-Maqadma, Adnan al-Ghoul, and Abdel Aziz al-Rantisi. The

---

83   Shaul Mishal and Avraham Sela, *The Palestinian Hamas: Vision, Violence, and Coexistence* (New York: Columbia University Press, 2006), 15–16.

84   Azzam Tamimi, *Hamas: Unwritten Chapters* (London: Hurst, 2009), 211.

85   Tareq Baconi, *Hamas Contained: The Rise and Pacification of Palestinian Resistance* (Stanford, CA: Stanford University Press, 2018), 73, 76.

86   Tamimi, *Hamas*, 210–11.

87   Baconi, *Hamas Contained*, 80.

88   Ibid., 80–4.

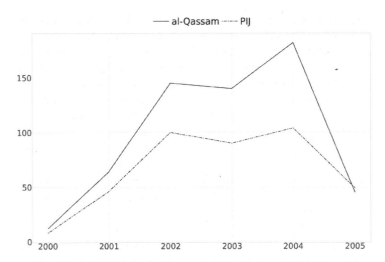

**Figure 5.4.** Number of al-Qassam and PIJ martyrs, 2000–5

void they left behind paved the way for a new generation of Hamas politicians who were predisposed to the feasibility of electoral politics.[89] Besides, the Qassam and Quds Brigades were effectively weakened in 2005 by the costs of protracted warfare and Israeli assassination campaigns. In 2001, sixty-four militants from the Qassam Brigades and forty-six from the Quds Brigades were killed. These numbers rose rapidly with Operation Defensive Shield in 2002. For PIJ, the annual number of killed militants stabilized on 2002 levels (noticeable for a group of its size). Fatalities in the Qassam Brigades continued to rise, however, with a peak of 182 militants killed in 2004. These casualties were in addition to those Islamist insurgents who suffered injuries or imprisonment. Although the Islamist armed wings were revitalized by a wave of new recruits from 2000 to 2004 (between 1,500 and 1,700 militants), two-thirds of that number perished in the same period. Accordingly, although the leadership of the Qassam Brigades vigorously protested the political leadership's decision to participate in the 2006 elections,[90] their objections were made ineffective by military weakness and a Palestinian popular notion that violence could not achieve Palestinian national aspirations.

---

89   Milton-Edwards, 'Prepared for Power', 317–18.
90   Sayigh, '*We Serve the People*', 124.

Hamas's decision to participate in the legislative elections revealed a crucial multifurcation within Palestinian Islamism. It was not just al-Qassam militants and Hamas hardliners who rejected the new approach. Also PIJ opposed any electoral participation. One reason for its electoral boycott stemmed from its concern about the legitimizing effects of participation. PIJ contended that, while the 1996 legislative elections took place under the Oslo agreements, Mahmoud Abbas's motivation for holding the 2006 elections stemmed from his desire to implement the Roadmap. As the differences now and then were merely cosmetic, any participation would still legally, practically, and realistically imply a recognition of Oslo. PIJ disagreed with what it termed Hamas's 'jurisprudence of interest' – maximizing its gains within the existing system – because in its view only armed struggle could liberate the occupied territories.[91]

PIJ also viewed the influence of political power with a certain suspicion. Shallah feared that Hamas would struggle to maintain a balance between participating in elections, governing, and persistence in its commitment to liberate all of Palestine, while also avoiding recognition of past agreements between Israel and the PLO.[92] That suspicion was strengthened by the structural deficiencies of Palestinian parliamentarian democracy, with the PA limiting the role of the Palestinian Legislative Council. PIJ concluded that no parliamentary bloc, no matter how strong, could change the PA's direction. The PLC was essentially like any 'parliamentary body in the Third World': instead of controlling, and holding those in power accountable, it merely concealed autocratic structures behind a veil of democracy and legitimacy.[93] Both Al-Hajj Muhammad and Shallah drove home their points by pointing to the Iraqi Hamas, which participated in Iraqi parliamentarian elections. Just as there was an American occupation there, they reasoned, there was an Israeli occupation in Palestine.[94] PIJ's opposition to electoral participation was thus partly based on a defence of democracy rather than a rejection.

Others have written extensively about Hamas's ascent to power in Gaza following its surprising electoral victory in 2006, when the movement obtained 74 of the 132 seats in the PLC.[95] Tensions between Fatah and

---

91  Muhammad, *al-Masira al-jihadiyya*, 99, 193.
92  Shallah, *Haqa'iq wa mawafiq*, 50.
93  Muhammad, *al-Masira al-jihadiyya*, 191.
94  Ibid., 193; Shallah, *Haqa'iq wa mawafiq*, 57.
95  See for example Beverley Milton-Edwards, 'Hamas: Victory with Ballots

Hamas escalated as Fatah, having accepted its electoral defeat with little grace, refused to participate in any government formed by the Islamist victor. In addition to a deepening Palestinian political rift, the Hamas-formed government was subjected to a widespread international boycott. By late 2006, clashes between armed Fatah and Hamas elements in Gaza began to escalate in intensity and in frequency. Just as the Strip had begun catching its breath after the Second Intifada, it now turned into yet another battlefield.

PIJ – so often betraying its reputation as one-sidedly radical – attempted to step in and de-escalate. Stressing the need for national unity in the struggle against the Israeli occupation, PIJ attempted to create an atmosphere of shared responsibility and criticized both Hamas and Fatah from the onset. Mahmoud Abbas was responsible for escalating the division in the Palestinian arena. Hamas had taken control in Gaza without establishing the required law and order.[96] PIJ attempted throughout the dispute to mediate between the warring factions by approaching the initiatives of Hamas with a conception of 'Yes, but', while avoiding to alienate Fatah when doing so.[97] When intra-Palestinian violence escalated in May 2007, it vowed to march down the streets of Gaza with the Quds Brigades to resolve the clashes and avoid further deterioration of the social fabric. PIJ worked actively with the PFLP and the DFLP to bring Fatah and Hamas to the negotiations table. If anything, they succeeded in persuading Fatah and Hamas to release the soldiers they had kidnapped from each other.[98]

Hamas's electoral participation also created new fissures. As the

---

and Bullets', *Global Change, Peace and Security* 19, no. 3 (October 2007): 301–16; Frode Løvlie, 'Explaining Hamas's Changing Electoral Strategy, 1996–2006', *Government and Opposition* 48, no. 4 (October 2013): 570–93; Manal A. Jamal, 'Beyond Fateh Corruption and Mass Discontent: Hamas, the Palestinian Left and the 2006 Legislative Elections', *British Journal of Middle Eastern Studies* 40, no. 3 (July 2013): 273–94; Tavishi Bhasin and Maia Carter Hallward, 'Hamas as a Political Party: Democratization in the Palestinian Territories', in Mary Beth Altier, Susanne Martin, and Leonard B. Weinberg, eds, *Violence, Elections, and Party Politics* (New York: Routledge, 2014).

96   Jihan al-Husayni, 'Masadir qariba min 'al-jihad al-islami' tahmal ala qiyadat Hamas wa Fatah', *al-Hayat*, August 5, 2007.

97   Asmaa al-Ghoul and Ibraheem Abu Mustafa, 'Islamic Jihad Takes Mediator Role between Hamas, Fatah', *al-Monitor*, January 26, 2015.

98   ''Hamas' wa 'Fatah' tuwasilan tabadul al-ittihamat', *al-Hayat*, November 15, 2013.

political leadership of Hamas worked hard for reconciliation with Fatah and save whatever was left of Palestinian unity, there was a growing concern within the Qassam Brigades that they were insufficiently prepared to counter the swift armament of Fatah loyalists in Gaza. They became convinced that Fatah security chief Muhammad Dahlan prepared his followers to violently seize power in Gaza.[99] The prevailing sentiment was that they had to choose between 'eat or be eaten'. On June 11, 2007, the Qassam Brigades in Gaza commenced a five-day military campaign against hundreds of Fatah members who in fear of their lives fled the Strip. Sweeping through Gaza, from the South to the North, Hamas's forces captured 'one Fatah stronghold at a time before moving on' to the next.[100] When the dust settled, Gaza found itself under new rulers.

For some in the Qassam Brigades, ousting Fatah was necessary to protect what they believed was rightfully theirs as the legitimate victors in the legislative elections. Others viewed it as necessary to end the chaos in Gaza and to restore social peace.[101] Some elements believed that Fatah was an obstacle to a more effective struggle against Israel,[102] while hardliners such as Nizar Rayan, a pivotal figure and strategist in leading Hamas forces against Fatah, were ideologically and religiously driven:

Today the struggle is between Islam and the infidels, and it will end with the victory of faith . . . How can we not fight against those who desecrate the sanctity of God, execute clerics, and sell out the Palestinian cause – those who blasphemed in houses of worship, burned mosques, Korans and [Islamic] education facilities and executed jihad fighters. We will hold dialogue with [these] people only through the barrels of our guns.[103]

Rayan's statement was especially revealing, as the swift brutality of the Hamas militants must have been driven, in part, by the personal tragedies they had experienced in the 1990s. Hamas's legislative victory occurred

99    Björn Brenner, *Gaza under Hamas: From Islamic Democracy to Islamist Governance* (London: I. B. Taurus, 2017), 37.

100   Milton-Edwards and Farrell, *Hamas*, 286.

101   Abu Tayr, *Sayyidi Umar*, 356.

102   Milton-Edwards and Farrell, *Hamas*, 281.

103   Quoted in Jonathan Fighel, 'The Mujaheed Sheikh – Dr. Nizar Rayyan: The Spiritual Mentor of Iz a-Din al Qassam Brigades' (Herzliya: International Institute for Counter-terrorism, October 2021).

just six years after PA–Israeli security cooperation collapsed. A number of them must have experienced – either directly or indirectly – arrests, detentions, violence, and torture at the hands of the PA. Reportedly, Rayan was himself betrayed to the Israeli army by someone in Fatah; a considerable contingent in the Qassam Brigades must have feared what would happen to them if the security forces of the PA re-established their security cooperation with Israel in Gaza.[104] For them, with scars and memories still fresh, the ousting was not merely political, it was deeply personal. As Muhammad Abu Tayr, newly elected parliamentarian for Hamas, asked rhetorically:

> Who killed Professor As'ad al-Saftawi? Who killed Hatim Abu Sha'ban? Who killed Ayman al-Razayna and Amar al-A'raj while waiting for the call to break their fast in Ramadan? Who killed seventeen worshippers in the Palestine Mosque massacre? Who killed Muhammad Raddad at al-Najah University as he defended the honor of Muslims?[105]

Although the masked assassins who liquidated al-Saftawi in 1993 remain unknown, Abu Tayr necessarily blamed the security forces of Yasser Arafat. The PIJ militants al-Razayna and al-A'raj were, as noted in chapter 4, assassinated by the PA intelligence services in 1996. The worshippers were similarly killed on November 18, 1994, when PA police forces opened fire on Palestinian protesters, killing twelve and wounding more than 200.[106] Finally, Raddad was an activist in Hamas's Islamic Bloc at al-Najah National University in Nablus. Also he was killed by the PA security forces on campus on July 27, 2007. For Abu Tayr, the PA security forces were guilty of perpetrating severe and unjustified violence, not merely against Hamas but against their own people. The Qassam Brigades' ousting of Fatah, he implied, was essentially the chickens coming home to roost.

There is nothing that indicates that Hamas's takeover in Gaza was centrally planned. Nor was it approved by the political leadership.[107] Khalid Mishal, one of the political leaders who had been sidelined,

---

104    Trevor Mostyn, 'Nizar Rayan', *Guardian*, January 3, 2009.

105    Abu Tayr, *Sayyidi Umar*, 362.

106    Clyde Haberman, '12 Die as Arafat's Police Fire on Palestinian Militants', *New York Times*, November 19, 1994.

107    Are Hovdenak, 'Hamas in Transition: The Failure of Sanctions', *Democratization* 16, no. 1 (2010): 75.

heavily implied his dissatisfaction with the Qassam Brigades, and Usama
Hamdan, Hamas's former representative in Lebanon, made it clear that
the outside leadership were not a part of the decision-making process in
June 2007.[108] Reportedly, fissures also extended within the Qassam Brigades. Muhammad Deif aimed to unite all Palestinians across factions in a
common armed struggle against the Israeli occupation, and he was irked
by Ahmad al-Ja'bari, the de facto head of the Qassam Brigades in Gaza,
who, together with Rayan, directed al-Qassam forces against Fatah.[109]
The fallout in Gaza essentially meant that everyone in Hamas was
aggrieved. The ousting of Fatah had markedly weakened the moderates,
who saw their strategy of fully entering PA institutions backfire. The
breakdown of the national unity government and the ensuing international boycott obliterated whatever authority remained to moderates such
as Ahmed Yousef, who had invested much of their political capital in
convincing their movement to accept compromises to secure international
recognition.[110] The internal elections for Hamas's consultative council
in August 2008 – the highest authoritative body in the movement –
mirrored that political eclipse. There, the proponents of the democratic
experiment were ultimately outvoted, paving the way for a younger generation of militants from the Second Intifada who became responsible
for reining in the pragmatists and remilitarizing Hamas throughout the
2010s.[111] Neither were the Qassam Brigades pleased, as the militants
quickly perceived a transition from unbridled manoeuvrability during
the Second Intifada to having the handbrake firmly engaged. They chafed
as the official leadership of Hamas strived to maintain a calm with Israel
in order to avoid new bombings of Gaza, which would worsen already
deteriorating living conditions.[112]

---

108    See for example Mouin Rabbani, 'A Hamas Perspective on the Movement's Evolving Role: An Interview with Khalid Mishal: Part II', *Journal of
Palestine Studies* 37, no. 4 (July 2008): 74–5; Frode Løvlie, 'The Institutional Trajectory of Hamas: From Radicalism to Pragmatism – and Back Again?' (PhD
thesis, University of Bergen, 2015), 274.

109    Nicolas Pelham, 'Hamas's Deadly "Phantom": The Man Behind the
Attacks', *Economist*, October 20, 2023.

110    Hovdenak, 'Hamas in Transition', 74.

111    Are Hovdenak, *Al-Qaida: A Challenge for Hamas?* (Kjeller: Norwegian
Defence Research Establishment, 2009), 37–8; Løvlie, 'The Institutional Trajectory of Hamas', 286.

112    Sayigh, '*We Serve the People*', 120.

Because the internal power equilibrium in Hamas was so severely disrupted, because uncertainties – as well as grievances – were left unaddressed, and because there was a plethora of conflicting expectations of what the governance project would – and should – entail, Hamas's rise to power created ripple effects within Palestinian Islamism. In the long-term, it sowed the seeds of October 7 by creating a decisive schism between Hamas moderates and hardliners. In the short-term, it strengthened a subcurrent within Palestinian Islamism which so far had found no natural place within the occupied territories: salafi-jihadism. This new subcurrent is where we turn next.

## Black banners in Palestine

And I say: Until now, you have not returned to Islam!!! Until now, you have not overcome the pressures of reality!!! And you are the ones who turned reality upside down by removing the accursed tyrant from Gaza. And still, you lack a faithful leadership . . . By the way, before I forget, which is harder? Applying Islamic law or defeating an apostate regime? I await the answer! – Abu Yunus al-Abbasi.[113]

Israeli authorities attempted to portray Hamas and PIJ as synonymous with al-Qaida after the terrorist attacks on the US on September 11, 2001. There were nevertheless significant ideological and practical differences between the main currents of Palestinian Islamism and the salafi-jihadism of al-Qaida and, later, the Islamic State (IS), on core issues such as nationalism, democracy, enemy hierarchy, and creedal purity.

Hamas and PIJ operated with Palestine as a clearly defined territorial unit from Ra's al-Naqoura in the north to the Gulf of Aqaba in the south, and from the Jordan River in the east to the Mediterranean in the west. None of them engaged in international terrorism against US and Western targets, nor did they attempt or support the toppling of 'apostate' regimes in the region. Hamas and PIJ thus differed from earlier Palestinian currents like the PFLP and Black September, or the Abu Nidal Organization,

---

113   Abu Yunus al-Abbasi, 'Limadha la tatbiq Hamas al-shari'a?', *Jannat* 54 (2008): 44.

which hijacked international flights and assassinated targets in Europe. There were differences between them, yet the main currents of Palestinian Islamism largely conflated religious and nationalist duties. The opinions of Hamas and PIJ differed on the feasibility of electoral participation under occupation, yet none of them were against democracy, elections, representation, pluralism, and a strict separation of power. Authority in both movements stemmed from democratic internal electoral processes and not from the religious capital of individuals.[114]

Al-Qaida and its associated groups, in contrast, dismissed the concept of nationalism and strove to foster global solidarity among Muslims. They advocated the use of violence on a global scale, eschewed all forms of democratic processes and mechanisms, and resorted to brutal methods such as beheadings.[115] Subsequent groups such as IS even rejected the elevation of the Palestinian struggle as akin to idol worship.[116] Hamas's electoral participation in 2006 irked al-Qaida, as it put human governance over divine command. Democracy was directly contradicting the unity of God, the sole legislative authority. Al-Qaida's annoyance was far from alleviated in September 2006, when Hamas reached a tentative agreement with Fatah to form a unity government, and then failed in enforcing Islamic law when controlling the Gaza Strip.[117]

There was similarly no love lost between al-Qaida and PIJ. Although Fathi al-Shiqaqi maintained contact with Egyptian radical currents such as Egyptian Islamic Jihad (which later joined al-Qaida) and al-Jama'a al-Islamiyya well into the early 1990s due to perceived pan-Islamist loyalties, Shallah effectively cut contact when he became secretary-general in 1995. 'We do not believe in the violence of these groups. Neither against the regimes nor against civil society,' Shallah declared. 'What does Islam benefit from killing foreign tourists, journalists, or policemen?'[118] In fact, Shallah – who had obtained a PhD in economics at Durham University

---

114   Gunning, *Hamas in Politics*, 138.

115   Reuven Paz, 'Jihadis and Hamas', in Assaf Moghadam and Brian Fishman, eds, *Self-Inflicted Wounds: Debates and Divisions within al-Qa'ida and Its Periphery* (West Point: Combatting Terrorism Center at West Point, 2010), 183–4.

116   Cole Bunzel, 'Gaza and Global Jihad', *Foreign Affairs*, 2 November 2023.

117   Barak Mendelsohn, 'al-Qaeda's Palestinian Problem', *Survival* 51, no. 4 (2009): 78.

118   Charbel, 'Shallah: Lam yu'ayyid qatl al-madaniyyin fi 11 Aylul'.

in 1990 and who pursued an academic career in Florida before rising
to become head of PIJ – had few qualms expressing his admiration for
the 'organization, administration, democracy, law, freedom, and level
of advancement and progress' in the US.[119] It is difficult imagining al-
Zawahiri harbouring such sympathies, and he lambasted Shallah in 1996
for stating that the battle was waged against the Israelis not because of
their Jewish faith but because they were occupiers.[120]

Salafism, the non-violent variant, had existed in the occupied territories since the 1970s. It was mainly an imported product brought by
Palestinian students returning from Saudi Arabia. The first salafi organization in Gaza, Dar al-Kitab wa-l-Sunna, was organized in Khan Younis
in 1975 and headed by one Yassin al-Astal. Contrary to the Muslim
Brotherhood, the Gazan salafis isolated themselves from society and
withdrew from Palestinian politics.[121] Like Hizb al-Tahrir, Gazan salafis
focused less on the liberation of Palestine and more on the transnational
unity of the *umma*; the one-sided focus on the minutiae of practising
faith gave them a marginal role in Palestinian society. What mattered
to them was creedal purity. Although the forerunner of Hamas, the
Muslim Brotherhood, proselytized as well, the Brothers argued that
religion required renewal instead of blindly emulating the generation of
the Prophet; it had to be 'adapted to the local context in which it [was]
being interpreted'.[122]

Salafi-jihadism materialized later in the occupied territories, not before
the mid-2000s, and became increasingly visible from 2006. The Gazan
salafi-jihadists did not seem to fall under an overarching organizational
umbrella. Instead, they were elements of a flourishing, yet loosely established, ecology with militants, firebrand clerics, and media outlets. The
militants attacked symbols of 'immorality and decadence' in Gaza like
internet cafés, video shops, Christian bookstores, hotels, and UNRWA,

119    Ghassam Charbel, 'Ziyara li-dhakirat al-amin al-amm li-harakat 'al-
jihad al-islami fi Filastin' 4. Shallah: Talabtuhu bi-tashkil tanzim wa hin kashaf
al-sirr baya'tuhu bay'at 'al-jihad' al-Shiqaqi an Hassan Nasrallah: Sayakun khumayni al-Arab idha 'ash', *al-Hayat*, January 10, 2003
120    Skare, *A History of Palestinian Islamic Jihad*, 157.
121    Yoram Schweitzer, 'Salafi Jihadism in Gaza as Opposition to Hamas
Rule', in Anat Kurz, Udi Dekel, and Benedetta Berti, eds, *The Crisis of the Gaza
Strip* (Tel Aviv: Institute for National Security Studies, 2018), 61–2.
122    Brenner, *Gaza under Hamas*, 69–70.

while clerics such as Abu Yunus al-Abbasi catered to an international audience on jihadi internet forums. Publishers of Palestinian jihadi journals further proclaimed the infidelity of the Hamas government, the threats of Shiism, and the noble path of Usama bin Laden and his al-Qaida organization.[123]

The plethora of Gazan salafi-jihadi groups and currents, and their unorganized nature, illustrate the different drivers at work. While one salafi-jihadi group was a de facto private clan militia, another was primarily preoccupied by the perceived spread of Shiism. A third could be aggrieved by Hamas's ceasefires with Israel and the slow pace of the government's Islamization efforts. By the same token, none of the groups agreed on who was an apostate. While one group deemed the Hamas government and everyone who worked in it an infidel, another agreed that the government was infidel, but this did not include every governmental employee. A third proclaimed that the issue of infidelity had to be assessed individually as government employment was not anathema to faith.[124] Though grievances and aspirations often overlapped, Gazan salafi-jihadism was a heterogeneous phenomenon from the onset.

To illustrate, one of the most visible salafi-jihadi groups in this period, the Army of Islam, was almost exclusively comprised of members of the Dughmush clan. One of the most powerful clans in Gaza, the Dughmush were infamous for their criminal activity and described as the 'Sopranos of Gaza'.[125] Their adoption of salafi-jihadism was, as such, intended to legitimize the clan's resistance to a Gazan central power attempting to control smuggling routes and levy taxes on goods the Dughmush imported.[126] Army of Islam kidnapped a number of Western journalists in Gaza between 2006 and 2007, with the hostages intended to provide the Dughmush clan with leverage in negotiations with the Hamas government.[127] As Nasr Yusuf, a former public security head, explained to Hovdenak: 'The Dughmush family just wanted money. In Palestinian society it is very shameful to kidnap somebody for money, therefore they

---

123    Hovdenak, 'al-Qaida', 24; Paz, 'Jihadis and Hamas', 194–5.

124    Brenner, *Gaza under Hamas*, 75.

125    Dag Tuastad, 'Hamas and the Clans: From Islamisation of Tribalism to Tribalization of Islamism?', *Third World Thematics: A TWQ Journal* 6, nos 1–3 (May 2021): 93.

126    Paz, 'Jihadis and Hamas', 195.

127    Brenner, *Gaza under Hamas*, 85.

claimed an exchange with this al-Qaida prisoner in the UK, but in reality they asked for — and got — money.'[128]

Other salafi-jihadi currents, such as al-Tawhid wa-l-Jihad in Nuseirat, were occupied by what it perceived as enjoining good and forbidding evil. As Brenner narrates, the Italian activist Vittorio Arrigoni was a popular figure in Gaza with his support for the Palestinian people under occupation. For conservative Gazans and for the salafi-jihadis, however, his Western lifestyle of smoking, drinking, and open social relations was seen as a provocation. When the leader of al-Tawhid wa-l-Jihad, Hisham al-Saydani, was arrested by the Hamas government in March 2011, his followers kidnapped Arrigoni on April 13 to use him as a bargaining chip, and, in their words, to 'teach him a lesson'. Hamas security forces discovered their hideout the following day, but they were too late.[129] Arrigoni was already dead, strangled with a plastic cord.

For others, Gazan salafi-jihadism was more anti-Hamas than it was pro-al-Qaida. As salafists and salafi-jihadists remained one of the few organized opposition forces in Gaza from 2007, a number of Fatah loyalists began attending their mosques because they could not, or would not, attend those controlled by the Hamas ruling power.[130] Just as droves of former Baathists joined IS in Iraq, '[Salafi-jihadism] provided a new identity and sense of usefulness to men whom Fatah had forbidden from working in Gaza and who had seen its military wing stripped of its arms by the new Hamas government'.[131]

The main driver of Gazan salafi-jihadism thus appears to be Hamas's rise to power in 2007 and the inconvenient responsibilities of governance. Hamas's electoral victory created serious fissures within Palestinian Islamism. A growing number were aggrieved by the changing opportunity structures in Gaza, imposed by Hamas security forces. Hamas did not merely restore law and order to end the anarchy of the Second Intifada and the street justice of the Gazan clans. Hamas security forces also began patrolling Gaza's borders to maintain calm with Israel and arresting militants attempting to carry out attacks or launch rockets. The aforementioned Murabitun Army, set up by the Qassam Brigades

---

128   Quoted in Hovdenak, 'al-Qaida', 29.
129   Brenner, *Gaza under Hamas*, 91–3.
130   Sayigh, 'We Serve the People', 15; Paz, 'Jihadis and Hamas', 194.
131   Brenner, *Gaza under Hamas*, 72.

to protect Gazan neighbourhoods from Israeli incursions, began instead protecting the borders. For a number of militants in the Qassam Brigades, the ceasefires with Israel were difficult to stomach and created confusion within a military body whose sole aim was fighting an external enemy.[132] Nizar Rayan was the embodiment of these tensions within Hamas. Described as an ideological product of Saudi-Wahhabi influence from his studies at the Islamic University in Medina, Rayan despised Shiite Islam. He even refused to give an interview to a reporter from Hizbollah's al-Manar channel in Gaza, citing the 'forbidden [religious] innovations' it represented.[133] Rayan similarly despised Fatah for its perceived secularism and promised to turn the headquarters of the National Security Forces into a mosque from which he would deliver a sermon. For him, the ousting of Fatah was just as much a religious victory over the infidels as it was a political one.[134]

Rayan was one of those in the Qassam Brigades who were aggrieved by Hamas's decision of first participating in the legislative elections – a form of heresy – and then forming a unity government with Fatah – a party of apostates and quislings. While other Hamas hardliners like Salih al-Aruri, who built the Qassam Brigades in the West Bank, could stress the need for armed struggle against Israel while being an ardent proponent of Palestinian reconciliation, Rayan opposed any dialogue with Fatah. For them, he proclaimed, there could only be the sword and the rifle.[135] As Sayigh points out, Rayan was particularly influential because he was one of few who were both a leader in Hamas's political wing and a field commander in the Qassam Brigades. Described as a mentor for the salafi-jihadi network in Gaza – often referred to as the Jaljalat – he 'tapped into the fear of many within Hamas that the movement's involvement in the mundane tasks of government and public service delivery would jeopardize its nationalist and Islamic purity and its commitment to armed resistance against Israel'.[136] Salafi-jihadism presented a significant ideological challenge for Hamas, because its appeal was particularly strong among one of its most influential groups: its own

132   Ibid., 71.
133   Fighel, 'The Mujaheed Sheikh – Dr. Nizar Rayyan'.
134   Ibid.
135   'Obituary: Nizar Rayan', BBC News, January 1, 2009.
136   Sayigh, 'We Serve the People', 17.

militants.[137] By 2010, 50 per cent of Gazan salafi-jihadis were former Hamas members.[138]

The ideological threat from salafi-jihadism both within and without the movement, Sayigh notes, may partly explain the Islamization efforts by Hamas in government, which have been more de facto in nature than de jure. Hamas security forces have, for example, reportedly implemented extra-legal measures, 'almost entirely to gender issues', such as imposing proper dress code, preventing gender-mixing, banning women from riding motorcycles, requiring female lawyers to wear hijab in court, preventing male hairdressers from working in women's hair salons, and banning females from smoking water pipes. There was a determination in Hamas 'to pre-empt and deflect doubts cast by more militant Salafists with respect to their Islamic credentials . . . Such behavior is probably also directed at Salafists and conservatives within their own ranks.'[139]

That is not to suggest that Hamas was lenient towards the salafi-jihadists. On August 14, 2009, the spiritual leader of Jund Ansar Allah, Abdel Latif Musa, delivered a speech to hundreds of salafi-jihadis in Gaza. In the speech, Musa criticized the Hamas government strongly for not implementing Islamic law and declared the establishment of an Islamic emirate:

> Let me give the Hamas government some advice . . . Either you enforce [God's] law and the punishments set out in the Quran [or] you become a secular party which is falsely described as Islamic, like Recep Tayyip Erdogan's. Our brothers in the Hamas movement know that it is the intimidation of other movements that drives them to clandestine activity. We hereby declare the establishment of a new-born entity, the Islamic emirate of Palestine. This emirate will implement hudud, the Islamic criminal laws and sharia.[140]

In the meantime, Hamas's security forces had surrounded the mosque and demanded the group's surrender. When that failed and the salafi-jihadists shot an al-Qassam commander sent into the mosque to mediate, Hamas's

---

137    International Crisis Group, *Radical Islam in Gaza* (Crisis Group, March 29, 2011), 5.

138    Brenner, *Gaza under Hamas*, 76.

139    Sayigh, 'We Serve the People', 94–8.

140    Quoted in Brenner, *Gaza under Hamas*, 92.

patience ran out, and they stormed the site 'leaving only a half-destroyed minaret standing'.[141]

Hamas's heavy-handed crackdown on Jund Ansar Allah revealed that the fissures within the wider Palestinian Islamist movement was not limited to that between Hamas and the salafi-jihadi currents in Gaza, nor within the Qasssam Brigades. The PIJ leader Abdallah al-Shami denounced the salafi-jihadis as having adopted a deviant and incorrect ideology; the declaration of an Islamic emirate in Gaza was premature and a sign that they lacked vision. However, al-Shami also noted that the growing extremism in the Gaza Strip had to be seen as a direct consequence of Hamas's electoral participation and the 'negative practices' it had adopted in power.[142] Essentially, PIJ had begun feeling the restrictions imposed by Hamas. This is where we turn next.

---

141   Ibid., 90.
142   'Mumarasat Hamas fi Ghazzah hiya allati Khalaqat hadhihi al-Jama'ah al-takfiriyyah', al-Shuruq, August 16, 2009.

# 6

# Prelude

When Hamas entered the 2006 legislative elections, the group sought to transform the institutions of the Palestinian Authority in support of the Palestinian resistance. After taking control over Gaza in 2007, it soon found itself policing the Gazan border and preventing other armed factions from firing rockets into Israel.

This chapter examines the prelude to the October 7 attacks. It explores the struggles with which Hamas contended as it governed the Gaza Strip, when it suddenly had to balance between being a responsible service provider and an armed resistance movement. While Hamas was blamed for the deteriorating situation in Gaza, PIJ's popularity surged for continuing to stress the need for armed struggle. Suffering from a diplomatic and political impasse with no end to the blockade and treated by Israel as a security issue rather than a possible negotiating partner, Hamas's hardliners prepared militarily. Manufacturing and smuggling weapons, and excavating the tunnel network under Gaza, they were setting the stage for the next phase.

## Law, order, and resistance

It was essential for Hamas to reinstate law and order after years of prolonged urban warfare, intra-factional disputes, and anarchy in Gaza. Not merely to consolidate its governance project but also to restore a semblance of normalcy for its inhabitants, who had endured years of conflict and disarray. This was easier said than done, given the constraints put on Hamas. The international boycott imposed on its newly established Gazan government did not just mean that Hamas lacked any sense of international backing and legitimacy, but also that the coffers required to administer life in the Strip ran dry. In its efforts to undermine Hamas, Mahmud Abbas and the PA in the West Bank ordered its public employees and police officers to stay at home and not report for duty, which effectively created a public sector vacuum.[1]

'More inclined to create faits accompli than submit to them', Hamas established the Executive Forces to counter Fatah in their power struggle, an adjunct police unit which by June 2007 consisted of 6,500 men.[2] They were assigned full responsibility for policing the Strip, and in the first months after Hamas took control over Gaza, they rounded up alleged rapists, thieves, clandestine liquor merchants, and money forgers. The Executive Forces also intervened in the Gazan informal economy and the hitherto open arms market while combatting criminal elements who engaged in kidnappings, car thefts, drug smuggling, and racketeering. While the police officers of the Hamas government proved capable in establishing long-sought security for the inhabitants of Gaza, local human rights organizations did protest at the use of torture and excessive force in the process.[3] Hamas's policing efforts in Gaza also included violently stomping down any unruly clan that engaged in criminal enterprises or posed an ideological challenge to its rule. The Dughmush clan and its salafi-jihadi outlet Army of Islam was one of them. The Fatah-affiliated Hillis clan was another.[4]

---

1   Benedetta Berti, 'Non-state Actors as Providers of Governance: The Hamas Government in Gaza between Effective Sovereignty, Centralized Authority, and Resistance', *Middle East Journal* 69, no. 1 (2015): 16.

2   Yezid Sayigh, '*We Serve the People*': Hamas Policing in Gaza (Washington, DC: Brandeis University, Crown Center for Middle East Studies, 2011), 50.

3   Ibid., 54–6.

4   Dag Tuastad, 'Hamas and the Clans: From Islamisation of Tribalism to

Intentionally or not, Hamas's quest to establish law and order effectively altered dynamics both within Gaza and within Hamas itself. Palestinian factions have traditionally tapped into their ties to supporting clans in the occupied territories to gain their support. Various Palestinian clans have been affiliated with political movements 'through a combination of membership, party position and support', and kinship clusters have, as such, developed and grown in the factional membership bases.[5] While the al-Dahduh family was seen as synonymous with PIJ after joining the movement in the early 1980s, the Hillis clan in Gaza similarly enjoyed close ties to Fatah.[6] These clan-faction alliances have neither been fixed nor constant, and Palestinian clans have historically switched sides if they have been offered a better deal by a rival faction; they have more often than not been prone to play off outsiders.[7]

Reflecting the historical interplay between political factions and kinship networks, Hamas's rise to power effectively shaped the membership base of the Qassam Brigades, as Gaza's new rulers strategically redefined their relationship with the Gazan clans. Just as Fatah had to ally with the most influential clans to consolidate its power in the 1990s, Hamas had to put its heel on the same groups to solidify theirs; one of the first things Hamas did in power was to crush the strongest clan groups. Yet despite the diminished political sway of the major clans, the kinship networks continued to exert significant social and political influence in Gaza. In fact, smaller clans welcomed Hamas's heavy-handed approach, given that they themselves could have become victims of unruly and stronger kinship groupings.[8] Clan-faction affiliation – and Gaza's political and social composition – was thus effectively altered as smaller clans sought protection and power under the wings of Hamas and the Qassam Brigades.

Tribalization of Islamism?', *Third World Thematics: A TWQ Journal* 6, nos 1–3 (May 2021): 93–4.

5    International Crisis Group, *Inside Gaza: The Challenge of Clans and Families* (International Crisis Group, 2007), 9.

6    Glenn E. Robinson, 'Palestinian Tribes, Clans, and Notable Families', *Strategic Insights* 7, no. 4 (2009); Erik Skare, *A History of Palestinian Islamic Jihad: Faith, Awareness, and Revolution in the Middle East* (Cambridge: Cambridge University Press, 2021).

7    Robinson, 'Palestinian Tribes, Clans, and Notable Families'.

8    Tuastad, 'Hamas and the Clans', 100–1.

Figures 6.1 and 6.2 capture the sociological changes within the Qassam Brigades in Gaza. While kinship clusters were conspicuously small and far apart among its fallen militants before 2007, they surged after Hamas's rise to power. From only five clusters with six or more fallen family members, there were nearly fifty post-2007.[9] They did not grow just in number but also in size, and the al-Masri and Hamuda clusters, for instance, would have been even larger had they not been distinguished by their respective districts (Gaza and North Gaza). Numerous fallen militants from prominent Gazan clans like al-Masri and al-Kafarna were now represented among the Qassam martyrs, along with the Mushtaha, the Abd al-Al, and the Hillis clans. The Gazan al-Dayri clan, known for its close ties to Hamas, is similarly represented in Figure 6.2.[10] It was not just Hamas that changed Gaza; Gaza changed Hamas.

Above all, Hamas's governance project put the movement between a rock and a hard place as it had to satisfy the contradictory demands of its Gazan constituency, on the one hand, and its own rank-and-file, on the other. As a government, Hamas had the responsibility of protecting and serving the Palestinians of Gaza. As a resistance movement, Hamas felt obliged continuing armed resistance against the Israeli occupation and blockade. This would inevitably provoke Israeli counter-bombings, however, harming the very constituency it sought to protect.[11] Already in September 2007, Prime Minister Ismail Haniyeh called on all Palestinian factions to avoid sending rockets and shelling the Gazan border crossings to preserve commercial movement, security, and stability in the Strip.[12]

From initially targeting criminal elements and unruly clans, Hamas therefore quickly had to expand its reach to curb the armed activity of other Palestinian factions. The Murabitun Army was repurposed to patrol

---

9    The Qassam Brigades experienced 2.3 times higher casualty numbers from 2007 on. The kinship clusters expanded by a factor of 9.31 in the same period, indicating that factors beyond casualty numbers contributed to this growth.

10    I do not suggest that membership variations can be reduced to kinship, as if a militant is bounded by a family's decisions. My point is instead that clusters presumably result from factors reinforcing kinship as a social network and recruitment structure.

11    Frode Løvlie, 'The Institutional Trajectory of Hamas: From Radicalism to Pragmatism – and Back Again?' (PhD thesis, University of Bergen, 2015), 264.

12    Fathi Sibah, 'Hukumat haniya tunashid fasa'il al-muqawama 'tajannub' qasf al-ma'abır al-hududıyya', al-Hayat, September 14, 2007.

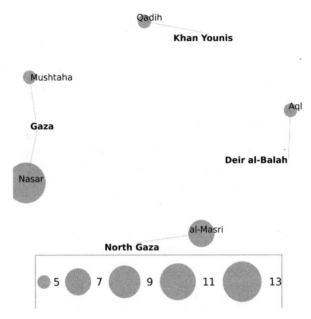

**Figure 6.1.** Gazan kinship clusters in the Qassam Brigades, 1988–2006 (> 4)

the borders. Although Hamas viewed its policies in Gaza as an existential mission to safeguard the broader Palestinian struggle, its biggest challenge was now 'curbing the resistance activities of other factions, including Islamic Jihad', and Hamas was accordingly 'very effective at limiting rocket fire into Israel, even establishing a police force to restrain armed operations'.[13] As one Hamas representative in Gaza described Hamas's policing of the other armed factions: 'Everything we've gained [from ceasefires with Israel] could be lost by the actions of a single idiot.'[14] Although the Qassam Brigades respected the outcome of the internal decision-making processes in Hamas, and its commanders played a crucial role in disciplining its militants, the new role irked several in the military wing. Ahmad al-Ja'bari, for example, complained to Mishal in 2009 that the military wing had been reduced to mere janitors at the borders.[15]

---

13    Tareq Baconi, *Hamas Contained: The Rise and Pacification of Palestinian Resistance* (Stanford, CA: Stanford University Press, 2018), 148, 151, 214.

14    Quoted in International Crisis Group, *Radical Islam in Gaza* (International Crisis Group, March 29, 2011), 4.

15    Sayigh, *'We Serve the People'*, 124.

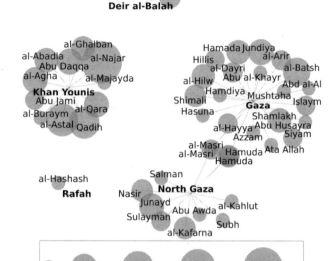

**Figure 6.2.** Gazan kinship clusters in the Qassam Brigades, 2007–22 (> 4)

Despite its ideological commitment to armed resistance, maintaining ceasefires became one of the few significant leverages Hamas could use in negotiations with Israel. A new status quo slowly established itself in the Gaza Strip, and a new normalcy developed between Hamas and Israel. Hamas's logic of violence adapted.[16] No longer adhering to maximalist positions in negotiations with Israel, Hamas now used force – either on the part of its own militants or by unleashing other factions – as a bargaining tool to ease the blockade.[17] While conditions for a truce with Israel during the Second Intifada included a full Israeli withdrawal from the occupied Palestinian territories or the return of all Palestinian refugees, the movement's demands in 2012 were limited to opening the Gazan border crossings or, at best, lifting the blockade.[18] This was favourable to Israel, as Hamas proved itself highly capable of maintaining law

---

16    Daniel Byman, 'Curious Victory: Explaining Israel's Suppression of the Second Intifada', *Terrorism and Political Violence* 24, no. 5 (November 2012): 67.

17    Baconi, *Hamas Contained*, 154–5, 195.

18    Joas Wagemakers, 'Legitimizing Pragmatism: Hamas' Framing Efforts

**Table 6.1.** Occupation distribution in the Qassam Brigades and PIJ, 2007–22

| Occupation | Number (%) | Occupation | Number (%) |
|---|---|---|---|
| Police officer | 189 (17.45%) | Student | 93 (24.67%) |
| Student | 132 (12.19%) | Labourer | 83 (22.02%) |
| Executive forces | 95 (8.77%) | Unemployed | 45 (11.94%) |
| Salesman | 71 (6.56%) | Governmental employee | 28 (7.43%) |
| Security forces | 68 (6.28%) | Tailor | 12 (3.18%) |
| Governmental employee | 67 (6.19%) | Farmer | 10 (2.65%) |
| Farmer | 60 (5.54%) | Salesman | 10 (2.65%) |
| Construction worker | 39 (3.60%) | Construction worker | 9 (2.39%) |
| Teacher | 27 (2.49%) | Driver | 9 (2.39%) |
| Tailor | 20 (1.85%) | Electrician | 6 (1.59%) |
|  |  | Iron worker | 6 (1.59%) |

and order while preventing other factions from launching cross-border attacks. Hamas was now a guarantor for maintaining calm and, at the same time, the trump card Israeli authorities employed to prevent any lifting of the blockade on Gaza ad infinitum: 2.3 million Palestinians were now effectively out of sight and out of mind as regards the Israeli occupation.[19]

The occupational backgrounds in the Qassam Brigade reflected the newly imposed raison d'être after 2007, which now combined credentials of both resistance and governance. The Qassam militants were no longer tailors, construction workers, or carpenters. Almost 40 per cent of al-Qassam martyrs with a known occupation were now engaged in governance, serving in roles within the Executive Force, police, security services, or other governmental institutions. PIJ, in contrast, persisted in recruiting students, the unemployed, and blue-collar workers.[20]

---

from Militancy to Moderation and Back?', *Terrorism and Political Violence* 22, no. 3 (June 2010): 371.

19  Baconi, *Hamas Contained*, 227–8.

20  For discussion on data gaps in the Palestinian Islamist martyr dataset, see the appendix. Table 6.1 calculates only the percentage of martyrs with known occupations to avoid deflating numbers. Although 1 to 2 per cent for PIJ occupations like construction worker and iron worker may appear insignificant,

These differences would inevitably exacerbate tensions between the two Palestinian Islamist movements in Gaza, tensions that had always existed although they had been subdued.[21] Signs of tensions surfaced in 2004, for example, when a videotape was leaked in which a member of Hamas's consultative council, Fathi Hamad, slammed PIJ for allegedly attempting to 'outmuscle' Hamas. Although Hamad focused on the perceived Shiite credentials of PIJ – claiming that the movement was only a proxy of Iran and Hezbollah, and that PIJ had no right to operate on the Palestinian street – the tape seemingly indicated the frustration of Hamas. Although Hamas was by far the larger organization, it resented PIJ being presented as equally important by the press:

> We outnumber them, we have many more mosques, and much more commitment, but they are ahead of us in the satellite TV stations, and their Web sites are much bigger than the group itself. They are stealing attacks from Hamas, exaggerate the number of their killed, and inflate the numbers of their street demonstrations as if they are a domestic group, even though they are supported by Hezbollah. The media has turned them into the equals of the Muslim Brotherhood.[22]

Such allegations should be taken with a grain of salt, as they were frequently traded by Palestinian factions throughout the Second Intifada. Husam Badran from the Qassam Brigades, for example, expressed similar grievances, while PIJ 'deeply [regretted] the adoption by some factions of many operations carried out by our heroic mujahedeen'.[23] Hamad's grievances nevertheless matter because they illustrate how competition between Hamas and PIJ persisted even though clashes diminished in

---

the subsequent occupations were almost exclusively blue-collar jobs, including mechanic, blacksmith, painter, and plumber.

21    The analysis of PIJ in this chapter is based on and draws text from Skare, *A History of Palestinian Islamic Jihad*, chs 5 and 9.

22    Quoted in Arnon Regular, 'Leading Hamas Preacher Warns of Clash with Islamic Jihad', *Haaretz*, December 15, 2004.

23    Husam Badran, *Katibat al-Shimal: al-Sabiqun ila al-janna* (n.p.: al-Maktab al-i'lami li-kata'ib al-shahid izz al-din al-Qassam, 2010), 56; quoted in Antonella Acinapura, 'A Framing-Sensitive Approach to Militant Groups' Tactics: The Islamic Jihad Movement in Palestine and the Radicalisation of Violence during the Second Intifada', *Critical Studies on Terrorism* 16, no. 1 (January 2023): 134.

frequency and intensity after the two signed the Charter of Brotherhood and Cooperation in 1992. These tensions, as illustrated by Hamad, were essentially connected to Hamas's perception of itself as the main Palestinian Islamic representative and of PIJ as its 'little brother'. During the strife with Fatah in 2007, for example, Hamas attempted to make PIJ declare its support and to position itself as an ally. As sources in PIJ stated at the time: '[Hamas] expects people to deal with it in the way that [Hamas] sees fit.'[24] Although PIJ attempted to de-escalate, the relationship between the two Islamic movements was inherently unstable once Hamas took control in Gaza.

As discussed earlier, Hamas spent its first year in government taking control over the administrative institutions in Gaza, gaining a monopoly on violence and re-establishing law and order.[25] Hamas pledged to keep the streets of Gaza safe and sent a signal to other armed Palestinian groups to respect its authority, including PIJ.[26] When Hamas attempted to stop PIJ members firing weapons into the air during a wedding, a practice on which Hamas had issued a ban one month earlier, clashes soon occurred. As the man who fired the weapon fled into the house of a PIJ official, violence ensued as Hamas attacked the building, wounding ten and killing one.[27] Two months later, in October 2007, further clashes erupted between PIJ and Hamas.[28]

The rapid changes Gaza underwent in this period contributed to the deteriorating relationship between the two Palestinian Islamic movements. As late as June 2013, Hamas police officers killed Raid Jundiyya, one of the field commanders in PIJ's rocket unit.[29] Less than two months later, PIJ members and Hamas security services clashed after a dispute over a sermon given by the imam of the PIJ-affiliated al-Tawhid Mosque in

24    Jihan al-Husayni, 'Masadir qariba min 'al-jihad al-islami' tahmal ala qiyadat Hamas wa Fatah', *al-Hayat*, August 5, 2007.

25    Berti, 'Non-state Actors as Providers of Governance', 17.

26    '2 Killed in Clashes between Hamas and Islamic Jihad', Associated Press, August 2, 2007.

27    Ezra HaLevi, 'Hamas Cracks Down on Fatah Media, Clashes with Islamic Jihad', *Arutz Sheva*, August 2, 2007.

28    Muhammad al-Jamal and Fayiz Abu Aoun, 'al-Hudu' yukhayyim Mujaddidan ala Rafah ba'd sarayan ittifaq li-waqf al-iqtital bayn 'Hamas wa-l-jihad', *al-Ayyam*, October 23, 2007.

29    Nasouh Nazzal, 'Palestine: Hamas and Jihad Trade Barbs as Clash Looms', *Gulf News*, June 23, 2013.

Beit Hanoun. Allegedly, the dispute was caused by the imam's criticism of the continuous power outages in the Gaza Strip and that one party, Hamas, led the country. Another claimed that the mosque was in possession of a substantial amount of Iranian food aid, which the security services attempted to confiscate.[30] In April 2014, a new dispute between Hamas and PIJ erupted when the imam of the Ibrahim al-Khalil Mosque, Murid al-Qanouh, was dismissed by the Ministry of Religious Endowments and Affairs. While al-Qanouh claimed that he had been fired for political reasons, the ministry stated that it was because he had not carried out his duties for two months. The dispute developed into a fistfight between Hamas and PIJ worshippers, with both leaderships quickly intervening in order to end the clashes. Then, in Rafah, another dispute erupted in Gaza when PIJ members physically assaulted a salafi sheikh.[31]

The fact that the clashes between PIJ and Hamas persisted (although sporadically) over seven years implies they were not isolated events, but rather symptoms of the underlying and developing contradictions between the two movements. The main cause for these contradictions was presumably Hamas's attempt to establish law and order in Gaza, and its need to walk a far more delicate line between maintaining the ethos of a resistance movement and the responsibilities of a ruling party. This was in sharp contrast to PIJ, which adhered to its mantra that only armed resistance could liberate Palestine, and Hamas arrested two members of PIJ in Khan Younis in 2013 after the latter had sent in mortars during an incursion of Israeli troops into the southern Gaza Strip.[32]

This was not limited to PIJ. Abu al-Saed, the military spokesperson of the Popular Resistance Committees (PRC) in the Gaza Strip, noted that Hamas security forces had arrested a number of members from the Palestinian factions for attempting to fire rockets into Israel.[33] The Palestinian artist Majida Shaheen certainly caught popular sentiment about the Gazan situation when she drew a caricature of Haniyeh nervously trying to tame

---

30    Asmaa al-Ghoul, 'Hamas, Islamic Jihad Clash over Mosque', *al-Monitor*, August 21, 2013.

31    Hani Ibrahim, 'Hamas' Growing Rivalry with Islamic Jihad', *al-Akhbar*, April 16, 2014.

32    'Hamas tawaqqaf unsurayn min 'al-jihad' ba'd itlaq qadha'if athna' tawaghul Isra'il', *al-Hayat*, November 15, 2013.

33    Hazem Balousha, 'Hamas a Spectator in Latest Gaza-Israel Clash', *al-Monitor*, March 14, 2014.

an angry dog with 'al-Quds Brigades' written on its collar.[34] While Hamas failed on multiple occasions to participate in military actions against the Israeli occupation, PIJ found itself at the forefront and pushing further. 'The decision of war is not in the hands of a government or an authority,' the senior PIJ member Muhammad al-Hindi defiantly declared in September 2014. 'Everyone knows that we are not a real state, that both the Gaza Strip and the West Bank are occupied and that the enemy is the one that started the hostilities. Is the resistance supposed to sit and wait for the war decision to be made?'[35]

This new Gazan reality, in which PIJ began to sideline Hamas in the armed resistance, could only add to these tensions. In the period following the Arab Spring and the regional shifts, PIJ enjoyed considerable growth in the Gaza Strip and became the second-largest military force there. In terms of military power, only Hamas surpassed it. PIJ also experienced a rapid growth in its public appeal. While 13.5 per cent of Gaza's population preferred PIJ in April 2014, 30.8 per cent of the same population supported the movement in September 2014 after the Israeli bombing campaign, Operation Protective Edge.[36] PIJ's ability to grow was partly connected to popular Palestinian sentiment. This was the case during its drought in the 1990s and its resurgence during the Second Intifada. Much indicates that the support for armed resistance was a factor explaining the rapid growth of PIJ under Hamas rule in Gaza from 2007. In Gaza, 60.3 per cent of the Palestinian population believed armed resistance was the most appropriate means to attain Palestinian rights in 2014, while only 6.5 per cent believed in negotiations. PIJ would therefore necessarily thrive as long as Hamas adhered to a restraining line as the ruling party.[37] As a merchant in Gaza explained, 'We have no other option; certainly no diplomatic option. That's why we support Islamic Jihad.'[38]

---

34    Asmaa al-Ghoul, 'Gaza Political Cartoonist Faces Censorship, Death Threats', *al-Monitor*, February 26, 2014.

35    Quoted in Asmaa al-Ghoul, 'Islamic Jihad's Popularity Grows after Gaza War', *al-Monitor*, September 25, 2014.

36    Rasha Abou Jalal, 'Islamic Jihad Gains Support in Gaza as Hamas Declines', *al-Monitor*, April 10, 2014; al-Ghoul, 'Islamic Jihad's Popularity Grows after Gaza War'.

37    Abou Jalal, 'Islamic Jihad Gains Support in Gaza as Hamas Declines'.

38    Quoted in Roni Shaked, 'And the Loser Is: Hamas', *al-Monitor*, March 21, 2012.

The increasing popularity of PIJ was also assisted by the development of the Arab Spring. As discussed in the next section, PIJ maintained relatively good relations with its foreign benefactors until about 2015. Similarly, the realignment of the political map in the Middle East does not seem to have initially favoured Hamas, as it grew closer to the so-called Sunni axis. Muhammad Hijazi noted that many Palestinians were suspicious of the 'moderation axis' of Qatar, Turkey, and the Muslim Brotherhood in Egypt, as many perceived it as Hamas getting closer to a 'US sphere of understanding'. PIJ, on the other hand, maintained its unequivocal positions such as never accepting a state on the 1967 borders.[39]

While Hamas according to some estimates had received up to $150 million annually from Iran, in addition to military support and training, the distancing of Hamas from Bashar al-Assad's Syrian regime resulted in a decline of Iranian financial support.[40] According to other sources, aid to Hamas was cut off completely while Iran increased its support for PIJ.[41] The financial imbalance in Iranian funding to Hamas and PIJ manifested itself through the military development of the latter in Gaza. In March 2012, PIJ managed to lead a four-day military battle of some magnitude against Israel for the first time in its history.[42] This development continued when PIJ developed into a more cohesive, organized, and flexible militant organization, as shown during the fighting with Israel two years later, in 2014.[43]

The military development and professionalization of PIJ between 2011 and 2014 had decisive intra-Palestinian repercussions. While PIJ stated in 2012 that it had won the battle against Israel, Hamas had effectively been pushed into a corner with increasing criticism of its rule with electricity and water-supply problems.[44] Even worse, the self-constraint of Hamas strengthened the image many Palestinians had of it as yet another version

39    Al-Ghoul, 'Islamic Jihad: "We Will Not Accept a State on the 1967 Borders"', al-Monitor, May 12, 2013, al-monitor.com.

40    Asmaa al-Ghoul, 'Hamas Isolated as Iran Boosts Ties with Islamic Jihad, Fatah', al-Monitor, February 12, 2014.

41    Shlomi Eldar, 'Hamas Trapped between Israel, Islamic Jihad', al-Monitor, March 14, 2014.

42    As'ad Talhami, 'Awsat Isra'iliyya ta'tabir 'al-jihad' al-rabih al-akbar wa wazir yad'u ila dars furas al-tafawud ma' Hamas', al-Hayat, March 15, 2012.

43    Al-Ghoul, 'Islamic Jihad's Popularity Grows after Gaza War'.

44    Shaked, 'And the Loser Is'.

of Fatah in the Gaza Strip.[45] The split between Hamas and Fatah was even reported to be a source of new members for PIJ.[46] The new circumstances in the Gaza Strip developed into a win–win situation for PIJ, as the movement continued its confrontations with Israel, which earned it increased support among Palestinians. Hamas was, meanwhile, blamed for the deteriorating situation in Gaza, accelerated by the Israeli bombing campaigns. As Baconi notes: 'Hamas's popular support is now shaped by the quality of its administration within the Gaza Strip and not by its commitment to resistance.'[47]

Coupled with PIJ's ability to maintain cordial relations with several Arab states at once, the increased importance and sophistication of its armed activity also sidelined Hamas diplomatically. Although some group leaders in Hamas voiced their support for the fighting in 2012, it showed itself unable to stop PIJ from firing rockets from the Gaza Strip and had to appeal to Egyptian authorities to broker a truce agreement.[48] Even worse, when PIJ fired a new round of rockets against Israel in 2014, the Egyptian intelligence services went as far as to broker a truce with PIJ without contacting Hamas, demonstrating the increasing impotence of the latter. As Ghazi Hamad, a Hamas senior official, noted, 'Egypt did not communicate with us about a return to calm, and limited its contact to Islamic Jihad. The Egyptians did not inform us of any agreements, despite the fact that they should coordinate with Hamas [regarding such matters].'[49]

## Iranian Palestine

Iran's entry into Palestine did not start with the Palestinian Islamists. Instead, it came through the Palestine Liberation Organzation (PLO). Ayatollah Ruhollah Khomeini was a principled pro-Palestinian and he was ardently against Israel. When he was exiled in Paris, the PLO provided Khomeini with bodyguards; leading personalities in the Iranian Revolutionary Guard Corps received training in the PLO camps in Lebanon.

45   Talhami, 'Awsat Isra'iliyya ta'tabir 'al-jihad'.
46   'Inqisam yankhur 'al-jihad al-islami', al-Akhbar, November 7, 2008.
47   Baconi, Hamas Contained, 234.
48   Al-Akhbar, 'Inqisam yankhur 'al-jihad al-islami'.
49   Quoted in Balousha, 'Hamas a Spectator in Latest Gaza-Israel Clash'.

In a highly symbolic move, Arafat became the first foreign leader to visit Iran after the Islamic revolution as the Israeli embassy in Tehran was handed to the Palestinians.[50]

Iran's support for the Palestinians had always been ideologically driven, given Jerusalem's religious significance, and the new Iranian constitution affirmed its duty to provide 'unsparing support for the dispossessed of the world', to wit, to export its revolution.[51] Yet, by the mid-1980s, the rationale had begun to shift. While Iran was still prepared to encourage regional opposition forces, the motivation was expanding Iranian interests rather than pursuing vague ideological aspirations. The shift was largely caused by the inevitable learning curve and adjustment process of revolutionary Iran coupled by its inability to win its war against Iraq.[52] By the 1990s, Iran had developed a security-centred foreign policy in which Palestinian armed groups were perceived as integral to contain and preoccupy Israel, which, along with the United States, was perceived as the greatest threat to its security and domestic stability.

Israel's deportations – described as a strategy to 'systematically wipe out' the indigenous Palestinian leadership in the occupied Palestinian territories and to physically eliminate leaders able to rally resistance – inadvertently facilitated Iran's cooperation with Hamas and PIJ.[53] Iranian officials first made contact with PIJ in Beirut in the late 1980s after Israel expelled Fathi al-Shiqaqi, Ziyad al-Nakhala, and other of the movement's incarcerated leaders to Lebanon. By this time Palestinian Islamists had concluded, like the PLO before them, that they needed a strong state sponsor to succeed in their struggle against Israel. This soon translated into financial and military support from Iran, with Palestinian militants receiving training in the Beqaa Valley in Lebanon, in camps run by the

---

50    Jørgen Jensehaugen, 'A Palestinian Window of Opportunity? The PLO, the US and the Iranian Hostage Crisis', *British Journal of Middle Eastern Studies* 48, no. 4 (August 2021): 601.

51    Abbas William Samii, 'A Stable Structure on Shifting Sands: Assessing the Hizbullah-Iran-Syria Relationship', *Middle East Journal* 62, no. 1 (2008): 34–5.

52    Shireen Hunter, 'Iran's Pragmatic Regional Policy', *Journal of International Affairs* 56, no. 2 (2003): 139; Gary Sick, 'Iran: The Adolescent Revolution', *Journal of International Affairs* 49, no. 1 (1995): 157.

53    Ann M. Lesch, 'Israeli Deportation of Palestinians from the West Bank and the Gaza Strip, 1967–1978', *Journal of Palestine Studies* (1979): 108.

Iranian-backed Lebanese group Hezbollah.[54] By 1993, al-Shiqaqi told *Newsday*: 'Iran gives us money and supports us, then we supply the money and arms to the occupied territories and support the families of our people.'[55]

Israel also used this strategy on Hamas, as 415 Palestinian Islamists (the majority Hamas) were deported to the Lebanese no-man's-land Marj al-Zuhur in 1992, a move that ultimately backfired. Left in limbo, the Islamist deportees refused relocating to Beirut, Damascus, or other diaspora capitals, which would have effectively made their exile permanent. Establishing the Camp of Return, the deportation turned into a blessing in disguise for Hamas, which rose to international prominence. Suddenly journalists and researchers arrived to interview Hamas senior members about the movement, what they stood for, and their aspirations. Senior figures such as Abdel Aziz al-Rantisi and Mahmud al-Zahar were regularly featured in international news outlets such as CNN. On Christmas night, Aziz Dwayk featured on *Larry King Live*, where he wished all Christians a merry Christmas.[56]

The Israeli decision to deport the Islamists also backfired because it bolstered Iranian–Palestinian ties. In addition to journalists, Hezbollah and Iranian Revolutionary Guard Corps representatives visited the camp, where they offered to help the Palestinians. Although the links were not considered high level in the 1990s, the meetings mattered for two reasons. First, they established direct communication channels between the parties, a foundation for further collaboration, and senior members from the Qassam Brigades were reportedly receiving training in Iran from 1993.[57] Second, the Palestinian Islamists' use of suicide bombings beginning in 1993 was likely influenced by their Lebanese counterparts, who willingly shared their experiences and know-how with the Palestinian camp dwellers. As Tamimi hypothesized: 'It could not have been a

---

54   Skare, *A History of Palestinian Islamic Jihad*, 107.

55   Quoted in Matthew Levitt, 'Sponsoring Terrorism: Syria and Islamic Jihad', Washington Institute, December 1, 2002, washingtoninstitute.org.

56   Azzam Tamimi, *Hamas: Unwritten Chapters* (London: Hurst, 2009), 69.

57   Elad Ben-Dror, '"We Were Getting Close to God, Not Deportees": The Expulsion to Marj al-Zuhur in 1992 as a Milestone in the Rise of Hamas', *Middle East Journal* 74, no. 3 (November 2020): 410–11; Beverley Milton-Edwards and Stephen Farrell, *Hamas: The Islamic Resistance Movement* (Cambridge: Polity Press, 2010), 224.

coincidence that the first martyrdom operation was carried out in Palestine in the year after the return of the Hamas and [PIJ] deportees from South Lebanon'.[58] Shallah similarly confirmed that PIJ's use of suicide bombings in the 1990s was influenced by Hezbollah's tactics.[59]

Hamas and PIJ always differed in how they perceived an alliance with Iran. The founding fathers of PIJ were accused by the Palestinian Muslim Brotherhood for being Shiites in disguise and Iranian agents when Islamist disputes were at their height in 1980s Gaza. There were correspondingly conflicting feelings within Hamas about the alliance with Iran. Just as the outside leadership opted for escalating military operations to avoid marginalization in the 1990s while the inside leadership sought accommodation with the PLO and the PA, so the outside leadership worked for rapprochement with Iran while the inside wished to strengthen relations with Arab (Sunni) countries.[60] Hamas's international portfolio was largely diversified for the next decade, and Iranian supplies of material support, finances, and weaponry only rose exponentially after Hamas's electoral victory when Western aid for Palestinian administrative institutions in Gaza dried up.[61]

PIJ had its own set of conflicts pertaining to Iran, and problems reportedly began to appear in 1990–91 because of growing contradictions within its leadership regarding its support for the Iranian revolution. Although al-Shiqaqi was unquestionably inspired by the example of the Iranian Revolution, he was nevertheless so 'within certain limits, given the difference of circumstances between Iran's Islamic revolution and the situation in the occupied territories'.[62] It was this political line that is thought to have made a number of PIJ cadres leave the movement, as they believed that the Iranian revolutionary line had to be fully emulated.

---

58   Tamimi, *Hamas*, 163.
59   Ghassan Charbel, 'Ziyara li-dhakirat al-amin al-amm li-harakat al-jihad al-islami fi Filastin 1. al-Jihad itlaqat awwal amaliyya istishhadiyya fi Filastin am 1993 wa-l-muqawama al-lubnaniyya iftahat al-amaliyyat al-istishhadiyya bi tafjir maqarr al-marinz fi 1983', *al-Hayat*, January 7, 2003.
60   Leila Seurat, *The Foreign Policy of Hamas: Ideology, Decision Making and Political Supremacy* (London: I. B. Tauris, 2022), 30–1.
61   Milton-Edwards and Farrell, *Hamas*, 225.
62   Zaki Shihab, ''al-Jihad al-islami' al-Filastini fi ghayab qa'idihi: shallah 'ala nahj al-Shiqaqi al-siyasa . . . wa 'amaliyyat intihariyya', *al-Hayat*, November 6, 1995.

Allegedly, al-Shiqaqi was forced in this period to exclude a number of senior members who had 'adopted the Iranian line', although it is unclear what this meant in practice.[63]

Although their approaches to Iran differed, strategic necessity meant that the outside leaderships of both Hamas and PIJ were based in Syria, an Iranian strategic ally, from the 1990s. Outside the reach of the Israelis, Syria offered a suitable environment for the outside leaderships of the Palestinian Islamist movements, as they could move freely within the region and host diplomats visiting the country. The Damascus platform was strategically important to both, and the eruption of the Syrian popular uprising in March 2011 thus posed a conundrum for them – particularly so by mid-2012, when the unrest developed into a full-blown civil war. Hamas and PIJ now watched haplessly as not just Syrians, but also Palestinians, were arrested, tortured, and executed by a regime whose sole aim was survival. It was practically impossible for either of them to criticize a regime that had provided them with unfailing diplomatic support and protection for over a decade.[64] The different strategies of Hamas and PIJ in the 2010s show how Palestinian–Iranian relations were a marriage of convenience because Palestinian Islamist groups shared Iran's anti-Israel sentiments but disagreed with its regional agenda. It also shows how Hamas failed in its gamble on changing diplomatic course while PIJ had few opportunities to do so because it had grown dependent on Iranian aid.

Initially, Hamas's Damascus-based leaders attempted to mediate between the Syrian regime and Sunni insurgents. The group's political leadership nevertheless refused Iranian demands to provide unconditional support for Syria's president, Bashar al-Assad, leading to a rift in relations. The rupture prompted a gradual evacuation of Hamas representatives starting in December 2011, culminating in the complete departure of its external leadership by February 2012. On September 30 of the same year, head of Hamas's political bureau, Khalid Mishal, publicly declared his support for the Syrian revolution.[65]

---

63    Jamal Khashoqji, Faysal al-Shaboul, and Abd al-Latif Furati, "Hamas' takhattat li-warithat al-munazzama. Mu'arada li-l-iqtital murfaqa bi-tahdhir li-l-shurta al-Filastiniyya ightiyal mas'ul fi 'fath' wa Ghazza takhsha al-rasasa al-ula', *al-Hayat*, September 27, 1993.

64    Seurat, *The Foreign Policy of Hamas*, 89.

65    Erik Skare, 'Iran, Hamas, and Islamic Jihad: A Marriage of Convenience', European Council of Foreign Relations, December 18, 2023, ecfr.eu.

The decision to break with Syria also adversely affected Hamas's relationship with Iran, a close ally of Syria. Iran had cut its annual funding to Hamas from $150 million to less than $75 million by mid-2012 and then reduced it by half again by mid-2013.[66] Anticipating a reduction in Iranian funding, Hamas gambled on the prospects of democracy in the region. The electoral victory of the Egyptian Muslim Brotherhood in June 2012, for instance, buoyed Hamas's hopes that Egypt might serve as a new patron. As Iran never completely severed its financial support for the movement, it allowed Hamas to enjoy a combination of Iranian military, financial and diplomatic support from regional allies of the US, such as Turkey and Qatar.[67] This strategy, as discussed later, proved untenable.

PIJ chose another approach. Its strategy was to claim neutrality, and the movement refrained from directing any criticism of the Syrian regime.[68] 'We do not interfere in what is happening in Syria,' Khadr Habib noted. 'This is an internal affair.'[69] When both Shallah and his deputy, Ziyad al-Nakhala, left Damascus in 2012, their departure came only after alleged consultations with Iran and Hezbollah, and it was stated that it was an issue of security and not of a political realignment.[70] With regime after regime falling in the Arab world, PIJ adhered to the same policy as it pursued in the Palestinian arena: complete neutrality. In the words of Shallah, PIJ adhered to a 'principled pragmatism' in order to preserve the movement's alliances in the Palestinian arena and in the region.[71] The rationale of its principled pragmatism was the perceived necessity of keeping the Palestinian struggle outside internecine regional struggles to avoid making Palestine 'just another regional flashpoint'. This could be achieved only if the Palestinian factions agreed that the Palestinian cause had to remain apart from regional struggles and that Arab and non-Arab actors recognized Palestine's 'specificity and circumstances'.[72]

---

66   Ibid., 90–6.

67   Byman, 'Curious Victory', 65–6.

68   'al-Jihad tanfi mughadarat mas'uli al-haraka bi-Dimashq', al-Resalah, July 21, 2012.

69   'Abna' an i'tiqal najl qiyadi fi 'al-jihad al-islami' bi-Suriya', CNN, June 17, 2012.

70   'Harakat al-jihad al-islami taghadar Suriya', al-Jazeera, August 3. 2012.

71   Ibrahim Humeidi, 'Islamic Jihad Leader Discusses Iran, Reconciliation, Syria', al-Monitor, May 22, 2014.

72   'Interview with Ramadan Shallah (Part II)', Journal of Palestine Studies 44, no. 3 (2015): 39–48.

PIJ had few illusions about the Arab regimes, and a member of PIJ's political bureau, Anwar Abu Taha, made its position clear:

These Arab regimes are authoritarian, they kill their people, they are the agent of the West, and they take their orders from the White House, from London and Paris. The presidents are not democratically elected, and we are for a democratic political life in the Arab world under free and fair elections and circulation of power. We are with economic independence and against corruption and theft . . . and [we are] not with the interests of those who want the oil. So we are with those who rose up, with the Arab revolutions, and with the Arab Spring.[73]

Yet PIJ understood that it was strategically sensitive to openly support the people's quest for freedom, recognizing that the Arab regimes represented a political reality the movement could not afford to ignore. In the case of the Syrian civil war, Abu Taha noted that any intervention by PIJ would not only fail to alter the course of the war, but it could exacerbate strife and undermine the movement's efforts against the Israeli occupation. Similarly, while the movement was ideologically opposed to the Egyptian regime of Abdel Fattah al-Sisi, the political and geographical realities of Gaza forced PIJ to adhere to neutrality in practice.

By 2013, PIJ had managed to keep out of the new political axes being formed in the region through its adherence to neutrality. This neutrality seemingly had an expiration date, however, as its relationship with Iran began to deteriorate by 2015. As civil war broke out in Yemen, and Saudi Arabia intervened in a bombing campaign, Iran reportedly asked PIJ to issue a statement on the crisis, supporting the Houthis while condemning the bombing campaign. PIJ defiantly refused.[74] When Iranian radio stations then subsequently stated that the leadership of PIJ supported the Houthis, PIJ strongly reiterated its opposition to intervention in the internal affairs of other Arab countries. Accordingly, Iran chose to cut funding for PIJ, and instead reallocated it for the newly established al-Sabirin movement in Gaza.[75] An anonymous PIJ leader noted, 'The

73   Anwar Abu Taha, interview with Erik Skare, March 19, 2018.
74   'al-Quds: Shallah yughadir Teheran wa khilafat kabira awqafat da'm Iran li-l-haraka', Amadnews, May 20, 2015; Kareem Asakira, 'Madha yahduth dakhil harakat al-jihad al-islami?', Ma'n News, May 16, 2015.
75   Fatima al-Smadi, 'Analysis: Hamas, Islamic Jihad, Redefining Relations with Iran', al-Jazeera, September 20, 2015.

Iranians are no longer accepting neutral positions, and they are starting to put pressure on the movement to adopt a clear and unambiguous position and to support them in all major regional issues, especially in the Syrian and the Yemeni issues.[76] Moreover, although Abu Taha rejected the claim that Iran had cut its funding to PIJ in its entirety, he nevertheless noted that the Arab Spring had affected their relationship negatively: 'The affected relationship did not reach the level of cutting Iranian financing, but the relationship is affected. If you have two friends, they will anger each other. Okay, so what? But, the relationship is not as it used to be.'[77]

Iran's choice to cut funding hit PIJ hard because it had no other major benefactor. Reports surfaced describing how PIJ had to lay off workers in its civic and research institutions.[78] The same applied to PIJ's West Bank employees working for the movement's news agency, Palestine Today, while its capacities in the Gaza Strip were constrained by financial difficulties.[79] By December 2015, PIJ had failed to pay salaries for three months.[80] During this period of strained relationship with Iran, PIJ attempted to solve the financial problem by looking for alternative sources of financial support. In 2015, reports surfaced that Algerian authorities had begun financing PIJ 'humanitarian projects'. Al-Hindi notably travelled to Turkey and Algeria to obtain financial support, and the movement also established direct communication channels with Saudi Arabia while moving closer to Egypt and Jordan to alleviate its financial difficulties. This support never exceeded that previously provided by Iran, and was limited to sporadic payments, 'according to the possibilities and circumstances' of the two parties.[81]

Then, somewhat unexpectedly, Iran renewed its financial aid to PIJ when the Iranian Revolutionary Guard pledged a $70 million transfer

---

76    Ali Wakid, 'Qiyadi fi al-jihad al-islami: 'al-Iraniyyun lam ya'udu yaqbalun mawaqif muhayida', al-Masdar, May 28, 2015.

77    Anwar Abu Taha, interview with Erik Skare, March 19, 2018.

78    Hazem Balousha, 'Islamic Jihad's Coffers Run Dry', al-Monitor, June 2, 2015.

79    Wakid, 'Qiyadi fi al-jihad al-islami'.

80    'Tawasul al-azma al-maliyya li-l-jihad al-islami', al-Masdar, December 28, 2015.

81    'al-Quds: Shallah yughadir Teheran'; 'Azmat al-jihad al-islami al-maliyya tatasa'ud: Hal hasalat al-haraka ala tamwil min al-jaza'ir?', al-Watan Voice, December 28, 2015; Adham Manasra, 'Intakhabat "al-jihad al-islami": Tiba'ud ma' Iran?', al-Mudun, September 30, 2018.

to the movement in May 2016.[82] This transfer was seemingly not a free lunch. One month later, al-Manar stated that PIJ stood with the Yemeni people against [foreign] aggression, and that to target Yemen was equal to targeting the Palestinian cause.[83] If true, it seems that one year was the approximate time required before PIJ was forced to renounce its principled pragmatism and neutrality. Whatever the true causes, the newspaper *al-Masdar* commented about this development: 'It is clear that [PIJ] is no longer the spoiled son.'[84]

Hamas's gamble on regional shifts also failed – mainly because of the counter-revolutionary wave hitting the region. Egypt, for example, never became the new patron of Hamas, as the government of Mohamed Morsi was ousted in a coup d'état on July 3, 2013. A decision by his successor, President Abdel Fattah al-Sisi, to reinforce Egypt's blockade on Gaza from July 2013 onwards made this short-lived reorientation politically and financially unfeasible for Hamas. Saudi Arabia, Egypt, and the United Arab Emirates also pursued a foreign policy in the region against the Muslim Brotherhood and its affiliates with a collective blockade of Qatar, the new headquarters of Hamas. While Hamas had broken off relations with Iran after it received Qatari promises of patronage and financial support for the reconstruction of Gaza, the movement soon discovered that the hereditary Gulf monarchy was unwilling to replace, or incapable of replacing, Iranian funding.[85] Despite sustained efforts, PIJ similarly failed securing alternative regional backing. Luckily for PIJ, Iran had no viable replacement in the occupied Palestinian territories. The short-lived al-Sabirin Movement, which Iran established in Gaza to compete with PIJ, was frail, and without any popular backing or military infrastructure it quickly died. Neither the Palestinian Islamists nor Iran could afford a divorce.[86]

The visit of Hamas senior member Khalil al-Hayya to Damascus in October 2022 effectively ended nearly a decade of hostility between

---

82    Maayan Groisman, 'Iran to Renew Financial Support for Islamic Jihad after Two-Year Hiatus', *Jerusalem Post*, May 25, 2016.

83    'Harakat al-jihad al-islami tu'akkid mawqifha al-thabit ila janib al-sha'b al-yamani didd al-'adw', *al-Manar*, June 1, 2016.

84    Wakid, 'Qiyadi fi al-jihad al-islami'.

85    Seurat, *The Foreign Policy of Hamas*, 132.

86    Afshon Ostovar, 'Iran, Its Clients, and the Future of the Middle East: The Limits of Religion', *International Affairs* 94, no. 6 (2018): 1247–8.

Hamas and the Syrian regime, demonstrating its return to the Iranian fold and the failure of its earlier regional manoeuvring and realignments. Having received insufficient support from Arab capitals, Hamas was forced to return to Damascus and Tehran in order to preserve its interests. Rapprochement also reflected the failure of Western policy insofar as the international isolation of Hamas pushed the movement back into the fold of the Islamic Republic.

The resumption of Iranian–Palestinian diplomatic ties added to the changing dynamics within Hamas. While the outside leadership of Hamas had been the dominant force within the movement for the last three decades, its command had slowly begun to deteriorate. Gradually, the influence and power of the Gazan leadership grew. One factor contributing to the strengthening of the inside leadership, Seurat notes, was Hamas's electoral victory and the emergence and growth of Gaza's tunnel economy under blockade. The revenues generated from trade and smuggling meant that the internal leadership of Hamas and the Qassam Brigades grew less dependent on the outside for funding. Another, she continues, was the diplomatic failure of Hamas in the 2010s, for which the outside leadership was responsible. While Mishal and his deputy Musa Abu Marzuq cut their ties to Iran, the inside leadership and the Qassam Brigades maintained strong links with the Islamic Republic.[87] Continued Iranian aid to Hamas's military wing added to the Qassam Brigades' autonomy and to strengthening its influence within the movement. The deputy of Muhammad Deif, Marwan Issa, reportedly travelled to Tehran whenever possible. The rising prominence of the militant wing translated into political influence; three Qassam militants joined Hamas's political bureau in 2013, as the Qassam Brigades now had a direct role in Hamas's political decision-making process.[88] Mishal, conversely, barely managed to secure re-election. Although the outside leadership had traditionally enjoyed the role of hardliners, the Gazan inside leadership had turned more uncompromising, more militant, and more intransigent. The experience of ruling Gaza under blockade and international isolation strengthened their sentiment that the democratic experiment of the Hamas moderates had failed.

---

87    Leila Seurat, 'Hamas's Goal in Gaza', *Foreign Affairs*, December 11, 2023.

88    Ibid.

If anything, the Arab Spring prompted a shift in Hamas's internal power balance from the outside to the inside, from Damascus to Gaza City. This shift was largely cemented when Ismail Haniyeh succeeded Mishal as the head of Hamas's political bureau in 2017. Partly to circumvent the restrictions the Egyptian blockade imposed on Gaza and to maintain diplomatic engagements, Haniyeh relocated to Doha, Qatar, in December 2019. Though unremarkable on its own, the move caused ripple effects within the movement, as it facilitated the rise of Yahya Sinwar, the former Majd militant, to the very top of Hamas in Gaza.[89]

## The Return of Sinwar

We feel that we have left our hearts behind. We have left many prisoners behind, from the Izz ad-Din al-Qassam and the al-Quds Brigades. We left Mohammed Issa behind. We left Hassan Salameh behind . . . I call upon the leaders of the resistance groups and the Izz ad-Din al-Qassam Brigades to take it upon themselves to free all the prisoners soon. I call upon those who have the ability to take part in doing so. – Yahya Sinwar upon his release from prison in 2011[90]

On June 25, 2006, eight Palestinian militants from the Qassam Brigades, the Popular Resistance Committee, and the Army of Islam dug their way out at the southern end of Gaza. Approaching silently, the militants took an Israeli tank unit by surprise and killed two Israeli soldiers. Another two Israelis were wounded; one of them, Sergeant Gilad Shalit, was dragged away through the border fence. The Israelis responded by shelling the Gaza Strip, killing 1,390 Palestinians, of whom 454 were women and children. When a ceasefire was reached four months later, in November, Shalit was still nowhere to be found.[91]

Negotiations for the release of Shalit persisted through the unofficial backchannels established between Hamas and Israeli authorities. After

---

89  Ibid.

90  Quoted in Avi Issacharoff, 'Rising New Hamas Leader Is All Too Familiar to Israel', *Times of Israel*, December 18, 2015.

91  Ronen Bergman, 'Gilad Shalit and the Rising Price for an Israeli Life', *New York Times*, November 9, 2011.

years of trust-building, both parties were ready to reach a settlement in 2011, Shalit in exchange for 1,027 Palestinian prisoners. Israeli Prime Minister Benyamin Netanyahu conveyed a readiness to compromise due to the intense domestic pressure he was facing, and Hamas was ready to accept, with the pressure its leaders were facing from the Arab Spring and the movement's uncertain future in Syria. There was also growing unrest within Hamas's political leadership about al-Qassam commander al-Ja'bari aiming to extend the negotiations indefinitely without commitment. When the negotiations succeeded, it was partly because the political leadership forced the final agreement on the Qassam Brigades.[92]

Yahya Sinwar had by then been incarcerated for twenty-two years. Having failed escaping prison twice, he remained a part of Hamas's leadership and was repeatedly elected to represent the movement in the prisoners' representative body.[93] He also planned several armed operations and kidnapping campaigns from the inside – albeit with the same success rate as his prison breaks. Sinwar was reportedly against the Shalit deal, although he himself was included, because he perceived it as providing too many concessions to the Israelis. In fact, when the negotiations reached a crucial stage, Sinwar was moved to solitary confinement for fear of his thwarting the prisoner exchange.[94]

We do not know what Sinwar must have felt when he returned to Gaza and witnessed the changes that had transpired over the past two decades. One thing was the desolation of the Gaza Strip, whose population had more than doubled from 589,000 in 1988 to 1.6 million in 2011.[95] The Israeli–Egyptian blockade against Gaza had destroyed its economy in a collective punishment of the Strip's population. They were effectively confined in what can only be described as an open-air prison. The de-development of Gaza persisted with unrelenting force throughout the 2010s. By 2022, nearly 80 per cent of Gaza's population depended on aid,

---

92    Ibid.
93    Motasem A Dalloul, 'The New Leader of Hamas in Gaza Is Yahya al-Sinwar', *Middle East Monitor*, February 13, 2017.
94    Ben Caspit, 'Why Some in Israel Are Wary of Hamas' New Gaza Boss', *al-Monitor*, February 15, 2017.
95    Wael R. Ennab, *Population and Demographic Developments in the West Bank and Gaza Strip Until 1990* (Geneva: United Nations, 1994), 64; Palestinian Central Bureau of Statistics, *Palestine in Figures 2011* (Ramallah: Palestinian Central Bureau of Statistics, 2012), 8.

with food insecurity reaching 65.9 per cent. Almost half of its population suffered from multidimensional poverty.[96] More than half of its population was unemployed by 2018, while the numbers for its youth population exceeded 70 per cent.[97] Almost half of Gaza's population were children, and a sixteen-year-old would by 2023 have experienced four wars and a countless number of skirmishes, airstrikes, and cross-border armed confrontations. The *Report of the United Nations Fact-Finding Mission on the Gaza Conflict* (also known as the Goldstone Report) stated in 2009 that the primary purpose of restricting goods into Gaza was 'to bring about a situation in which the civilian population would find life so intolerable that they would leave (if that were possible) or turn Hamas out of office, as well as to collectively punish the civilian population'.[98]

It is also unclear what Sinwar thought about the changes taking place within his own movement, Hamas. As Issacharoff notes, when Sinwar was imprisoned in 1988, Hamas was a clandestine movement, and its military apparatus was a small network of military cells. Now, Hamas was the government and responsible for the social welfare and administration in Gaza. The Qassam Brigades was the de facto security service in the Strip. Sinwar had been personally close to the spiritual guide of Hamas, Ahmad Yasin, and militants like Salah Shahada. Now, the upper echelons of the movement were filled by a professional class of politicians 'who had forgotten what it was like to be on the run or in prison'.[99] While Hamas oversaw the administration of the Strip and was blamed for its deteriorating conditions, PIJ – unencumbered by the inconvenient responsibilities of governance – could keep stressing the need for armed struggle to achieve its maximalist aspirations.

Sinwar rapidly rose in the Hamas hierarchy. Seniority, his credentials from the armed Palestinian struggle, and the time he had served in prison meant that Sinwar's influence on the military wing, and their loyalty

96    Yazan Ajamieh et al., *West Bank and Gaza: Selected Issues* (Washington, DC: International Monetary Fund, 2023), 5–6.

97    'Food Insecurity in the oPt: 1.3 Million Palestinians in the Gaza Strip Are Food Insecure', United Nations Office for the Coordination of Humanitarian Affairs, December 14, 2018, ochaopt.org.

98    United Nations, *Human Rights in Palestine and Other Occupied Arab Territories: Report of the United Nations Fact-Finding Mission on the Gaza Conflict* (Geneva: United Nations, 2009), 256–7.

99    Issacharoff, 'Rising New Hamas Leader Is All Too Familiar to Israel'.

in return, were unquestionable. His brother, Muhammad, served as a prominent military commander in the Qassam Brigades, which created an important communication channel between the wings. By 2015, Sinwar was the de facto security minister of Hamas, with the responsibility for conducting negotiations with Israel for the release of Hamas prisoners in Israel in exchange for the bodies of two killed Israeli soldiers and the release of two Israelis, Mengistu and al-Sayed, who had wandered into Gaza and been captured.[100]

The position of Sinwar also strengthened within the Qassam Brigades. Senior al-Qassam leader al-Ja'bari was assassinated in November 2012, which meant Muhammad Deif had to retake the leadership role in the military wing. Still, Deif was reportedly physically weakened after surviving at least five assassination attempts between 2001 and 2014. In the first assassination attempt, Deif lost an eye and part of his arm. He was also severely wounded the second time, in 2006, with reports of losing additional limbs, and Deif was forced to undergo a series of orthopaedic treatments and vacate his position to al-Ja'bari. Paralyzed and with prolonged periods of rehabilitation, his deputy Marwan Issa took control of the daily affairs. On August 18, 2014, during Operation Protective Edge, the Israelis dropped a one-ton bomb on Deif's home. After one minute, they dropped another one. His wife, his seven-month-old son, and his three-year-old daughter were killed. Deif survived.[101] His miraculous survival against overwhelming odds – a sign, according to some, of divine protection – gave Deif a legendary status. His severe disabilities and the debilitating headaches from the shrapnel lodged in his head meant that Sinwar and Issa were the ones who effectively held daily command over the Qassam Brigades. As the 'liaison between the military and political wing', some also reported that it was Sinwar who actually pulled the strings in the military wing.[102]

Another factor contributing to the rise of Sinwar was the success with which he framed himself as the polar opposite of other political leaders in Hamas. Mishal frequented luxury hotels, talked with the international press, and lived a relatively affluent life compared to Gazan standards.

---

100    Shlomi Eldar, 'Why Hamas Refused to Return IDF Remains', al-Monitor, July 5, 2016.

101    Caspit, 'Why Some in Israel Are Wary of Hamas' New Gaza Boss'.

102    Shlomi Eldar, 'How Hamas' New Gaza Leader Came to Power', al-Monitor, February 14, 2017.

Sinwar, conversely, remained an ascetic, 'scrupulous about keeping his hands clean' of corruption, and exercised his political capital under modest conditions in Khan Younis refugee camp while shunning the media.[103] Blessed with charisma and a 'flare [*sic*] for the dramatic', Sinwar boldly declared at the end of a live, televised speech in 2021 that he would walk home; he openly challenged the Israelis to assassinate him. As he casually walked through Gaza's streets, Sinwar greeted shopkeepers and stopped to take selfies with enthusiastic admirers.[104] In the internal elections of 2017, Sinwar was elected Hamas's leader in Gaza, succeeding Haniyeh, who moved on to replace Mishal. Observers interpreted the elections as a protest against Hamas's leadership and economic and social policies in Gaza, in addition to the failure to capitalize on the 2014 Gazan war, which instead brought widespread destruction.[105]

The formalization of Sinwar's authority effectively cemented the shift in Hamas's internal power balance. While the external leadership had controlled the Qassam Brigades since the 1990s by overseeing funding, the growth of Gaza's tunnel economy and the strategic redirection of Iranian aid to the military wing bolstered the Gazan leadership's autonomy. By the mid-2010s, reports emerged that the Qassam Brigades had become the de facto rulers, with Muhammad Deif, Marwan Issa, and Yahya Sinwar holding ultimate authority over all decisions.[106] Beyond Sinwar's formal ascension in Hamas's hierarchy, the influence of the Qassam Brigades was also bolstered as its militants swept the local elections in several areas of Gaza.[107] After operating with strict separations between Hamas's political and military wings for almost twenty-five years, the lines had now become increasingly blurry.[108] The guns, which Mao Zedong had warned against, had begun commanding the party.

---

103    Peter Beaumont, 'Election of New Hamas Gaza Strip Leader Increases Fears of Confrontation', *Guardian*, February 13, 2017; Caspit, 'Why Some in Israel Are Wary of Hamas' New Gaza Boss'.

104    Ben Hubbard, 'Key Hamas Plotters of Oct. 7 Elude Israel's Grip on Gaza', *New York Times*, December 21, 2023.

105    Rory Jones and Abu Bakr Bashir, 'Hamas Puts Militant Yahya Sinwar in Charge of Gaza', *Wall Street Journal*, February 13, 2017; Beaumont, 'Election of New Hamas Gaza Strip Leader Increases Fears of Confrontation'.

106    Eldar, 'Why Hamas Refused to Return IDF Remains'.

107    Kifah Ziboun, 'Hamas Elects Yahya Sinwar New Leader in Gaza Strip', *Asharq al-Awsat*, February 14, 2017.

108    Eldar, 'How Hamas' New Gaza Leader Came to Power'.

There are thus two ways to view Hamas's effort to revise its charter in 2017. On the one hand, it was obvious that its 1988 charter did the movement few favours. Hamas had, as noted, moderated key positions from the early 1990s, and Hamas leaders and senior members seldom if ever referred to the 1988 charter to explain movement positions. By then, the movement had already shifted away from framing the conflict as part of a global Jewish-crusader conspiracy against Islam.[109] Instead of reflecting Hamas's new position, which distinguished between Judaism as a religion and Zionism as a political movement, the 1988 charter was used by critics to portray the group as intransigent, fundamentalist, and, not least, supposedly anti-Semitic.

On the other hand, the process to revise the charter was also caused by the rise of Hamas's hardliners in the internal elections. Mishal, its architect, hoped that the document would create consensus on all declared Hamas positions and commit 'the new leadership to those positions regardless of any hard-line tendency that some of its members may have'.[110] The polemical language from its 1988 charter was toned down. The anti-Semitic tropes were removed; so was the religious determinism. Its Islamist credentials were softened, and its Palestinian nationalist ones strengthened. Instead of justifying its normative claims with references to religious texts, it now referred to human rights and international law. Its affiliation with the Muslim Brotherhood was now gone. Most important in this context, although Hamas proclaimed that it would never compromise an inch of Palestinian land, it nevertheless opened up for a two-state solution along the 1967 borders by stating that it was part of a Palestinian national consensus.

True, rather than considering the charter a moderation of Hamas, as was the common perception in 2017, it would be more accurate to regard it as flexible given how it operated with a number of grey zones that provided Hamas the necessary flexibility to adapt its political and military strategies in response to changing realities on the ground. As Hroub notes, the 2017 charter was carefully worded and with the deliberate inclusion of opacities on those aforementioned key issues such as a two-state solution and the legitimacy of the State of Israel; the Oslo Agreement and

---

109    Khaled Hroub, *Hamas: Political Thought and Practice* (Washington, DC: Institute for Palestine Studies, 2000), 49.

110    Khaled Hroub, 'A Newer Hamas? The Revised Charter', *Journal of Palestine Studies* 46, no. 4 (2016–17): 108.

the legitimacy of the Palestinian National Authority (PA); and, equally important, the diversification of means and tools of resistance.[111] Also PIJ also reshuffled its upper echelons after the health of its secretary-general, Ramadan Abdallah Shallah, deteriorated, and his deputy, Ziyad al-Nakhala, was elected the new leader. Al-Nakhala had as a young militant joined PIJ from prison and, upon his release, organized the military wing of the movement. Once deported to Lebanon, he became PIJ's representative in Beirut before he ascended as Shallah's deputy after the assassination of al-Shiqaqi in 1995. Reportedly, al-Nakhala was per-sonally close to Qasem Soleimani, commander of the Iranian Quds Force, and politically close to Iran, although he did not display any aspirations to emulate the Iranian line.[112] How ideologically driven his affinity was is nevertheless uncertain. It could just as well come out of the realization that PIJ had no other viable alternatives. Having acted under Shallah's leadership, al-Nakhalah knew all too well from 2015–16 that a light purse was a heavy curse for a movement unfamiliar with self-sufficiency. His leadership, described as hardline and rhetorically fierce, did not signif-icantly alter PIJ's trajectory. His elected deputy, Muhammad al-Hindi, seemed, then, a suitable compromise, as he was reportedly politically closer to the Muslim Brotherhood and Hamas.

The emergence of a hardliner supposedly balanced by his moderate peer – Sinwar and Haniyeh in Hamas and al-Nakhala and al-Hindi in PIJ – was one trend within Palestinian Islamism from the late 2010s. Another one was the overall shift in the Islamist movements' politi-cal centre of gravity, which now moved from the diaspora to the Gaza Strip. Historically, the external leadership of Hamas had overseen both financial resources and the Qassam Brigades since the early 1990s. This control now began to wane in favour of Gaza's leadership due to a series of adverse events, the mismanagement of political leverage within the organization, and unsuccessful bets on regional alliances in the early 2010s. The election of the Gaza resident al-Hindi mirrored a similar tran-sition within PIJ. While only two out of eleven members of PIJ's political bureau were from Gaza before the 2018 internal elections, there were now five. The diaspora held two seats, the West Bank one, and the prisons held

111   Ibid., 100, 109.
112   Ahmad Abu Amer, 'Has Iran's Influence Increased in Palestinian Arena?', al-Monitor, October 15, 2018.

one, with two members remaining undisclosed for security reasons.[113] Above all, this shift illustrates how the blockade on Gaza suffocated its civilian population while providing its armed factions with the required autonomy to learn, strategize, and coordinate with increased operational manoeuvrability.

Because Sinwar was perceived as both 'extremely hardline and at the same time ruthlessly pragmatic', widely differing predictions were traded over the next years.[114] Several referred to his military credentials and predicted that his ascent increased the likelihood for another Gazan–Israeli war. Yet Sinwar quickly declared that he embraced peaceful popular resistance against the Israeli occupation, that he sought a long-term truce with Israel and pushed for negotiations, that another war was not in Hamas's interests, and that he would work for political reconciliation with Mahmoud Abbas and the PA in the West Bank. In fact, Sinwar actively held back, which was interpreted as a dawning realization that Gaza had more to lose than the Israelis.[115] Although he also defended the use of violence to draw attention to the Palestinian cause, he ostensibly proved a more complex political player than initially assumed.[116] Sinwar showed how one could be both moderate and hardliner depending on the issue, and external drivers were key to the political line adopted.

Much indicates that the Israeli suppression of the Great March of Return in 2018 was a crucial turning point. Aspiring to 'revive the peaceful marches as a [Palestinian] tactic of mass resistance' and aiming to initiate an independent, refugee-led protest, the organizers set up tents along the Gazan border. Rallying Palestinians of all ages, genders, and political and social groups, the unifying element was from the onset a shared principle of being unarmed and peaceful. Explicitly referencing the 1948 dispossession of Palestinians, the protesters demanded the right to return to the villages and towns from which they were displaced during the *nakba*.[117]

---

113  Manasra, 'Intakhabat "al-jihad al-islami"'.

114  Quoted in 'The Leader of Hamas in Gaza Is the Most Influential Man in Palestine', *Economist*, May 26, 2018.

115  Raf Sanchez and Abu Bakr Bashir, 'Why Hardline Hamas Leader Yahya Sinwar Is Gambling on an Unlikely Truce with Israel', *Telegraph*, October 3, 2018.

116  'In Interview with Israeli Paper, Hamas Chief Defends Group's Terror Tactics', *Times of Israel*, October 5, 2018.

117  Shourideh C. Molavi, *Environmental Warfare in Gaza: Colonial Violence and New Landscapes of Resistance* (London: Pluto Press, 2024), 81–2.

Initially pervaded by a sense of optimism, national songs were sung, lunches were prepared for families and children, and young girls were dressed in traditional embroidered dresses. Prayers and football matches were performed alike.[118] The encampments also operated with field clinics, food vendors, and cultural activities. Clown shows, live music shows, acrobat shows, dabke dancing, poetry readings, and even wedding celebrations were organized as the encampments developed into sites of cultural production.[119] For many Gazans, the march was initially a reprieve from the suffocating conditions in the Strip.

In its February 2019 report, the independent international commission of inquiry concluded: 'In the commission's view, the demonstrations were civilian in nature, had clearly stated political aims and, despite some acts of significant violence, did not constitute combat or a military campaign.'[120] Notwithstanding, Israeli soldiers were ordered to shoot anyone within several hundred metres of the fence and used considerable force to suppress the protests. Israeli forces, most of whom were snipers, shot and killed 223 Palestinians during the march. Forty-six of them were minors. Amnesty International observed how 'Israeli soldiers shot unarmed protesters, bystanders, journalists and medical staff approximately 150–400 meters from the fence, where they did not pose any threat.' They also fired teargas at the tent encampments set up 400 to 600 metres away from the fence, despite the distance and peaceful nature.[121] By the end of the protests, at least 10,000 people were injured, including nearly 2,000 children.[122] If Sinwar did, in fact, embrace paths of peaceful resistance with genuine hopes they could break the impasse, then the Israeli response to those means decidedly closed that door.

118   Maram Humaid, '"We Want to Return to Our Lands without Bloodshed or Bombs"', *al-jazeera*, March 30, 2018, aljazeera.com.

119   Bram Wispelwey and Yasser Abu Jamel, 'The Great March of Return: Lessons from Gaza on Mass Resistance and Mental Health', *Health and Human Rights Journal* 22, no. 1 (2020): 180; Molavi, *Environmental Warfare in Gaza*, 86.

120   UN Human Rights, 'Report of the Independent International Commission of Inquiry on the Protests in the Occupied Palestinian Territory', February 25, 2019: 5.

121   'Military Fired Teargas at Family Tents Far from Fence during Gaza Protests, Injuring Hundreds', B'Tselem, April 20, 2018, btselem.org.

122   'Six Months On: Gaza's Great March of Return', Amnesty International, October 19, 2018, amnesty.org; see also 'And Now for the Whitewashing', B'Tselem, May 24, 2021, btselem.org.

Ultimately, it must have been clear to Sinwar by the late 2010s that Hamas's governance project had become a net loss for the movement. After over a decade, Hamas was no nearer to lifting the blockade. Its population still suffered from the politically willed poverty, unemployment, and aid-dependence. Israel did not even bother approaching Hamas as a political actor, but instead viewed Gaza as a security issue, an excess population to be pacified indefinitely.[123] Hamas's relationship with Iran had begun to normalize, but even this was a return to the pre-2012 status quo. There were no signs of the reconciliation efforts with the PA in the West Bank bearing fruit. From 2020, the Abraham Accords initiated a normalization process between Israel and several Arab states, while Palestinian–Israeli negotiations remained at an impasse. As the blockade of Gaza normalized and the West Bank remained pacified by the Israeli infrastructure of control, it was clear that the Palestinian cause simply did not seem to be prioritized by the international community.

Hamas's popularity was also declining, and there was growing popular unrest caused by the government's inability to improve living conditions. In March 2019, protests erupted with the slogan 'We want to live', which developed into one of the most serious anti-government protests in Gaza since 2007. 'We're not political and we don't want to change political systems. We just want to get our rights,' one Gazan activist proclaimed. 'We want jobs, we want to live. We want equality, dignity and freedom.'[124] Hamas's answer was to violently crack down on the protesters.

The political costs notwithstanding, the blockade allowed Hamas to develop its military capabilities and infrastructure. Smuggling tunnels in Gaza had existed since 1981, when Bedouin clans on both sides of the Egyptian–Gazan border sought to bypass the demarcation imposed by Egyptian and Israeli authorities. Expanded in the 1990s, the Gazan tunnels were primarily used for smuggling drugs, gold, and other goods earning the smugglers a decent profit. It was with the blockade on Gaza from 2007 on that the tunnels turned into a lifeline, as they were increasingly used to smuggle food, medicine, fuel, and any product required to sustain life beyond the bare minimum.[125] Another, military, tunnel

---

123    Baconi, *Hamas Contained*, 159.

124    Yolanda Knell, 'Gaza Economic Protests Expose Cracks in Hamas's Rule', BBC News, March 18, 2019.

125    Michael Barak, *The 'Tunnel Strategy' among Palestinian Armed Factions in the Gaza Strip* (Herzliya: International Institute for Counter-Terrorism, 2019), 9.

network was also constructed once Hamas ousted Fatah from the Strip, 'a maze of underground concrete bunkers connected with tunnels and multiple entrances and exits underneath the residential areas of Gaza'.[126] Realizing that the Palestinians could not defeat the Israeli occupation military at sea, in the air, or on land, the developing tunnel strategy allowed Hamas to move freely, conduct training exercises, and test weapons far from the gaze of Israeli drones hovering above.[127] As al-Qassam commanders began to understand how Israeli intelligence intercepted their communication, they installed hardwired phone lines in the tunnel networks or returned to the stone age by avoiding laptops or mobile phones. By 2021, Hamas had reportedly dug an underground network exceeding 500 kilometres, with some passages sufficiently large to drive a car through.[128]

The tunnel network was also used to secretly manufacture weapons, and – although far from self-sufficient – Hamas produced a large part of its own arsenal, developed drones and unmanned underwater vehicles, and engaged in cyber warfare.[129] The effort was partly facilitated by Hamas's own efforts and developed over decades of trial and error. Demonstrating remarkable resourcefulness, the movement utilized everything at its disposal, from scrap iron and leftover electrical wiring to undetonated Israeli munitions, to craft improvised explosive devices and rocket tubes. 'Necessity is the mother of inventions', one Hamas member declared to this author when queried about the movement's developing cyber capabilities.[130] The weapons that Hamas could not produce itself were smuggled into Gaza from Iran either by sea or by land, first via Yemen and Sudan and then through the Egyptian desert with the help of Bedouin

126    Eado Hecht, 'Gaza: How Hamas Tunnel Network Grew', BBC News, July 22, 2014.

127    Pelham, 'Hamas's Deadly "Phantom"'.

128    Adolfo Arranz et al., 'Inside the Tunnels of Gaza', Reuters, December 31, 2023; Pamela Brown and Zachary Cohen, 'Hamas Operatives Used Phone Lines Installed in Tunnels under Gaza to Plan Israel Attack over 2 Years, Sources Familiar with Intelligence Say', CNN, October 24, 2023.

129    Madjid Zerrouky, 'Hamas's Relentless Efforts to Build up Its Military Arsenal in Gaza', Le Monde, October 11, 2023; Erik Skare, 'Digital Surveillance/ Militant Resistance: Categorizing the "Proto-state Hacker"', Television and New Media 20, no. 7 (November 2019): 670–85.

130    Quoted in Erik Skare, Digital Jihad: Palestinian Resistance in the Digital Era (London: Zed Books, 2016), 112.

smugglers.[131] Components for ballistic missiles were smuggled into Gaza, where trained al-Qassam personnel constructed them. Engineers in Hamas also travelled to Iran, where they received training in developing more advanced systems.[132] Politically and diplomatically at an impasse, Hamas still managed to strengthen militarily.

In July 2023, an Israeli intelligence officer warned her commanders that Hamas had completed a series of training exercises in which the armed wing simulated raids against Israeli kibbutzim and army outposts on the Israeli side of the Gazan border. Her superiors dismissively brushed off her warnings as 'imaginary'.[133] After all, although there had been the occasional military conflagration during the last sixteen years, they had never threatened the Israelis. Moreover, this was not the first time Hamas had trained on surprise raids on the Israeli side of the border. Such exercises had been reported as early as June 2015, when Israeli newspapers noted that 'it is possible that . . . Hamas will attempt in the next war to raid an Israeli community or army base, killing as many civilians or soldiers as possible'.[134] Still, training exercises remained training exercises.

Then, on Saturday, October 7, 2023, at 6:30 a.m., Hamas launched 2,200 rockets from the Gaza Strip towards southern and central Israel. As air raid sirens warned Israelis to find cover, 3,000 soldiers from Hamas's special forces stormed the Gaza border wall and crossed into Israel by land, air, and sea. As the wall was breached, a video was released showing Deif claiming responsibility: 'Today, the people reclaim their revolution, correct their path, and resume the march of return.'

---

131    Adnan Abu Amer, 'Report Outlines How Iran Smuggles Arms to Hamas', *Al-Monitor*, April 9, 2021.

132    Brad Lendon, 'How Does Hamas Get Its Weapons? A Mix of Improvisation, Resourcefulness and a Key Overseas Benefactor', CNN, October 12, 2023.

133    Amos Harel, 'Chilling Warnings Picked up by Israeli Intelligence Months before October 7 Massacre', *Haaretz*, November 27, 2023.

134    Issacharoff, 'Hamas Masses Troops on Israeli Border, Trains for New Round of Fighting', *Times of Israel*, June 28, 2015.

# 7

# Road to October 7

October 7 happened because the moderates in Hamas had few, if any, victories to show after the movement won the legislative elections in 2006. Politically, Hamas had not brought the Palestinians any closer to liberation. A status quo had been effectively established in Gaza, with the Strip remaining isolated, impoverished, and fully aid-dependent under blockade. There was always the occasional flareup. The Israelis would assassinate a Palestinian leader or militant, and the factions would respond by sending rockets into Israel. Or the Palestinian factions fired rockets in protest against Israeli policies, and the Israelis would respond by bombing Gaza. These escalations did little to disturb Israeli daily life or shake the perception that pacifying and containing 2 million Palestinians indefinitely was feasible. The Gazans were out of sight and out of mind, while Hamas proved surprisingly adept at ensuring law and order in the Strip.

The political and geographical division between the West Bank and the Gaza Strip similarly persisted after 2007, and there were no signs of genuine Palestinian reconciliation efforts between Fatah and Hamas.

While the Israelis paid lip-service to the two-state solution, the settler population increased by over 50 per cent between 2006 and 2023 – from approximately 460,000 settlers to over 700,000.[1] If there ever was a realistic chance of establishing a viable Palestinian state in the archipelago known as the occupied territories, it had dwindled by the day. From 2020, Israel normalized relations with numerous Arab states – the United Arab Emirates, Bahrain, Morocco, and Sudan. Their shared fears of the Iranian threat similarly drove unofficial cooperation and normalization talks between Israel and Saudi Arabia, while Omani leaders advocated normalization. The Palestinian cause was no longer on the international agenda, as policymakers appeared bored with the impasse in peace negotiations. The Palestinians were effectively sidelined and forgotten.

The failure of Hamas moderates was partly caused by their own naivety. Hamas gambled that its participation in the 2006 legislative elections would underscore the movement's democratic intentions and its acceptance of shared international political norms. By demonstrating that it was a responsible political actor, Hamas aspired to normalize its relationship with Western politicians and policymakers. Yet the Quartet (the United Nations, the European Union, the United States, and Russia) would never have accepted Hamas in power while armed resistance remained at the core of its identity. Hamas remained designated a terrorist movement, which limited meaningful diplomatic interactions beyond unofficial backchannels.

Hamas was also naive in believing that ideological purity would prevent the movement from making the same mistakes and concessions as Fatah had done before them. Once in power, Hamas faced the same inconvenient constraints of reality. Instead of turning the Palestinian Authority institutions into ones in the service of the resistance, the Islamist movement was reduced to bureaucrats – janitors of the border, as the Qassam leader Ahmad al-Ja'bari complained to Khalid Mishal. The legitimacy of Hamas in Gaza no longer derived solely from its status as an armed resistance movement, but now as a service provider to the Gazan populace as well. Although Hamas attempted to maintain ceasefires with Israel to

---

1  B'Tselem, *Human Rights in the Occupied Territories: Annual Report 2007* (Jerusalem: B'Tselem, 2008), 46; United Nations, 'Human Rights Council Hears That 700,000 Israeli Settlers Are Living Illegally in the Occupied West Bank', press release, March 28, 2023.

prevent a complete halt in aid and imports, other factions like Palestinian Islamic Jihad (PIJ) could keep stressing the need for uncompromising violence without any associated costs. While Hamas was blamed for the deteriorating living conditions in Gaza, PIJ's popularity surged as belief in a negotiated settlement with Israel dwindled. While Hamas security forces violently crushed popular peaceful Palestinian popular protests for improved living conditions in Gaza, PIJ never had to make those choices. It became increasingly clear that Hamas's governance project was turning into a slow suicide.

The failure of Hamas moderates – those who opposed suicide bombings, who vocally criticized the Qassam Brigades, who argued that legal political work and communal activities should be prioritized, and who argued that the movement should accept a two-state solution – cannot be attributed solely to their naivety or incompetence, although they played a role.[2] 'It is fashionable nowadays to speak of a victim's agency,' Finkelstein observes, 'but one must be realistic about the constraints imposed on such agency by objective circumstance.'[3] Indeed, the moderates fought an uphill battle from the beginning.

The EU's boycott of the Hamas government had a devastating impact. Although it encouraged Islamist participation in the political process prior to the 2006 elections, the EU nonetheless refused to accept the outcome of the people's vote. Instead of adhering to its declared goal of promoting democracy in its neighbourhood, the EU decided to join the UN, the US, and Russia in boycotting the Hamas government. Hamas had invested no expectations of the US, Are Hovdenak notes, but there was palpable surprise and disappointment regarding the response of European leaders. Its response to the boycott – showing steps of moderation by granting the PLO and Mahmoud Abbas the mandate to negotiate with Israel, accepting the establishment of a Palestinian state on the 1967

---

2   See, for example, Nicolas Pelham and Max Rodenbeck, 'Which Way for Hamas?', *New York Review of Books*, November 5, 2009; Adnan Abu Amer, 'Former Hamas Official Speaks Out', *al-Monitor*, May 20, 2015; Sara Roy, *Hamas and Civil Society in Gaza: Engaging the Islamic Social Sector* (Princeton, NJ: Princeton University Press, 2011), 88; Gianluca Pacchiani, 'As IDF Advances in Gaza, Hamas Chief Haniyeh Claims to Seek "Political Negotiations" ', *Times of Israel*, November 2, 2023.

3   Norman G. Finkelstein, *Gaza: An Inquest into Its Martyrdom* (Oakland: University of California Press, 2018), xi.

borders, and accepting past agreements – was futile. Instead of encouraging further pragmatic steps and influencing Hamas in a strategic direction, the EU doubled down and demanded an immediate compliance with the Quartet's principles.[4] Although it is stressed as one of the most important foreign policy assets of the EU, dialogue remained conspicuously absent in its approach to Hamas.[5]

The political collapse of a Palestinian unity government engendered deep-seated resentment within Hamas, which was seen as a direct outcome from the Quartet's sanctions. Although the Quartet aspired to weaken Hamas as a whole, it instead undermined one specific faction in the movement: the moderates who first convinced the rest of the movement to participate in the legislative elections, and then to accept compromises in order to secure international recognition. Their political capital was effectively shattered when Hamas's initiatives yielded no tangible results. The erosion of the political leadership's authority contributed in large part to the violent takeover by al-Qassam militants who had reached the end of their patience.[6]

Regional dynamics after 2010 had a detrimental impact, as well. The relationship between Hamas and Iran was always a marriage of convenience driven by mutual interests. The Palestinian Islamists reasoned, like the PLO before them, that they were in need of a state sponsor if they were to succeed in their struggle, while Tehran sought to enhance its regional influence. They correspondingly adjusted their external relations according to their own strategic calculations. The eruption of the Arab Spring in 2010, and the rise of Islamist parties in the region, made Hamas overconfident. Expecting that the regime of Bashar al-Assad would fall like those in Tunisia, Libya, and Egypt, Hamas left Damascus and publicly endorsed the Syrian uprising at the expense of Iranian patronage. Hamas's gamble on Cairo, Ankara, and Doha failed. Mohamed Morsi of the Egyptian Muslim Brotherhood remained president for merely a year before Egypt returned to 'pre-uprising politics' from July 2013, and Abdel Fattah al-Sisi – a sworn enemy of the Brotherhood – renewed the

---

4   Are Hovdenak, 'Hamas in Transition: The Failure of Sanctions', *Democratization* 16, no. 1 (2010): 60.

5   Erik Skare, 'Staying Safe by Being Good? The EU's Normative Decline as a Security Actor in the Middle East', *European Journal of International Security* 8, no. 3 (2023): 338.

6   Hovdenak, 'Hamas in Transition', 75.

Gazan blockade from the Egyptian side of the border.[7] The Qataris, on the other hand, were unable, or unwilling, to make up for the shortfall in Iranian funding. Hamas was effectively forced back into Iranian orbit to preserve its own interests.

Hamas's gamble did not merely alienate Tehran. It also shifted the power dynamics within the movement, as Hamas in Gaza and its armed wing, the Qassam Brigades, maintained regular contact with the Iranians and received continued backing. It gave the hardliners greater autonomy, as they no longer depended on the outside leadership for funding.[8] Traditionally, the external leaders were seen as the more hardline faction. From the 2010s, the Gazan internal leadership turned more uncompromising, more militant, and more intransigent. Governing Gaza under a blockade and international isolation deepened their conviction that the experiment of the Hamas moderates was in vain and that there was no political or diplomatic solution. Iran was a proven ally on their path of armed resistance.

Hamas's revision of its charter in 2017 did little to change the position of the international community, although it addressed the most common criticisms levelled against Hamas over the past thirty years. Severing its affiliation with the Muslim Brotherhood never convinced the Egyptians to lift the blockade. Hamas's insistence that the PLO remained the national framework for the Palestinians did not bring forth reconciliation with Mahmoud Abbas and the PA. The EU did not change its stance, although Hamas legitimized its normative claims with references to human rights and international law rather than religious texts. The US and Israel remained similarly unconvinced that the new document signified a new, more moderate Hamas. Palestinian Islamic Jihad (PIJ), on the other hand, criticised Hamas for abandoning the core principles of the Palestinian struggle.[9]

If the hardliners within Hamas believed that only violence could liberate the Palestinians – arguing that the outside world would always oppose them as Palestinians and as Muslims – then the continued isolation of the movement only reinforced their stance. This view was further solidified

---

7   Khaled Hroub, 'A Newer Hamas? The Revised Charter', *Journal of Palestine Studies* 46, no. 4 (2017): 106.

8   Leila Seurat, 'Hamas's Goal in Gaza', *Foreign Affairs*, December 11, 2023.

9   Ibid., 100.

during the Great March of Return in 2018, when Israeli forces responded
to thousands of peaceful Gazan protesters with gunfire.[10] Indeed, if Hamas
had enjoyed any victories over the past seventeen years, they came from
the use of force. The kidnapping of the Israeli soldier Gilad Shalit led to
the release of 1,027 Palestinian prisoners. Easements in the blockade
typically resulted from violent escalations and negotiated ceasefires with
Israel. Diplomatic interactions with the outside world also increased.
Immediately after Operation Cast Lead in 2008–9, for example, there was
a notable rise in contact with the US and the EU. The continued threat of
violence – either from Hamas itself or from unleashing the other armed
factions in Gaza – meant that Qatari aid kept coming with Israeli consent
in the hope that it would maintain the lull.[11]

Even when we ignore the immense human costs, it is evident that the
Gazan blockade was an utter policy failure. Originally aimed at turning
the Palestinian population against Hamas through collective punishment,
it merely impoverished them and cemented Hamas's power in the Strip.
Rather than dissuading Gazans from militancy and violence, it created
a lost generation whose desperation and hopelessness bred unprecedented radicalism. Instead of weakening Hamas through isolation, the
strategy allowed the movement to avoid the frequent Israeli incursions
endured by the West Bank, thereby providing it with time to prepare and
strengthen itself. Constructing a 500-kilometre tunnel network beneath
Gaza, Hamas was able to smuggle, manufacture, and stockpile arms and
rockets. The blockade could never produce Israeli security, only immense
Palestinian suffering.

There were numerous warnings that the unsustainable situation in the
occupied territories would come at a cost. Deprived of the most basic
human rights, livelihood, and protection, decades of occupation facilitated
the dehumanization enabling October 7. With the complete destruction

10    Gilles Paris and Hélène Sallon, 'How Hamas Became the Leader of the
Palestinian National Movement', *Le Monde*, November 26, 2023; Loveday Morris
and Hazem Balousha, 'Israelis Kill More Than 50 Palestinians in Gaza Protests,
Health Officials Say', *Washington Post*, May 14, 2018; Human Rights Council,
'Report of the Independent International Commission of Inquiry on the Protests in the Occupied Palestinian Territory', United Nations, February 28, 2018,
ohchr.org.
11    Tareq Baconi, *Hamas Contained: The Rise and Pacification of Palestinian
Resistance* (Stanford, CA: Stanford University Press, 2018), 161, 234.

of the Gaza Strip, the professed aim is now to dismantle Hamas. As of this writing, it is clear that this is, and always would be, a failure.

Indeed, if this brief history of Palestinian Islamism demonstrates anything, it is that its appeal has never been its religious doctrine – although it certainly resonates with a segment of Palestinians. It has proven potent only as a prism through which Palestinian nationalism is expressed. Hizb al-Tahrir failed because it refused to fuse its idealist theology with nationalist aspirations; it could never become popular as long as it refused to address Palestinian grievances. Salafi-jihadism did gain some support among conservative Gazans, but its primary strength lay in the perception that Hamas's focus on governance came at the expense of its resistance. PIJ, like Fatah before it, was a product of the nationalist aspirations espoused by the Brotherhood's young guard, who were aggrieved by their movement's quietist stance towards the Israeli occupation. Hamas was founded by leading Brotherhood members because they realized the movement would be sidelined by the First Intifada if they restricted themselves to proselytizing and social services.

The Israeli–Palestinian conflict did not commence with the foundation of Hamas, nor with the emergence of Palestinian Islamism. In the hypothetical absence of Hamas, other outlets of Palestinian nationalism will necessarily appear. Although external drivers will always influence preferred choices and tactics in the Palestinian resistance, whether opting for violence or non-violence, such nationalism will persist if these grievances remain unaddressed. And it will do so with or without the phenomenon to which we refer as Palestinian Islamism.

# Appendix

## On transliteration and spelling conventions

This text is not a philological or linguistic analysis; therefore, transliteration has been minimized to enhance readability. I have adopted a simplified transliteration standard similar to that used by the *International Journal of Middle East Studies* (IJMES), which omits macrons over long vowels and diacritics, and includes the representation of 'ayn and hamza only when they appear mid-word. All Arabic names are transliterated according to this simplified IJMES system unless a more widely recognized version of the name exists. For instance, I use 'Gamal Abdel Nasser' instead of 'Jamal Abd al-Nasir'.

## On the availability of sources

Digitization of historical sources presents certain challenges for citing materials. This is particularly the case with URLs. They are often lengthy, aesthetically displeasing, give certain typesetting and proofreading difficulties, and, most importantly, are often changed by the website hosts, intentionally or otherwise. Arabic URLs are notably cumbersome due to their length and complexity, and are often difficult to format, as the script is frequently converted into a lengthy series of encoded characters, which make them less intuitive to use and reference. URLs and other cumbersome citation elements have for this reason been excluded. A full bibliography can be found at erikskare.no/resources for those interested.

The reproducibility crisis – the inability across disciplines to replicate empirical results and scientific findings – profoundly affected how various fields perceived themselves and led to numerous recommendations aimed at enhancing the process of establishing and building scholarly consensus about different types of knowledge. My own discipline, the humanities, has proven particularly resilient to critical introspection, however, although the core issues of the crisis are endemic to our field.[1] Inspired by the Active Citation standard developed by Andrew Moravcsik, and to assure transparency and replicability in the selection, presentation, and preservation of qualitative evidence, I have published excerpts of cited primary sources together with the full bibliography. This enables readers to assess in real time whether the evidence cited in this book provides a prima facie case for my interpretative or theoretical claims, and the hope is that the Active Citation standard will 'encourage, enforce, and reward higher standards in historical and qualitative analysis.'[2]

## On the Palestinian Islamist martyr dataset

The Palestinian Islamist martyr dataset referred to in this book contains data from 4,037 martyr biographies published by the Qassam Brigades and PIJ, and encompasses all Palestinian Islamist militants who were killed between 1985 and 2022, as reported by the movements themselves. Of these martyr biographies, 2,851 were from the Qassam Brigades and 1,186 were from PIJ. All militants in the dataset were either killed or killed themselves in suicide bomb operations within the Occupied Palestinian Territories or within Israel. The dataset begins with the first recorded martyr of each respective movement (1985 for PIJ and 1988 for Hamas) and ends in 2022. It was not feasible to continue data-gathering beyond 2022 at the time of writing, given the backlog of unpublished biographies following the October 7 attacks.

---

1   Andrew Piper, *Can We Be Wrong? The Problem of Textual Evidence in a Time of Data* (Cambridge: Cambridge University Press, 2020), 15.

2   Andrew Moravcsik, 'Active Citation: A Precondition for Replicable Qualitative Research', *PS: Political Science and Politics* 43, no. 1 (January 2010): 32.

I gathered data based on eleven categories: (1) surname, (2) first name, (3) sex, (4) governorate/district, (5) neighbourhood, village, or city, (6) date of birth, (7) date of death, (8) marital status, (9) level of education, (9) educational specialization, (10) occupation or type of employment, and (11) year in which the militant joined the organization. While home governorates follow the official geographic boundaries of the OPT (such as Hebron, Jenin, North Gaza, Rafah, Deir al-Balaha, and so on), neighbourhood is applied only to Gaza City – Shuja'iyya, Rimal, and Sabra, to mention just three. For smaller cities like Bethlehem, or villages such as Silat al-Harithiyya or 'Anza, among others, the city/village is listed. The level of education has five categories: elementary school (first to seventh grade), intermediate school (eighth to tenth grade), secondary school, university, or vocational programme. I have listed vocational programmes as a distinct category instead of aggregating them with secondary education, insofar as it signifies a form of non-academic education. Type of specialization lists either what type of vocational diploma the militant obtained (plumbing, electricity, automobile mechanics, etc.) or their area of academic specialization (Islamic law, journalism, or social sciences).

A number of martyr biographies were excluded from this analysis. For example, I excluded subjects under sixteen years of age, as both movements laid claim to a small number of casualties in their early adolescent years. Since these were mostly civilian victims and not militants, data about the children – some as young as three years old – would be of little analytical value. I also do not include fallen members of Hamas's political wing because it was difficult to determine their actual affiliation – there were sometimes few additional sources to substantiate claims made in the martyr biographies. Militants from the Qassam Brigades, Hamas's military wing, on the other hand, participated in armed clashes covered and confirmed by media sources. Although it would be ideal to incorporate all fallen members of Hamas and to compare the political and military wings, the data for the former proved too unreliable. For PIJ, the fallen militants are almost exclusively militants in the traditional sense of the word, as the separation between the movement's military and political wings is not as clear as in the case of Hamas. Third, if actual membership in the movements was in doubt, the militants were excluded from the dataset. This could be the case if both Hamas and Fatah claimed a particular fallen militant, for example.

The reliability of the data varies depending on subject matter. According to the martyr biographies, all militants were smiling, respectful to their parents, prayed regularly, and had a positive impact in their local communities. No biography asserted, for example, that a particular militant suffered from an off-putting persona. The martyr biographies are thus ill-suited for studying the personality traits of Palestinian Islamist militants. Evidence does not suggest any tweaking or doctoring of the socioeconomic backgrounds of the militants; reports from both PIJ and the Qassam Brigades reveal a variety of occupations and educational achievements. One martyr biography highlights a militant's unemployment, while another details specialized labour such as teaching. Similarly, the reports diverge in educational backgrounds. One describes a militant's education ending after elementary school due to the economic hardships of his family, whereas another reportedly pursued higher education, with university studies in political science. There is thus both a behavioural uniformity and socioeconomic diversity in the data.

The dataset has an inherent military bias, given that it does not include any socioeconomic data on killed members of Hamas's political wing. It is possible that the 'politicos' in Hamas enjoy a different socioeconomic background to fallen militants in the military wing. Another limitation is

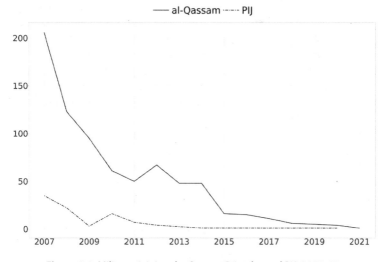

**Figure 8.1.** Militants joining the Qassam Brigades and PIJ, 2007–22

the fatality bias, as the dataset includes only those who died. This means that the data becomes increasingly unreliable the closer we come to the present. Figure 8.1 illustrates the problem: There is little to suggest that PIJ's or the Qassam Brigades' pools of recruitment dried up after 2007. Instead, the decrease can be attributed to the Qassam and PIJ militants still being alive, and the figure would presumably look quite different if it included militants killed in the fierce fighting in 2023 and 2024. There are few information gaps on fallen militants from PIJ. Of the 1,186 PIJ militants, information about the level of education was missing for 39 of them and professional information was missing for 251. A larger information gap pertains to university specializations, as this information is missing for 138 out of the 330 PIJ militants who commenced university studies. Detailed employment information about the Qassam martyrs is notably scarce; the occupations of 1,272 Hamas fighters remain un-identified, approximately 40 per cent. This gap should not be overstated, however. Given that all individuals in the Qassam Brigades are recog-nized as soldiers and militants, it is reasonable to infer that they received financial compensation from the Qassam Brigades. Notably, 914 of the 1,272 al-Qassam martyrs who lacked specified occupations died after 2007 following Hamas's rise to power in Gaza. This era overlaps with the enforcement of a strict blockade on Gaza, suggesting that involvement in militancy could have served as a significant source of income due to limited alternative job opportunities. Some martyr biographies have no other job description than 'serving' in the Qassam Brigades as soldier or field commander. Others worked in the Brigades as tunnel diggers, which reportedly provides a monthly income of $250 to $400.[3] In documenting all martyrs whose sole listed occupation is the Qassam Brigades, their occupation has been noted as 'NA' to circumvent the indiscriminate use of the term 'al-Qassam soldiers'. Although it would be technically feasible to label every individual in the dataset as an 'al-Qassam soldier', doing so would inflate the number of those under that designation.

---

3    Avi Issacharoff, 'Hamas Spends $100 Million a Year on Military Infrastruc-ture', *Times of Israel*, September 8, 2016.

# Index

Page numbers in **bold** refer to figures,
page numbers in *italic* refer to
tables.

Abbas, Mahmoud 152–3, 165, 194,
  201, 203
Abbasi, Abu Yunus al- 160
Abid, Hani 81
Abraham Accords 196, 200
Abu Ali Mustafa Brigade 136, *137*
Abu Marzuq, Musa 25, 33, 33–4, 109,
  186
Abu Nidal Organization 157
Abu Shanab, Ismail 33, 109–10, 110,
  138–9, 139, 142, 150
Abu Taha, Anwar 7, 70, 74, 91, 117–18,
  119, 183, 184
Abu Tayr, Muhammad 8, 35–6, 97,
  106, 155
Afghan–Soviet War 67
aid workers, casualties 2
aid-dependence 1, 188–9, 196
Alami, Musa 46
al-Aqsa Martyrs' Brigades 136, *137*,
  138
al-Aqsa Mosque 69
Algeria 84, 184
al-Jama'a al-Islamiyya 158
al-Jura 31

al-Kanz Mosque 34
Alliance of Palestinian Forces (APF)
  107
al-Najah University 81
al-Qaida 140–1, 157–9, 160
al-Sabirin Movement 185
al-Tawhid wa-l-Jihad 161
al-Yarmuk refugee camp 116
Amman 22
anticommunism 28–9, 46
Aql, Adil 98
Aql, Imad 98–9, 100, 102–3
Aql, Walid 98n17
Arab Liberation Forces 82
Arab nationalism 52
Arab Spring 184, 188, 202
Arab-Islamic identity 86
Arab-Israeli war, 1948–49 19, 20
Arafat, Yasser 27, 40, 83–4, 86, 103,
  112, 113, 119, 140, 150
A'raj, Amar al- 112, 155
Army of Islam 160–1, 165, 187
Arrigoni, Vittorio 161
Aruri, Salih al- 111, 162
Ashkelon 94
Assad, Bashar al- 181, 202
assassinations, cost–benefit calculations
  140
Astal, Yassin al- 159

Augusta Victoria Hospital, Jerusalem
    81
Awda, Abdel Aziz 33, 74–5, 77, 78–9
Ayash, Yahya 93, 103, 104
Azhar University, Egypt 45
Azzam, Abdallah 8–9, 43, 116
Azzam, Nafidh 62

Baath Party 52–3
Badran, Husam 8, 113, 131, 146, 172–3
Banisadr, Abolhassan 116
Banna, Hassan al- 12–15, 17, 19, 32–3,
    62
Baraka, Sayyid 82
Battalion of Right 26, 27
bin Laden, Usama 141, 160
biographies 7–8
Black September 38, 157
border crossings 170
Brahma, Issam 82
B'Tselem 144–5

Cairo 63
caliph, the 49–51
Caliphate, the 47
Camp David Accords 40
Camp David talks, collapse of 131
Camp of Return 179–80
casualties 8, 100n24
    aid workers 2
    bombing campaign 2
    children 20
    defeat of PLO guerrillas, 1969–72
        30–1
    foundation of Israel 20
    geographical distribution 8
    Great March of Return 195
    Great Palestine Revolt 18
    June 25, 2006 187
    massacres, 1956 34
    Palestine War, 1948 45
    Palestinian Islamic Jihad (PIJ) 8
    Qassam Brigades 151, **151**, 168n8
    Quds Brigades 151, **151**
    Second Intifada 130, 135
    socio-economic data 8
ceasefire maintenance 170
child labour 130

civil society 116–17
clan-faction alliances 165–6
class realignments 21
class struggle 47
collaborators
    Majd, struggle against 88, 95–8
    moral collaborators 98
collective punishment 204
colonialism 48, 66–8, 104
communism 48
communists, Islamist cooperation with
    27
counterinsurgency 131
    1990s 113–15
culture war 11–12, 41

Dahlan, Muhammad 154
Damascus 93, 181, 185–6
Dar al-Kitab wa-l-Sunna 159
Dawr, Ahmad al- 55
decolonization 84
deculturalization 47–8, 67
dehumanization 204
Deif, Muhammad 102–3, 103, 104, 110,
    128, 142, 156, 190, 191
democracy 115, 120–1, 123–5, 158, 182
Democratic Front for the Liberation of
    Palestine (DFLP) 38, 84, 107, 135
deportations 94
de-secularization 4
domicide 2
double speech, Israeli 3
drug dealers 98
Dukhan, Abdel Fattah 90
Durham University 158–9
Dwayk, Aziz 179

ecocide 2
economic decline, 1992–2000 130
economic development 47
education 26
education levels 79
Egypt 139, 177, 184, 185, 202
    administration of Gaza 21–2, 23–40,
        30, 36
    al-Azhar University 45
    declaration of independence 12–15
    Free Officers Coup, 1952 24

Muslim Brotherhood 23, 24, 182
and origin of Muslim Brotherhood
    12–15
Palestinian student circles 62–6
Revolutionary Command Council
    (RCC) 24
role of the state 118
al-Sisi regime 183, 185
Egyptian Islamic Jihad 158
Egyptian–Palestinian ties 17
elections 120–1, 123–5
environmental factors 47
epistemic framework 9–10
Europe, rise of 47–8
European Union 200, 201–2, 204
executive authority 119
Executive Forces 165
executive powers 122–3

Fatah 36, 40, 82, 85, 86, 107, 161, 165,
    199
clan-faction alliances 165
formation 27
founding members 26
general elections, 1996 150
ousting of 154–5, 156
reconciliation with Hamas 154
and religion 83–4
Second Intifada 131–2, 135
tensions with Hamas 152–3
youth movement 83–4
First Intifada 60, 89–90, 98, 106, 107,
    119, 139, 205
foreign benefactors 176, 177
Free Officers Coup, 1952, Egypt 24
fundamentalism 116

Gaza Strip 1, 16
adolescence in 95
al-Banna visits 17
childhood in 95–6
economy devastated, 1949 20
Egyptian administration 21–2,
    23–40, 30, 36
Hamas takeover 154–7
isolation 21, 23, 199
Israeli occupation, 1956 27
life, 1960s to the 1980s 8

occupation, 1967 29–30, 30
Palestine War, 1948 19
Palestinian Islamic Jihad (PIJ) attacks
    87, 88–9
political opportunity structure 71
population 20, 21, 188–9
refugees 20, 21, 26
secularizing impact of Egyptian rule
    25–6
settler population 130
suffering 1, 2–3
See also Muslim Brotherhood,
    Gazan
general elections, 1996 150
genocide 2
Ghannouchi, Rachid al- 116
Ghoul, Adnan al- 142, 150
God 50, 51
Goldstone Report 189
governance project, Hamas 5, 165, 168,
    196, 200–1, 205
Great Britain 18, 19
Great March of Return, Israeli
    suppression of 194–5, 204
Great Palestine Revolt 15–16, 17–18

Habib, Khadr 80, 182
Hajj Muhammad, Yusuf Arif al- 7, 65,
    113, 115, 141–2, 152
Hamad, Fathi 172–3
Hamad, Ghazi 177
Hamas 11, 25, 29, 36, 71, 157–8, 199
al-Qaida and 158
appears to renounce unilateral terror
    145–6
approach to governance 149–50
approach to power 119
attempt to maintain calm 7
blame 164
break with Syria 181–2
casualties 8, 100n24
ceasefire maintenance 170–1
charter 146–8
clan-faction alliances 165
constraints of reality 200–1
consultative council elections, 2008
    156
cooperation with PA 149

Hamas (*continued*)
  and counter-insurgency, 1990s 113
  crackdown on Jund Ansar Allah
       163–4
  criticism of rule 176–7
  electoral participation 4
  emergence of 88–92, 147–8
  enmity against Israel 148–9
  EU boycott of government 201–2
  evolution 6
  Executive Forces 165
  failure of moderates 200, 201
  formal independence from
       Brotherhood 90
  Gaza-centred 144, *145*
  general elections boycott, 1996 150
  genocidal ideology 4
  governance project 5, 165, 168, 196,
       200–1, 205
  ideological challenge of Salafi-
       jihadism 162–3
  ideology 91, 170
  infidelity 160
  influence of external contacts 148
  internal competition 109
  internal power balance 186–7, 191
  Iranian support 178, 179–80, 181–2,
       186, 191, 196, 202, 203
  Islamization efforts 163
  jurisprudence of interest 91
  leadership 111, 121, 148, 156–7, 181,
       186, 190–1, 193
  leadership class background 109
  legislative elections 128
  legislative elections, 2006 129,
       151–3, 158, 162, 200
  legitimacy 200
  military wing 98–103, *100, 101,*
       113–14, 132, 189–90
  moderate/hardliner balance 110–12,
       150–1, 157
  moderation 148
  municipal elections, 1996 150
  *Muslim Palestine* (journal) 92
  opposition to Oslo Accords 103–8
  organizational structure 115
  Palestinian Islamic Jihad (PIJ)
       sidelines 175

Palestinian Islamic Jihad (PIJ)
     suspicion of 149
  patience 111
  policy of stages 149–50
  political behaviour 91
  popular support 131, 176–7, 196
  power dynamics within 203
  Quartet sanctions 202
  rapprochement with Syria 185–6
  reconciliation efforts with the PA
       196
  reconciliation with Fatah 154
  recruits and recruitment 148
  re-establishment of law and order
       165–9, 173, 174–5, 199
  relationship with Palestinian Islamic
       Jihad (PIJ) 90–2
  research on 5
  retaliatory violence 107
  Revised Charter 192–3, 203
  rise of Sinwar 187–91, 193
  search for new patrons 185
  Second Intifada 131, 138–9, 140,
       142, 143, 145, 150, 156
  security forces 161–2, 163
  shift to social services 114–15
  Sinwar elected leader 191
  Sinwar's leadership 194–6
  social practices 72
  social services 8, 131, 148
  strategy of temporary settlement
       111
  structural changes 108–12
  suicide bombings, 1990s 93–4,
       109–10, 113, **114**
  takeover in Gaza 154–7
  tensions with Fatah 152–3
  tensions with Palestinian Islamic
       Jihad (PIJ) 172–4
  tensions within 161–3
  tunnel strategy 196–8
  two-state solution 138–9
  vacillates in its approach 4
  weapons 197–8
  welfare infrastructure 8
  West Bank *145*
Hamdan, Usama 156
Hamdan, Yusra 41

Haniyeh, Ismail 168, 174–5, 187, 191, 193
HaSharon Junction suicide bombing 103–4
Hayya, Khalil al- 185–6
health-care institutions 39
Hebron 55, 57, 102, 134
Hezbollah 179, 180, 182
higher education, access to 79
Hindi, Muhammad al- 62, 116, 175, 184, 193
Hizb al-Tahrir 42, 52, 65, 205
  cause of failure 57
  formation 53–4
  hierarchical system 54
  insistence on intellectual and ideological purity 56
  Jordanian general elections, 1954 55
  lack of interest in Palestine 49
  lack of tactical flexibility 53, 56
  limited appeal 58
  optimism 54–5, 56–7
  Palestinian following 54–5, 57, 58
  Palestinian Islamic Jihad (PIJ) critique of 65
  purpose 43–4
  repression 55–6
  research on 5
  vision of Islamic state 49–51
Hobbes, Thomas 120
Houthis 183
human nature 49, 120
Husseini, Hajj Amin al- 14–15, 17, 18, 52–3

ideological fissures 129
ideological purity 200
Ijzim 44–6
imperialism 48
infidelity 160
international boycott 156, 165
intimidation campaigns 39
intra-Palestinian competition 6, 90–1, 106, 107
intra-Palestinian violence 39–41, 153
Iran 9, 174, 176, 177–81, 183–5, 186, 191, 193, 196, 200, 202, 203

revolution, 1979 66, 71, 85, 178, 180
Revolutionary Guard 179, 184–5
Iraq 152
Irgun 18
Islam
  as both religion and state 13–14
  mobilization of 83–5
  and Palestinianism 71, 84
Islamic community 48–9
Islamic Complex, the 37–8, 39–40, 53, 73–5, 88, 90
Islamic dress code 41
Islamic identity, building 35–6
Islamic ideology 49
Islamic Jihad Brigades 87, 169
Islamic law 51, 119, 125
Islamic Mujahid Forces 87, 112
Islamic state, the 49–51, 53, 119
Islamic State (IS) 158
Islamic thought 50–1
Islamic University of Gaza 40–1, 79, 86, 96, 102
Islamic values 119, 124, 126
Islamic way of life 49
Islamic world, spiritual decline 13
Islamism 82, 85–6, 95
Islamist identity 58
Islamist liberation theology, turn to 85–6
Islamization 71
Ismailia 12, 12–13
Israel
  Abraham Accords 196, 200
  bombing campaign 2–3
  defeat of PLO guerrillas, 1969–72 30–1
  deportations 178, 179–80
  destruction of 70
  double speech 3
  establishment of 20, 45–6, 67–8
  exaggerated use of force 130
  Great March of Return suppression 204
  intelligence 197, 198
  Islamic movement in 8
  nation-state building project 142–3
  PA security cooperation with 112–13, 155

Israel (*continued*)
  Palestinian community 20
  suppression of the Great March of
    Return 194–5
  targeted killings 139–40, 142
  view of Gaza 196
  violence and repression 6
Israeli Southern Command 94
Israeli–Egyptian blockade 188
Issa, Marwan 190, 191
Italian Communist Party 73
Izz al-Din al-Qassam Brigades. *See*
  Qassam Brigades

Ja'bari, Ahmad al- 156, 169, 190, 200
Jamal, Muhammad Sa'id al- 82
Jenin, Battle of 110, 136, 143
Jerusalem 16, 57, 70, 129, 178
  Augusta Victoria Hospital 81
  Mutasarrifate of 44
Jewish insurgency 18
Jibril Agreement 86
Jordan 21–2, 55, 56, 184
  coup plot, 1949 52
  Interior Ministry 53–4
judicial authority 122–3
Jund Ansar Allah 163–4
Jundiyya, Raid 173
justice 123

Kerem Maharal 46
Khalaf, Salah 26, 84, 86
Khalidi, Ismail Abdel Aziz al- 16, 18,
  25, 27, 28, 35, 41, 44, 45
Khalil, Sami al-Shaykh 82
Khan Younis refugee camp 29, 95, 159,
  174, 191
  massacre, 1956 34
Khatib, Omar Arafat al- 138
Khatib, Taysir al- 71–2, 79
Khawaja, Mahmud al- 74, 101, 104
Khomeini, Ayatollah Ruhollah 66,
  177–8
kinship clusters 165–6, **169**, **170**

*Larry King Live* (TV show) 179
law and order, reinstatement of 165–9,
  173, 174–5

Lebanon 179
legislation, source of 116
legislative elections, 2006 150–1, 162,
  200
  Hamas victory 129, 151–3, 158
Lehi 18
Lenin, V. I. 117, 122–3

Majd 88, 96–8
Majdal 94
Mao Zedong 85
Maqadma, Ibrahim al- 28, 33, 37, 98,
  100, 104–5, 142, 150
Mardawi, Thabit 8, 136, 141
Marj al-Zuhur 179
martyrdom 132
Marxists and Marxism 27–8, 46, 84
*Masdar, al-* (newspaper) 185
massacres
  foundation of Israel 20
  Gaza, 1956 34
  medicide 2
Minawi, Abdel Aziz al- 84
Mishal, Khalid 16, 90, 111, 155–6, 169,
  181, 186, 187, 190–1, 192, 200
missionary schools 48
modernity, and religious tradition
  71–2
Morsi, Mohamed 185, 202
Mossad 62, 93, 104
Muhammad, the Prophet 14, 69, 70,
  104
Muhanna, Ahmad 82
Mujhat al-Quds Foundation 8
municipal elections, 1996 150
Murabitun Army 145, 161–2, 168
Muru, Muhammad 64
Musa, Abdel Latif 163
Musa, Abu Samir 84, 86
Muslim Brotherhood 8, 64, 66, 76–7,
  78, 176, 182, 202
  1980s 58–9
  anticolonial stance 13
  becomes more confrontational
    39–40
  centrality of Islam 13–14
  culture war 11–12
  dissolution, 1954 26–7

dissolution decree, 1948 21
Egyptian–Palestinian ties 17
first official Palestinian branches 16
inability to embrace new ideas 72
Jordanian 22–3
main adversary 11–12
Mandate Palestine activity 15–17
membership 14
mobilization for war 18
mosque-building phase 37
al-Nabhani and 51–2
Nasserist crackdown on 24–5
origins 12–19
orthodoxy 72
Palestine War, 1948 19, 99–100
Palestinian membership 17
pro-Palestinian fervour 15
proselytizing 11, 16, 17, 37, 159
repertoire 11
as revivalist movement 13
social services 11, 16, 17, 58
spread across Egypt 14
spread of influence 14–15
Muslim Brotherhood, Gazan 23–40,
    147–8
anticommunism 28, 46
arrogance 91
communal activism 37–8
confrontation with Palestinian
    Islamic Jihad (PIJ) 75–6
cooperation with communists 27–8
and deculturalization 48
Egypt bans 23
engagement of women 39
growth 24
hierarchical structure 75
independence 24
insular turn 26
Islamic identity building 35–6
Islamic University of Gaza imprint
    40–1
mid-1950s passivity 26–7
mosque-building phase 37
Nasserist crackdown on 24–5
old guard honorably discharged 35
opposition to Oslo Accords 107
organizational framework united 29
policy of stages 149–50

quietist activism 70
status 41–2
transformation into Hamas 88–92
wedding ceremonies 39
Yassin as leader 34–8, 39
Muslim Brotherhood, Jordan 22–3
Muslim Brotherhood, West Bank
    22–3, 24, 29, 37
Muslim Palestine (journal) 92

Nabhani, Taqi al-Din al- 43, 67
background 44–6
death 56
education 45
elitism 48
expelled from Jordan 56
and Hizb al-Tahrir 53–9
idealist trend 47
ideology 47–8
insistence on intellectual and
    ideological purity 56
interpretation of Islam 52
and Islamic community 48–9
lack of interest in Palestine 49
and Muslim Brotherhood 51–2
pan-Islamism 49–51
Saving Palestine 52
vision of Islamic state 49–51
Nablus 55, 57, 81, 134
Nahal, Yahya al- 74
nakba, the 46, 105, 194
Nakhala, Ziyad al- 82, 87, 178, 182, 193
Namruti, Yasir al- 98n17
Nashar, Isa al- 90
Nasser, Gamal Abdel 24, 25, 38, 57, 84
national identity, Palestinian 22
National Liberation Front, Algeria 84
national unity government, breakdown
    of 156
nationalism 47–8, 52, 83, 158, 205
Negev, the 19
Netanyahu, Benyamin 188

Occupied Palestinian Territories 6
October 7 attacks 1–2, 7
causes 199, 204–5
Israeli intelligence 198
reactions to 4

October 7 attacks (*continued*)
    rocket attacks 198
    training exercises 198
Operation Cast Lead 204
Operation Defensive Shield 151
Operation Protective Edge 190
Operation Yoav, 1948 32
Organization for Jihad and
    Proselytizing. *See* Majd
Oslo Accords 93–4, 111, 112
    breakdown of 128–46
    constructive opaqueness 129
    disillusionment with 131
    Islamist opposition to 103–8, 119
Ottoman Empire 44–5, 46, 67

Palestine
    ideological stance on 104–5
    prominence of 69
*Palestine* (journal) 92
Palestine Communist Party 27–9
Palestine Liberation Army (PLA) 30,
    82
Palestine Liberation Front (PLF) 82
Palestine Liberation Organization
    (PLO) 73, 74, 81–5, 105, 177–8,
    180, 201
    defeat of, 1969-72 30–1
    gives up violence 139
    Islamic University of Gaza 40
    loss of faith in 4
    rise of 30
    Ten-Point Programme 71, 85
    weakened after Black September 38
Palestine Mandate 15–17, 19
Palestine Piaster campaign 16
Palestine War, 1948 19, 24, 32, 45–6,
    61–2, 99–100
Palestinian Basic Law 122
Palestinian General Strike 16
Palestinian Islamic Jihad (PIJ) 4, 6, 25,
    27, 33, 157–8, 163, 203
    Algerian funding 184
    al-Qaida and 158–9
    and Arab regimes 183
    Battle of Jenin 110, 143
    break with Syria 182
    bureaucratization 112

call for armed struggle 73
casualties 8
confrontation with Muslim
    Brotherhood 73–6
and counter-insurgency, 1990s 113
critique of Hizb al-Tahrir 65
declaration 60–1
and deculturalization 48
emergence of 4
and the emergence of Hamas 88–92
Gaza attacks 87, 88–9
Gaza-centred 144, *145*
growth 175
ideological formation 62–73
ideology 91, 92
and the influence of political power
    152
and intra-Palestinian violence, 2007
    153
Iranian support 9, 178–9, 180–1,
    182–5, 185
Islam, Jihad, and Palestine slogan 61
Islamist ideology 66
justification 92
leadership 71–2, 181, 193–4
leadership deported 112
martyr biographies 134
martyrs class background 79–80, *80*
martyrs geographical distribution
    76, **76**, 81, **83**
military development 176–7
military wing 86–8, 101, 112, 115,
    132–3
occupational backgrounds 171
opposition to electoral participation
    152
opposition to Oslo Accords 103–8
*Palestine* (journal) 92
as peacemakers 129
PLO fighter recruitment 81–5
popular support 131, 164, 175–6,
    177, 201
project 73
recruits and recruitment 76, 78–84,
    100, 101
refusal to change course 128
relations with foreign benefactors
    176, 177

relationship with Hamas 90–2, 149,
172–4, 175
and religion 68–71
research on 5
restructuring 112
return to Gaza Strip 73–8
revitalization 128, 132–3, 133–4
*Revolutionary Palestine* (journal) 92
rocket attacks 177
Second Intifada 132–3, 136, 141,
143, 145, 175
Second Intifada justification 141–2
sidelines Hamas 175
slogans 102
social practices 72
social profile 80–1, *80, 81*
spectacular violence 6
suicide bombings 93–4, 113, **114,**
143
suspicion of Hamas 149
tensions with Hamas 172–4
West Bank 144, *145*
West Bank recruitment 81
worldview 73
Palestinian Legislative Council 152
Palestinian Marxists 11–12
Palestinian National Authority (PA)
109, 180, 193, 203
authoritarian turn 116
democratic deficiencies 118, 121–2
democratic potential 123
establishment of 106
Hamas cooperation with 149
Hamas's reconciliation efforts with
196
Legislative Council 121
Second Intifada 131–2
security cooperation with Israel
112–13, 155
targeted killings 155
Palestinian Popular Struggle Front
(PPSF) 82
Palestinian-Islamic movement 24
Palestinianism, and Islam 84
pan-Arabism 25, 38
pan-Islamism 49–51
partition 19
patience 111

Peel Report, 1937 15
piety and morality 48
policy of stages 149–50
political legitimacy 123–4, 131
political opportunity structure 71
political pluralism 125
Popular Front for the Liberation of
Palestine (PFLP) 38, 39, 41, 83,
107, 135, 157
Popular Front for the Liberation of
Palestine-General Command
(PFLP-GC) 38, 87
Popular Resistance Committees (PRC)
174, 187
poverty 130, 189, 196
power balance 6
power outages 174
Preservation Association 51
prisoner exchanges 188, 190, 204
proselytizing 11, 16, 17, 37, 48, 159
proto-nationalism 38

Qanouh, Murid al- 174
Qasim, Abdel Karim 57
Qassam, Izz al-Din al- 8–9, 15, 99
Qassam Brigades 8, 110, 111–12, 129,
188, 189, 193, 202
Aql's legacy 102–3
casualties 151, **151,** 168n8
de facto annihilation of 114
early violence 101–2
establishment of 98–100
fissures within 156
funding 109, 186
influence 191
Iranian support 203
kinship clusters 165–6, **169, 170**
leadership 102
martyrs *76,* **77**
occupational backgrounds 171, *171*
organizational infrastructure 102
ousting of Fatah 154–5, 156
policing role 169
raid June 25, 2006 187
recruits and recruitment 100–1, *100,
101,* 132, **133**
revitalization 128, 131, 133–4
rise of Sinwar 190

Qassam Brigades (*continued*)
  Second Intifada 131, 132, 133–4,
    143, 143–4, 145–6
  tensions within 161–2
Qatar 176, 185, 187, 202
Qiq, Abdel Rahman al- 83
Quartet, the 200, 202
Quds Brigades 8, 87
  casualties 151, **151**
  formation 132–3
  recruits and recruitment 132, **133**
  Second Intifada 132, 143
Quds Force 193
Qur'an, the 14, 17, 35, 69–70, 116, 125
Qutb, Sayyid 62

Rabin, Yitzhak 104
Raddad, Muhammad 155
Rafah 61–2, 174
Rafah camp, massacre, 1956 34
Rajoub, Jibril 111
Rantisi, Abdel Aziz al- 8, 33, 34, 37, 90,
  140, 142, 150, 179
Rayan, Nizar 110, 154–5, 161–2
Razayna, Ayman al- 112, 155
Red Crescent 40
refugees 20–1, 26, 129
religion, role of 124–6
religious observance 71
religious tradition, and modernity
  71–2
Revolutionary Command Council
  (RCC) 24
*Revolutionary Palestine* (journal) 92
rocket attacks 168, 169, 177, 198, 199
Russia 200, 201

sacred jihad group 19
Sa'di, Lu'ay al- 143
Saed, Abu al- 174
Saftawi, Imad al- 83, 155
Salafi-jihadism 129, 157, 157–64, 205
Salafism 58, 159
Saqr, Muhammad 40–1
*Sarih, al-* (newspaper) 54
Saudi Arabia 159, 183, 184, 185, 200
*Saving Palestine* (al-Nabhani) 52
Saydani, Hisham al- 161

scholasticide 2
Second Intifada 7, 87, 128, 150, 156,
  170, 175
  Battle of Jenin 110, 136, 143
  casualties 130, 135
  causes 129–31
  ceasefire 145
  costs 144–5
  distribution of Islamist militants
    133–4, **134**, **135**
  Hamas peace offerings 138–9
  inter-faction cooperation 136, *137*,
    138
  Israeli targeted killings 139–40, 142
  justification 141–2
  popular support 131–2
  suicide bombings 132, 134–6, 140,
    142–3, 143, 145–6
  unsustainability 143
  West Bank 133–4, 144
secularism 27–8, 116, 117
September 11, 2001 terror attacks
  140–1, 142
settlements, Israeli
  expansion 129–30
  population 130, 200
Shafi, Haydar Abdel 40
Shafiq, Munir 85
Shahada, Salah 90, 132, 139, 142, 150
Shalit, Gilad 187–8, 204
Shallah, Ramadan 62, 65, 74, 77, 78–9,
  110, 113, 141, 152, 158–9, 180, 182,
  193
Sham'a, Muhammad 77, 90
Shami, Abdallah al- 65, 74, 79, 102,
  116, 141, 163
Sharon, Ariel 130, 140
Shawa, Zafer al- 23
Shiite Islam 159, 160
Shin Bet 104
Shiqaqi, Fathi al- 25, 33, 43, 49, 78, 92,
  112, 158
  arrest, 1983 82
  assassination 62, 93, 104, 112
  background 61–2, 105
  and colonialism 66–8
  confrontation with Muslim
    Brotherhood 73–6, 76–7, 78

'Fundamentalism and Secularism'
    115–19, 122–7
ideological formation 62–73
Iranian support 178, 179, 180–1
and Israel 67–8, 70
joins Muslim Brotherhood 64
*Khomeini: The Islamic Solution and*
    *Alternative* 76–7
and necessity of armed struggle 70–1
opposition to Oslo Accords 103, 105
political project 62
political theory 115–19, 122–7
religious analysis 68–71
return to Gaza Strip 73–8
rhetoric 76–7
turn to religion 64
West Bank recruitment 81
Shrine of Hussein's Head 31
Sinwar, Muhammad 190
Sinwar, Yahya 8, 33, 94–8, 101, 102,
    187, 187–91, 193, 194
Sinwar, Zakariya 41
Sisi, Abdel Fattah al- 183, 185
Six-Day War, 1967 29, 38, 57, 63, 71,
    95
smuggling 196–7
social services 11, 16, 17, 58, 114–15,
    131, 148
socialism 48, 84
societal patterns and developments 4
socio-economic data 8
Soleimani, Qasem 193
Sons of al-Aqsa 60
Sons of the Islamic Uprising 60
Sons of the Quran Movement 60
spectacular violence 6
spiritual decline 13, 25
starting points 3–4
state, the, role of 115–27
state-building 121
structural conditions 79
structural patterns 4
Suez Canal Company 13
Suez Crisis, 1956 25
suicide bombings 106
    1990s 93, 109–10, 113, **114**, 179–80
    logic of 94
    opposition to Oslo Accords 103–4

Second Intifada 132, 140, 142–3,
    143, 145–6
Sumaya bin Khattab 69
Sunni axis, the 176
Suri, Misbah al- 82, 87
Sword of Islam Brigades 87
Syria 176, 181–2, 185–6
Syrian civil war 181, 181–3, 183, 202

Tawalba, Mahmud 143
Tawhid Association 23, 24
Tel Aviv 15
Temple Mount 130
Ten Resistance Organizations (TRO)
    107
Togliatti, Palmiro 73
tunnel economy 186, 191, 196–7
tunnel strategy 196–8, 204
Turkey 176, 184
two-state solution 4, 116, 138–9, 192,
    200

*umma*, the 124, 125, 159
UN–Egyptian relocation plan 27
unemployment 1, 130, 189, 196
United Arab Emirates 185
United Nations 200, 201
    Resolution 181 19
United States of America 178, 200,
    201, 204
    September 11, 2001, terror attacks
        140–1, 142
urbicide 2

violence 6–7
    loss of potency 146
    Palestinian popular support for 132
    spectacular 6

Wazir, Khalil al- 26, 27, 84, 86
We want to live protests, March 2019
    196
West Bank 194, 196, 199
    institutional development 22
    Israeli reconquest 143, 144–5
    Jordanian administration 21–2
    Muslim Brotherhood in 22–3
    occupation, 1967 29–30

West Bank (*continued*)
    Palestinian Islamic Jihad (PIJ) 144,
        *145*
    Palestinian Islamic Jihad (PIJ)
        recruitment 81
    parliamentary elections 52
    political culture 22
    population, 1949 21
    refugees 20–1
    Second Intifada 133–4, 144
    settler population 130
    size 21
    Westernization 67, 68
    women 39, 41

Yassin, Ahmad 30, 43, 49, 53, 59, 64,
        67, 75, 90, 96, 99, 101, 109, 111,
        138, 140, 141, 149, 189
    arrest 88
    assassination 142, 150
    birth 31
    early life 31–2, 105
    everyday theology 33
    first recruits 33–4
    Islamic identity building 35–6
    leadership of Gazan Muslim
        Brotherhood 34–8, 39

opposition to Oslo Accords 105
Palestine War, 1948 32
photos, 1950s 32–3
preaching style 32–3
spinal cord injuries 32
vision for correct practice 37
Yazouri, Ibrahim al- 37, 40, 90
Yemen 183
Yishuv, the 18
Young Muslim Women's Association
    39
Yousef, Ahmed 110, 156
Youth of Revenge 26, 27
Yusuf, Nasr 160–1

Zahar, Mahmoud al- 25, 37, 111–12,
    179
Za'im, Husni al- 52
Za'nun, Salim al- 26
Zarnuqa 61–2
Zatma, Mahmud al- 112, 132
Zawahiri, Ayman al- 141, 159
Zionist movement, territorial
    aspirations 18
Zuhri, Zuhair al- 35
Zurayk, Constantin 46